LIBRARY PROGRAMS

How to Select, Plan
and Produce Them

SECOND EDITION

by
John S. Robotham
and
Lydia LaFleur

THE SCARECROW PRESS, INC.
METUCHEN, N.J., & LONDON
1981

Library of Congress Cataloging in Publication Data

Robotham, John S., 1924–
    Library programs.

    Bibliography: p.
    Includes index.
    1. Libraries—Cultural programs. I. LaFleur, Lydia.
II. Title.
Z716.R62 1981   021   81-2149
ISBN 0-8108-1422-6   AACR2

Copyright © 1981 by John S. Robotham
and Lydia LaFleur

Manufactured in the United States of America

★ ACKNOWLEDGMENTS

A great many of our colleagues around the country have again given their time and knowledge most generously. It would be impossible to name them all, but we are obliged to acknowledge those who contributed time and material far beyond the call of courtesy. Although some of these people are friends, many of them we have never met and special thanks go to them.

What follows is a list of generous people from all specialties of library service and from all parts of the country. We certainly couldn't have done it without them: Coni Dyckman, Hendrick Hudson Free Library, Montrose, N. Y.; Carey Jacobs, Port Washington (N. Y.) Public Library; Grace Carney, Manhasset (N. Y.) Public Library; Barbara Porte, Nassau County (N. Y.) Library System; Marion L. Carter, Salt Lake City (Utah) Public Library; Sharon Orienter, Rochester (N. Y.) Public Library; Jan Van Wyk, Seattle (Wash.) Public Library; Karl Beiser, Millinocket (Me.) Memorial Library; Tish Andresen, Boise (Idaho) Public Library; John Peters, Natrona County (Wyoming) Public Library; Jeanne Dornfeldt, Fox Lake (Wisc.) Correctional Institution; Cecilia Pizzi, Berkeley Heights (N. J.) Public Library; Bobbie Taylor, Grand Prairie (Tex.) Memorial Library; Grace Shanahan, Brooklyn (N. Y.) Public Library; Kaley Uyematsu, Caldwell (Idaho) Public Library, Julia Losinski, Prince George's County (Md.) Memorial Library; Susan B. Madden, King County (Wash.) Library System; Beatrice Lynch, Kettle Moraine (Wisc.) Correctional Institution; Irene Schell, Gloucester City (N. J.) Library; Samuel L. Simon, Finkelstein Memorial Library, Spring Valley, N. Y.; Barbara Webb, Baltimore County (Md.) Public Library; Susan F. Tait, Seattle (Wash.) Public Library; William Sloan, Michael Miller, Ed Riley, Susan Rappaport, Louise Spain, Marcia Purcell, Marjorie Marciano, Hannah Nuba Scheffler, Ruth Rausen, Rhonna Goodman, Jerome Hammond, all of The New York Public Library.

If, in error, we have left anybody out, thanks to them, too.

iii

★ TABLE OF CONTENTS

Acknowledgments   iii

Introduction to the First Edition   vii

Introduction to the Second Edition   xiii

PART I: KINDS OF PROGRAMS   1

1. Discussion Groups   2
2. Film Showings   25
3. The Performing Arts   61
      Poetry Readings   61
      Drama   65
      Music   69
      Dance   72
4. Talks, Demonstrations, Instruction   82
5. Workshops   105
6. Children's Programs   118
7. Programs for Special Needs   168
      Senior Citizens   168
      The Handicapped (General)   175
      The Deaf   177
      The Mentally Retarded   182
      The Emotionally Disturbed
        and Neurologically Impaired   187
      Prisoners   188
8. Radio and Television   194
9. Miscellaneous Programs   205

PART II: FINDING AND SELECTING PROGRAMS   211

10. Program Sources   212
11. Choosing the Right Program   223

PART III: PRODUCING THE PROGRAM   239

12. Planning, Scheduling, Supervising   240

13. Publicity   264
14. One Exemplary Library Program   285

APPENDICES

A. Sample Lists of Books for Discussion   293
B. Some Films for Discussion   303
C. Sample Film Programs (Adults, Teenagers,
      Children)   306
D. Video Programs   315
E. Film and Videotape Sources   317
F. Sample Flyers and Posters   321

Bibliography   332

Index   343

★ INTRODUCTION TO THE FIRST EDITION

In late summer 1973, the fact that libraries not only lent books but also put on puppet shows, showed films, and conducted discussion groups was front-page news for The New York Times (Sept. 17, 1973, p. 1). It was not, however, news to the hundreds of librarians who had struggled to do such things for many years. Still, many librarians do not have programs, or they do programming in a tentative, halfhearted way as though it is a frill that they flutter when they have time. There are many reasons for this attitude. Libraries are short of money, staff, space, and time. If they had more money, they would buy more of the materials they lack. If they had more staff, they could better do the jobs for which they now have so little time. And few libraries have sufficient space even for the books, not to mention programs. Furthermore, some librarians don't think programming is part of the library's function. We do! We also think the other problems can be overcome.

There are several reasons for having programs in a library, or, as so many libraries are now doing, producing library-run programs outside the library. The traditional reason--and the reason given by many librarians in the New York Times article--is to lure people into the library. It is a good reason. Many people never enter a library. Some of them have the wrong idea about what is inside; they think public libraries are for children--that they're an adjunct to the schools; or they think it's only a place to get best sellers and mystery stories; or, for a variety of reasons, they think it is too forbidding. Libraries never enter the consciousness of some people. They are surprised when it is suggested that they try the library for an answer to their questions. So, programs are a form of publicity. People are enticed into the library, discover all the things libraries have to offer, and begin to use them. Programs sometimes work in this way (we will give examples) and sometimes they create ripples that spread out, as ripples will, in all directions:

vii

ripples that lead to other programs or exhibits; ripples that
create good will, and that spread the library's fame by word
of mouth. However, librarians who produce programs, at
the cost of some hard work and some valuable time, are often disappointed when a lot of the people who come to the programs don't start using the library; many times they do not.
Others who come to programs are people who were using the
library anyway.

Those librarians should not be disappointed. There
are other reasons for having programs; they are extensions
of the material on library shelves. A film on Karel Appel
or Robert Frost, a rock or jazz concert, modern or interpretive dance programs, poetry readings, plays, a speaker
on spiders, a discussion group dealing with ecology or war
all add dimensions to the books, periodicals, pamphlets and
recordings that are the library's stock in trade. Such an
extra dimension (the performance of a play, the reading of
a poem) is often necessary to complete the experience or
understanding that comes from reading a book (a play or
poem). Is it not ideal to have the components of this experience available in one place? We do not suggest compet-
ing with other institutions, commercial or public, but a library can often be more flexible and offer more variety than
other institutions.

Furthermore, we, as a society, are beginning to realize that people learn in different ways. A macrame demonstration or a film on the population explosion might be more
meaningful to some people than reading about those subjects,
and we, as librarians, must learn to use any medium to
achieve our goals. As one librarian put it, "We are in the
business of information and ideas--whether they come in
printed form (books, magazines) or audio- (records, cassettes, musical programs) or visual (films, exhibits, etc.)
or human (personal contact, rapping, programs)...." [Young
Adult Alternative Newsletter, Oct. 15, 1973, pp. 7-8].

There is another reason to do programs. In many
places, little or nothing of a cultural nature is available, or
is being offered to the general public. Even in places such
as New York City that do offer many cultural experiences
there is a need for many kinds of programs. There are a
lot of films, for example, that are rarely, if ever, seen by
the general public, and most people are probably not even
aware they exist. Even in colleges, or large cities with
museums and film associations, one's chances of seeing them

are few. A beautiful film, such as White Throat (Dan Gibson Productions), that follows a white-throated sparrow through the woods, and Wholly Communion (Contemporary/McGraw-Hill), that captures the excitement of a poetry reading by Ginsberg, Ferlinghetti, Voznesensky and many others in London's Albert Hall, are only two examples of many kinds of films that would be enjoyed by many people, if they could be seen. Dance programs and discussion groups, lectures, and poetry readings may, in some places, be difficult to find, if they are given at all. For all of these reasons, library programs can, if they are well presented, provide a valuable free public service.

Presenting a program may well sound easier, or harder, than it is. It is our intention, therefore, to describe the techniques we have learned and the pitfalls we have encountered--and sometimes fallen into--on the way to successful programming. We have also tried to describe as many kinds of library programs as we have been able to find or to dream up. By the phrase "library program" we mean any activity, in or out of the library, in which a librarian and two or more members of the public are involved. (We are reminded by a children's librarian that she has more than once read to only one child. That is also a program.)

Programs in libraries now cover a tremendous range of activity. Libraries are not only engaged in the traditional activities of telling stories to children, showing films, and leading discussion groups; they are flying kites, demonstrating karate, teaching people how to repair motorcycles, and doing anything that seems important to any group of people.

To gather the information presented in this book, we have talked to many librarians, written them letters, and visited their libraries. We have also read all the published or unpublished material on the subject we could find in books, pamphlets, periodicals and reports. But, most importantly, we have been through the mill. During the last twenty years, we have led discussion groups and planned and produced film programs, poetry readings, plays, musical programs, lectures, and workshops, and worked out combinations of these as well. We have learned much, and we hope we can pass on what we have learned to those who would like to do some programs but who feel that because of one limitation or another they cannot.

The emphasis in this book is on public libraries and

they are the ones that will do the most programming. The
material should be useful, however, to schools, colleges,
museums and other organizations and institutions that have,
or want to have, programs. It should also be useful to library school students who will do the programs in the future,
and who will be free of the fixed ideas of the past about library service.

In organizing the material, we followed a logical sequence of events. That is, we thought of the librarian who
wanted to begin having programs or the librarian who wanted
to do more programs. He or she would first try to think of
all the possible programs. So, in the seven chapters of
Part I we describe every kind of program, or variation on
a program, that we could think of, or find out about. In
this part, we also describe how libraries handled many of
the different programs, because we wanted to give actual experiences wherever possible, and because we thought it useful to describe the entire experience of some programs in
one place. With this method, we have included some material in this part that might have more properly belonged in
Part III--on producing and publicizing the program. The material in those chapters is more general in nature and applies
to all kinds of programs.

Once a librarian has thought of all the kinds of programs possible, he must then think about where he can get
them; usually, he must think about where he can get them
for nothing. We have indicated in Chapter 8 of Part II the
kinds of places from which one can get successful programs,
and we have told how we, and others, have gone about getting them. These are mostly free sources, but we have included ways to raise money, if you want to go into programs
on a larger scale, or on a regular basis.

When you know the kinds of programs there are, and
what is available in the community, you then have to think
about which programs are suitable for your library. In Chapter 9 of Part II we describe a variety of techniques for finding out what programs would interest the library's users as
well as others in the community. We discuss the demograph-
ic factors that must be taken into account. We discuss how
to find out what is already being done (and what is not being
done) in the community. And we talk about practical matters:
such things as staff, space and equipment must be considered.
We conclude Part II by discussing the reactions of the community, or segments of the community, to the programs (and how

to elicit those reactions); there may be complaints and librarians will want to be ready for them.

After the program has been selected, it must be planned and produced. Part III is mostly devoted to mundane, but important, details. First one faces the decision of whether to have the program in the library or somewhere else in the community. Then there is the complicated business of scheduling, the necessity for checking up on equipment and other details, the importance of audience comfort, and the planning of the format of the program. We also discuss related exhibits, introductions, receptions and other things one does or can do at a program. There is also a discussion of the problems that can arise and what can be done about them--mainly, foreseeing them.

Publicity properly belongs with planning and producing the program and is discussed in Chapter 11. Planning the publicity, its kind and distribution, is discussed first. Then we describe the easiest and least expensive ways to have publicity designed and reproduced. (Appendix E contains numerous samples of flyers and posters.) The writing and use of press releases is discussed at some length. We then describe other means of publicizing the program, ways of getting publicity distributed, and the use of tickets in publicity.

For the convenience of those readers who want a handy recapitulation of steps to be taken in planning and administering a program as given in the various chapters on various subjects, and for users who are in the midst of actual preparation for a library program and do not have time to read the general advice of the chapters, a "summary and checklist of preparations" is provided at the ends of chapters 1, 2, 3 (four different ones for the four different performing arts covered), 4, 5, and 10.

We thought it would be helpful to have one program described from beginning to end. Chapter 12, at the end of Part III, is a case history of the Paul Zindel program, which brings out many of the problems involved in programming. It also shows how successful a library program can be.

Appendix A presents three lists of books suitable for discussion groups; Appendix B gives a brief list of films suggested for discussion groups; Appendix C gives sample film programs arranged as to suitability for teenagers, adults and children; Appendix D lists sources for both free loan and com-

mercially distributed films. All materials and sources suggested in the Appendices have been successfully used in library programs. A Bibliography cites articles and books that
are further sources of ideas or information on library programs in general, plus three brief sections of specific refer-
ences on film programs, puppet shows, and storytelling. In
addition a section on materials relating to videotaping has
been included.

In the Index you will find all the kinds of programs
mentioned anywhere in the text.

★ INTRODUCTION TO THE SECOND EDITION

       The first edition of this book, published in 1976, has been well-received by our colleagues across the country and we have been encouraged to revise it. Furthermore, much has happened in libraries since that book was written. They are taking programs to more and more places, having programs on every conceivable subject, and including practically every group of people. This book could have been expanded to twice its size, but we were limited by both space and time. Nevertheless, we think the significant trends are included here.

       Many new sections have been added this time. These include programs for the deaf, the mentally retarded, the emotionally disturbed and neurologically impaired, the elderly, the very young, and prisoners. Several new sections (storytelling with props, discussion groups, science programs) have been added to the chapter on children's programs. Other kinds of new material have been added throughout the book. For the rest, we have tried to update the examples. There has also been some reorganization. Radio and television programs have been brought together, for example, as have the previously mentioned programs for the mentally retarded and some other special interest groups. Some parts of the first edition have, perforce, been left out of this one. We would have liked to include them, but publishing costs would have made that prohibitive.

       Since our basic view of programming remains the same, we have left the introduction to the first edition in this one. Starting to write a book is like setting out to walk across the Sahara Desert--what used to be called "the trackless wastes" seems endless. Whether or not there will be a third edition is problematical--but there probably will be. At any rate, here is the second edition. We hope it will prove to be as useful as the first has been.

J. S. R.
L. L.

PART I: KINDS OF PROGRAMS

The kind of program one can have in a library is only limited by one's imagination--plus such mundane matters as money, staff, space, and equipment. The important thing to remember is that one should not be limited by what has been done. Librarians need to think freely about programming and to explore the needs and possibilities, both in form and in content. We will describe many of the programs that have been presented in libraries, and will suggest some things that might be done. We hope librarians will use these ideas as launching platforms for their own imaginations, thereby developing programs that fit the needs of their own libraries.

1 ★ DISCUSSION GROUPS

Discussion groups were probably the earliest kind of library program for adults, and they used to be the most common. They usually consist of a series of sessions, although it is possible to have a one-session discussion. It is desirable to have more or less the same people attend all sessions, but it is not always possible and is not absolutely necessary. The ideal number of discussants is from ten to twenty-five, but discussions can be held with five or six and in some programs, especially the one-shot discussions, the number has been much larger.

There are usually one or two trained leaders--often a librarian and/or a member of the community. In some cases, when special information is needed, a guest expert, to act as a resource person, may be desirable. It is important that such a resource person not be regarded as a teacher, because they can easily, if unintentionally, inhibit discussion.

Discussion groups can be centered around any medium of communication. Any printed material, such as books, pamphlets or periodicals, can be used, or one can use combinations of these. Recordings (discs, cassettes, tapes), films, filmstrips, or videotapes can be used. Or any combination of media might be tried. The choice should be dictated by which media best illuminate the subject, and which stimulate thought and provoke discussion. The potential discussants will also incline you to one medium or another.

One thing about library discussion groups should be stressed; one should not expect, or necessarily even want, to convert the participants to a particular point of view, or to teach them anything; they are not classes. They can, however, stimulate the participants and give depth to their thought, and they can be intellectually exciting and rewarding for both the participants and the leaders.

A discussion group is a very flexible kind of program. It can be used in any library from the largest to the smallest, with almost any age, deal with many kinds of subjects, and can engage many kinds of people.

THE LEADER is an essential ingredient in a discussion group; without him, a discussion will quickly degenerate and you might as well have a group of people talking in your living room--which is all right, but it will not be a discussion. It is sometimes useful to have two leaders, especially if they are inexperienced; they can give each other support, and if one is sick, or otherwise unavailable, the other will be there. An experienced leader, however, can easily handle a group alone.

Leading a group is something one learns to do mainly through experience. There are some pointers, though, that can help the beginner. The leader may first have to inform the group that he is not a teacher; people often think they are attending a class in whatever it is you are discussing. A leader should have a relaxed, friendly attitude which encourages people to talk. He will also, at times, have to be firm. People always wander off the subject (a little bit is all right), talk too long or too much, don't talk at all, become belligerent, and do other things that hinder good discussion. The leader must, in a firm but friendly way, stop them from doing these things, and he must lead them back, or on, to a good discussion. Beginning leaders are most afraid of silences. This fear is usually unjustified. If there are short silences, that is all right; people need time to think when they are seriously discussing something.

The preparation of questions is important. The questions should not be long or involved. They should require more than a yes or no answer. The leader should be prepared to follow up answers with more probing questions, so that the discussion will go deeper; many discussions remain on a superficial level. ˉˍ ˍˍˌˍˌˌa have some provocative questions ready when the discussion lags. Occasionally the entire group will be of the same opinion about something. Then the leader must ask questions that will bring out arguments for the other side.

A discussion should not be allowed to die; if it has gone on for an hour or more, and the topic seems to be about used up, end the session; participants are left with a better feeling about the session, and will look forward to the

next one. Finally, the leader does not enter the discussion.
He may supply factual information, but he doesn't express
his own opinions. He also doesn't allow himself to talk too
much; if questions are unnecessary, he doesn't ask them.

Two sets of tips for discussion leaders follow. The
first was written with adult groups in mind, and the second
was written for those leading discussions of young adults.
They shouldn't be memorized, or taken as sacred. However,
they may be helpful to go over both before a discussion and
afterward--to learn from your mistakes.

Some Do's and Don't's for Discussion Leaders

1. Use questions only; don't make statements or answer
   questions.
2. Don't ask too many questions and keep them short.
3. Ask questions to get the author's ideas expressed (Level
   1), examined (Level 2) and evaluated (Level 3).
4. Be a gadfly by probing cautiously the ideas of the author and participants for clarification, defense, conse-
   quences, and consistency.
5. Get the author's ideas applied to imaginary situations or
   current events.
6. Use provocative questions that divide the group into
   camps of pros and cons.
7. Don't let the discussion wander from the point.
8. Stop splinter discussions.
9. Redirect the question from the monopolizer and the non-
   reader.
10. Ask the participant who says "It's all through the book"
    for one example.
11. Don't let the group bring in outside information about
    the author's time and place.
12. Don't let the group attack the character of the author
    but only his ideas.
13. Don't let the group cite outside authorities.
14. Don't dispute facts, either disregard them or assume
    they are true and try to find out what they imply about
    the reading.
15. Get the definitions of important words out of the text,
    not from the dictionary.
16. Get the group to keep one foot in the text but not two.
17. Don't introduce or sum-up a discussion.
18. Avoid saying: "I'll tell you where it is."
19. Adjust to your co-leader by listening carefully to where
    he is going with his questioning.

20. Don't take things for granted.
21. Don't cling too closely to an outline; relax and let the discussion go if it is relevant to the text.
22. Encourage everyone to question one another.
23. Get the group to remember and compare the authors.
24. Keep an open mind; entertain any notion as possible and probe it impartially.
25. Get the group to avoid strong emotions like anger, impatience, and shouting.
26. Show patience and use humor; be leisurely in attitude.
27. Don't fear small silences.
28. Don't take a vote to determine an issue.
29. Ask questions not only about what the author says but how he says it ... his style.
30. Don't reduce the plot of a play to an issue.
31. Get the group to examine closely passages from works of fiction for effect and overtones.
32. Don't stop with agreement, go on to find out why.
33. Don't try to cover the whole book; cover about four issues, but get the group to look for a while at the book as a whole.
34. Get everyone into the discussion early.

Some general advice for discussion leaders is offered below by Ruth Rausen, of The New York Public Library. They are offered here with her permission and in a slightly amended form.

Keep the group small. Have them sit in a circle on the floor or around a table. Informality is the keynote. Put the group at ease by individual introductions and a little conversation with each one.

Keep a conversational tone throughout--a meeting of friends who like books and enjoy talking about them.

Don't let any individual gain control of the discussion. Everyone should feel relaxed and ready to give opinions on every aspect of the book.

Assure them that even if one person has given an opinion or answer that seems to coincide with what they were going to say, they should say it anyway.

Encourage those who do not speak up readily, but do not "call on" people with direct questions.

Keep the discussion moving. Use either a written plan,
or have a mental outline of those points you would
like to cover. The leader should know the material
thoroughly.

Try to avoid digressions which produce their own discussions. It's difficult to get back on the track without being autocratic. The leader can subtly direct
the group by saying things like, "We're getting away
from the discussion," and thus underscore his presence.

The leader must be firm, however. Participants should
not converse with the person next to them, or to
someone across the table. Talk is always directed
to the whole group.

Participants should listen to each other, and reply to
each other. The leader's questions should grow, or
seem to grow, out of the discussion.

Keep the discussion vital and keyed-up to the end. Don't
let it languish. If it seems to run out of possibilities,
introduce a wrap-up question, and then call a halt.
An hour is the maximum time.

Following the introductions and conversation, slip into
the discussion gently with general questions about
reading, the weather, school, the book. Relate the
book and its characters--whenever you can--to the
lives of the participants.

One way for the leader to help promote a good discussion is to hand the participants a list of discussion techniques. Any such list should be concise, covering only the
main points. It could be given out when people register and
pick up their first reading. Some will disregard it, but it
will help others. It may also help them to quickly recognize
the difficult member, and to come to the aid of the leader.
A beginning leader sometimes feels he needs all the aid he
can get. No deaths of leaders have been reported, however,
and--after the initial nervousness--it can be a very enjoyable
and stimulating experience. One possible list of techniques
for group members follows:

Let's Participate*

Some Suggestions on
Book Discussion Skills

A good discussion is somewhat like a game. There are
rules for the correct play, and definitions of what makes a
"foul." A good discussion depends partly on the skill we
develop as participants. You and your group may find it a
good idea to talk over these "rules of the game."

SPEAK UP! Group discussion is like a conversation; everyone takes part in it. And each speaker hinges his
say on what the man before him has said. There are
no prepared speeches, but a spontaneous exchange of
ideas and opinions. The discussion is your chance
to say what you think.

LISTEN thoughtfully to others! Try hard to get the other
person's point of view--see what experience and
thinking it rests on. Don't accept ideas which do not
seem to have a sound basis. Remember: On almost
every question there are several points of view.

BE BRIEF! SHARE the discussion with others. Speak for
only a few minutes or so at a time. Making your
point in a few words is more effective in group discussion. Be ready to pass the ball to someone else.
A good discussion keeps everyone in the conversation.

SHARE YOUR VIEWPOINT AND EXPERIENCE! Don't wait
to be called on before speaking, but enter into the
discussion with your comment of agreement or dis-
agreement. When you find that you're on the other
side of the fence in the discussion, say so and tell
why, in a friendly way. Considering all points of
view is important to group discussion.

COME WITH QUESTIONS IN MIND! As you read and re-
read the selection in preparation for discussion,
think over the points on which you would like to hear
the comment of the group members.

_____
*The New York Public Library Book Discussion Program.

HOW TO READ A BOOK---

Mortimer Adler says there are three questions to ask of every book as you read it: What does the author say? What does he mean? and How true is it? The last question cannot be answered until the first two have been answered.

Two readings of the selection for discussion are almost essential--but it needn't take twice the time!

MAKE YOUR FIRST READING RAPID. Discover the plan of the book, the major arguments or structure of thinking. Find out what is important to the author and what he is getting at.

THE SECOND READING will be a time to fit these ideas together carefully, seeing how they relate to one another. Decide which ideas need further study; find questions that will illustrate the important ideas.

AFTER THE SECOND READING you will be better able to judge critically how true the arguments are, and whether the author's ideas have importance to you and to our society.

THE NUMBER OF SESSIONS will depend on the content and on the potential interest of the participants. Groups have lasted from one session to fifteen or sixteen, and some groups have continued year after year. One-session discussions would probably use films or recordings, since readings must be done in advance. And they would be best used with some particularly hot topic, which would be fairly narrow in scope. Sometimes one book or narrow subject area would call for a series of three or four sessions. These short-term groups are also useful if one wants to test the validity of having discussion groups or of discussing a particular subject; if it works, a longer series can be planned. If there is reason to believe the interest of the participants will wane, one would not want to plan a long series. In an area where people get into their gardens with the approach of good weather, Plato may lose the battle to petunias. The possibility of blizzards and the certainty of Christmas are some other factors that may limit the number of sessions. In any case, go over the calendar and do some forecasting from what you know of your public and your area. The number of available staff members and the preparation time required will also be a factor, as will the availability of materials.

THE SPACING OF SESSIONS must be considered.

Spacing is partly related to the number of sessions and to the content. If it is a long series, or if long readings are used, every other week is good spacing. Having sessions further apart then two weeks makes it difficult to maintain continuity of either people or ideas. Weekly sessions are good for use with films, for short series, and when the subject is of immediate interest. Meetings would not be scheduled more often than once a week, in most cases.

Notice the phrases, "in most cases," "probably," and others that are used throughout this book: there are always exceptions to rules.

THE SIZE of the group can vary from as few as six or seven to twenty-five or more. And some, particularly the one-shot groups, have had much larger attendances. More than twenty-five, though, gets to be unwieldy. Not everybody will be able to participate and the discussion probably won't get into any depth. Also if books must be charged out, the mechanics become difficult with a large group. Small groups have other problems. People stimulate each other and a small group runs out of ideas too quickly. That might be a good test of your leadership ability, but you have to ask yourself if it will benefit the participants. It also may not be desirable for the library to invest so much time and effort in a small group. But, if no extra scheduling is involved, if materials can be used that are already in the library, and if the group doesn't take up needed space, one could justify spending time with five or six people: certainly the time is justified if the participants derive something of great value from the discussion. Sometimes they do. The best size, allowing for a full participation and a lively discussion, seems to be about twelve to fifteen.

THE AGES of the participants must be considered. There have been discussion groups for senior citizens, for young teenagers, for older teenagers and for all ages. Although libraries don't usually keep anyone out of a program-- unless she is a drunk, or otherwise obstreperous--some librarians feel that it is best, if possible, to limit some groups to the same age category. Both teenagers and the elderly have been said to feel more comfortable with their age peers. There is evidence both for and against this idea, and the choice probably depends on the subject, the sophistication of the participants, and their relationship to the librarian or leader. The Los Angeles Public Library has a general policy regarding teenagers: "Young Adult Services

ordinarily discourages adults and parents from attending the
programs in order to encourage good discussion participation
from the young people. "[1] The New York Public Library has
no hard and fast rule, but if because of the subject, or because there might not be enough room, there are indications
that adults will interfere with the teenagers' enjoyment of a
teenage program, they also discourage the adults from attending. In a program on venereal disease, for example, some
adults monopolized the discussion. In another program, on
sex, however, some adults did attend and the teenagers still
entered fully into the discussion: in this case, the adults--as
well as the leader--were young, and that may have made a
difference. Other programs that included adults and teenagers have been very successful. A program for parents
about the problems of dealing with teenage children was attended by a number of teenagers and an excellent discussion
took place. A poetry discussion group was attended mostly
by elderly people and teenagers and it was very successful.

A science fiction discussion group has also brought
adults and teenagers together, this time at the Salt Lake
City (Utah) Public Library. One of the librarians involved
reports that, "From its inception, a unique feature of the
group has been that young adults and adults have participated
and shared ideas on an equal basis. In respect to communication between Science Fiction and Fantasy buffs, age differences seem to have little relevance" [from a letter to the
authors].

The group was formed in 1974 and is continuing at
this writing (1979) which is an indication of its success.
Thirty-six persons attended the opening meeting. It was decided to meet once a month, and the group would decide on
the readings. Discussion leaders also came from the group.
When it was learned that a local planetarium was planning
something similar, a cooperative effort was decided on.
Thus, the Utah Society of Science Fiction was born, with
that organization and the Library as co-sponsors. Auxiliary
programs are presented by the group and a newsletter is
published. This is a good example of the way programs
have ripple effects.

The format of the series varied. Sometimes the works
of an author, such as Samuel R. Delany, were discussed, and
sometimes they used a group of works by an author, such as
The Foundation Trilogy by Isaac Asimov. At other times,
single works by different authors comprised the series.

Frederick Hoyle, Keith Laumer, Terry Brooks and Larry
Niven were among the authors discussed. Occasionally a
film or a speaker spiced the pot.

ADVANCE REGISTRATION is a useful device for discussion groups. For one thing, it will give you some idea
of how many will attend: always figure in a certain amount
of attrition, when estimating potential attendance. If registration is becoming too large, one can then cut it off when
an agreed-upon point is reached: some groups do this because a large enrollment is not usually conducive to good
discussion or to participation by most members. On the
other hand, if registration is going slowly, one can grind
out more publicity. Advance registration allows you to give
the participants the first title for a book discussion. Regis-
trants can also be urged to attend all meetings: such continuity makes for more meaningful and less superficial discussion.

Discussion groups can, of course, he held without
any registration, and with people drifting in and drifting out
from meeting to meeting. Much depends on the kind of
people you plan to attract and on the materials you select.
If you are trying to attract a group of new library users,
you may prefer an informal arrangement. Or, if the materials in each session can be discussed independently, it is
not so important to have the same people each time. It is,
however, usually better to have the same group; they get
to know each other and to talk more freely, and there will
be continuity. Even if there is advance registration, don't
be too rigid about it; it is only a guideline, and people are
there for pleasure, after all.

If there is registration, and other rules, put them in
the publicity. A registration form can be part of the publicity flyer. It is also a good idea to describe a discussion
group on the flyer. People often arrive at a first session
thinking it is a class and you are the teacher. This is what
one library put on its flyer:

PLEASE NOTE:

Register in advance; enrollment is limited.
Books are provided by the Library.
Participants are expected to attend each session
    thoroughly prepared by having read completely
    the book to be discussed.

Discussion is limited only to the material assigned.
No outside sources are permitted.

The use of the word "assigned" and the general tone of this
flyer were, perhaps, unfortunate, since an image of school
is evoked. Another flyer was less formal:

This book discussion program is open to people who are interested in the Black man's part in
the nation, his future, his rights, and discussion
of methods by which he may attain his goals. It
is based on readings in old and new books and is
concerned with questions of power, priorities and
dissent in the United States.
During the discussion each person is invited
to express fully his reactions, opinions, beliefs on
the ideas and questions raised by the reading.
In the library discussion programs, the leader
encourages the exchange of ideas, he does not
lecture. Members of the group are expected to
prepare reading assignments in advance and to play
an active part in the discussion. Copies of all
readings will be supplied by the Library.

There is that word "assigned" again, or in this case "assign-
ment," which brings on visions of homework. But the tone
is good and seems likely to appeal to the independent learner.

The form, the content, the problems and the audience
aimed at will vary somewhat with the medium used for discussion, and we will now describe discussion groups using
books, films, recordings, other media, and combinations of
these.

Book Discussion Groups

These have been the most common kind. In this
format, a copy of the book is loaned to each participant, and
it is returned and discussed at the following session. Paperbacks are usually used now, since they can be inexpensively
purchased in quantity. Readings are chosen by the availability of quantities of the titles, and the discussability of the
material.

Clearly, not all books are useful for discussion purposes. So, as librarians are always doing, we must select

the books we are going to use. Some books are too long: it
is too much to expect a normally busy person (people who
attend programs are usually those who do a lot of other
things) to read and digest a thousand pages in a week or two.
You could, of course, devote a whole series to one book. Or
you could have the group read passages from a long book.
One of the series of Great Books readings, for example,
lists six chapters of Veblen's Theory of the Leisure Class,
three chapters of The Education of Henry Adams, and two
books of Plato's Republic. Rarely, on the other hand, are
readings too short. Beginning discussion leaders are often
afraid the discussion will peter out. But since, in everyone's experience, people can talk for hours about nothing,
they can also talk for hours about something; that is, they
can if the discussion leaders keep digging in. Short readings
can also be packed with ideas, and only one or two fruitful
ideas are needed to keep a discussion going. The Declaration of Independence can keep a group going all night. This
kind of discussion is probably the most fruitful, because the
ideas can be explored in depth--something that is rarely
done, even in the best of circles.

More important than the length are the contents; that
is, the book or other material must raise some question that
is not subject to scientific proof--some metaphysical, moral,
artistic, or socioeconomic question. It may be something as
vital to the life of the discussants as welfare rights or the
right to have an abortion. It may be on a somewhat more
removed plane, such as secrecy in government. Or it may
by something that doesn't really affect our lives, but is still
fascinating, such as free will versus determinism. Some
books are particularly apt, because they raise questions that
touch on current situations. Such a book is Robert Bolt's
A Man for All Seasons which raises questions of individual
conscience in relation to governmental power. George Orwell's 1984, too, seems more appropriate with every passing
year.

The difficulty of the material must also be considered;
if a reading requires a background in physics, you must
think whether your potential group might have such a background. The readability of the material is important. No
matter how difficult are the ideas, they can be expressed in
a way that is clear, concise and interesting. If the writing
is turgid or dull, the group will tire of it. The bias of the
writing must be examined: the presentation should not be
slanted or distorted (as nearly as this is possible). You

might, of course, want to discuss slanted writing; an examination of propaganda can be very interesting and could be the basis for an excellent discussion.

The form of the reading in a book discussion group can be anything. Plays, poems, novels, short stories, essays, biographies, journalism and anything else you can think of can be used if it illuminates the subject or fuels the fires of discussion. Book discussion groups (maybe they should be called printed materials discussion groups) can also use pamphlets, newspaper clippings and magazine articles. A reading list for a particular subject--say, the destruction of the environment--might well include several of these forms.

Book discussions take many forms. They can be on subjects, forms of writings, countries, ideas. The familiar Great Books series, with its fifteen years of readings (see Appendix A), was probably the earliest book group. Selections cover thousands of years, many parts of the world, and a great variety of ideas. Subjects such as the American Heritage and the American Idea later became popular. Now all kinds of subjects and ideas are discussed. Significant Modern Books is a useful title for a discussion group that The New York Public Library has developed. The list of readings (see Appendix A) is revised regularly so that important new titles or subjects can be included. Novels, plays, poetry, essays, biographies and books dealing with social issues are used. The Feminine Mystique, Clockwork Orange, Ceremonies in Dark Old Men and Cat's Cradle are examples.

Any debatable topic can be used--even broad subjects such as war and education. All the current problems have been discussed; among them are drugs, youth in America, dissent in America, women's rights, mental health, the black experience, American Indians, ecology, advertising, and foreign affairs. Among the forms of writing that have been bases for discussion series are science fiction, poetry and plays. Series involving broad philosophical or moral questions have centered around the Eastern religions, science and modern man, and such a catchall as "Love or Will? Questions of Morality." Variations on, and parts of, these large subjects can be used. Play discussions have used "Significant Modern Plays" and "The Tragic Theme in Greek Drama and Shakespeare." Modern poetry, American poetry or almost any subdivision could be used.

If there is a sizable group in the community that speaks a language other than English, it might be possible--

and desirable--to hold a discussion group in that language.
Discussable books exist in any number of languages. Since
Spanish-speaking persons are now residents of the United
States in large numbers, and since much fine literature is
coming out of Latin America, Spanish seems an obvious
choice for an example. Furthermore, there are books worth
discussing that are coming from most of the Spanish-speaking
countries in the hemisphere. A discussion group that uses
materials from a specific country or area would also be interesting to have with English translations, so that people of
other ethnic groups could broaden their experiences. How about
running both groups concurrently? It's worth speculating about.

The New York Public Library has developed a lecture series on books from a variety of Spanish-speaking countries, and the following list could be useful for a discussion
group. There are many more titles available.

> La Carreta (The Oxcart) by Rene Marques--Puerto Rican
> Cien Años de Soledad (A Hundred Years of Solitude) by Ga-
> briel Garcia Marquez--Colombian
> Los Cachorros (not trans.) by Mario Vargas Llosa--
> Peruvian
> El Señor Presidente (same in English) by Miguel Astur-
> ias--Guatemalan
> Señas de Identidad (Marks of Identity) by Juan Goytisolo--
> Spanish
> Rayuela (Hopscotch) by Julio Cortazar--Argentine
> La Muerte de Artemio Cruz (The Death of Artemio Cruz)
> by Carlos Fuentes--Mexican
> El Monte (not trans.) by Lydia Cabrera--Cuban

Although there have not been as many book discussion
groups for teenagers as there have for adults, there have
been some successful ones. The Racine, Wisconsin, Public
Library has had a lot of success with a Great Books group
for seventh and eighth graders. [2] The program began in
1960 and had run for a number of years at last report. It
was conceived to try to keep the teenagers reading independently before they became too involved in high school and to
acquaint them with some books they might not read on their
own. Teenagers also need to be able to express themselves
freely, away from a structured school, and the program was
geared to that purpose. A different leader was used for each
session, to give flexibility and to make the discussions seem
less like school. The leaders, as in discussion groups for
any age, were asked not to lecture; the opinions of the teenagers were considered most important. And an informal at-

mosphere was the goal "to achieve a free flow of ideas and
exchange of opinions." This goal was apparently achieved;
"although the meetings frequently have begun stiff and formal,
the participants soon realize that no one is being graded or
degraded for what he says, and the ice melts."

Participants were chosen from lists submitted by librarians and English teachers. Selection was made on reading capability and interest. There was a seventh-grade series of five sessions and an eighth-grade series of six.
Groups met every other week, to allow reading time. Paperbacks were used and were furnished by the library. Each
session lasted 50 to 80 minutes, depending on enthusiasm.
Teachers, librarians and other community residents were en-
listed as leaders, and many found it a rewarding experience.
The following books were used:

Seventh grade	Eighth grade
London. Call of the Wild	Crane. Red Badge of Courage
Twain. Huckleberry Finn	Shaw. Pygmalion
Poe. Great Tales	Dickens. Oliver Twist
Crane. Red Badge of Courage	Ullman. Banner in the Sky
Shaw. Pygmalion	Thoreau. Walden
Frank. Diary of a Young Girl	Stowe. Uncle Tom's Cabin

Some of the most successful were Call of the Wild,
Huckleberry Finn, Red Badge of Courage, Pygmalion, Diary
of a Young Girl and Poe's short stories. Although the Great
Books Foundation puts out a Junior Great Books list, this
library found that its own selections worked well, and did
not use it.

A less traditional discussion group for teenagers was
held in New York City. Using The New York Public Library's
Books for the Teenage as the basic reading list, the teenagers selected the subject they wanted to discuss, and read
a book from that section of the list. Espionage, Africa and
art were some of the subjects discussed. Guest experts
were sometimes invited and the librarian who ran the
group says they added a good deal of vitality to the sessions. Among the guests were a staff member who had been
a member of the O. S. S. during World War II, two teenage
art students from the neighborhood who demonstrated painting
and sculpture, and a young woman who was a native of
Dahomey.

A very successful teenage book discussion group is currently going on in a New York Public Library branch in Harlem. It is being conducted by a librarian at the branch library and the librarian from the local junior high school. Both are well liked by the teenagers, a key factor in the program's success. The teenagers range in age from thirteen to seventeen. Each person gets a copy of the book ahead of time (paperbacks are used whenever available) and reads it before the meetings, which take place on alternate Mondays. The librarians try to select books that present positive values. To date they have discussed Roll of Thunder, Hear My Cry by Mildred D. Taylor, A Hero Ain't Nothin' But a Sandwich by Alice Childress, and Let the Lion Eat Straw by Ellease Southerland. The teenagers were thrilled when Ms. Southerland came to join them in the discussion of her book. The group is planning to discuss other books dealing with the Black Experience, by authors such as Walter Dean Myers, Rosa Guy, Brenda Wilkinson, James Baldwin and Sharon Bell Mathis, but they will not limit themselves exclusively to black authors.

A branch library in the Bronx, New York presented another variation for young teenagers. This was a summer program running for four consecutive weeks. The first session was devoted to "Witchcraft and the Occult." Four books were used: Tituba of Salem Village by Ann Petry; The Witch of Blackbird Pond by Elizabeth Speare; A Candle in Her Room by Ruth Arthur; and Lois Duncan's Summer of Fear. As it turned out, discussion centered on the first two, which seems to be the usual experience when a group of books is used. The same thing happened in the second session, entitled "Runaways." Again, four titles were used. Felice Holman's Slake's Limbo was the book they talked about most, in this case. The other titles were Run, Shelley, Run by Gertrude Samuels, My Side of the Mountain by Jean George and E. L. Konigsburg's From the Mixed-up Files of Mrs. Basil E. Frankweiler. The third session included a film, Jade Snow Wong (Films Inc.), and for the fourth session the teenagers each talked about his or her favorite book, and discussed it with the others.

A discussion group for teenagers at the Port Washington (N.Y.) Public Library, in three sessions, dealt with books wherein the teenage protagonist had serious problems. Ordinary People by Judith Guest, a book about a 17-year-old former mental patient, was the topic of the first session. That was followed by Winning by Robin Brancato (about a para-

lyzed football player) and A Day No Pigs Would Die by Robert
Newton Peck.

Film Discussion Groups

With this type of program, the group views and then
discusses the film on the spot. Film discussions have some
advantages over books: you don't have to supply the reading
material; no preparation time is necessary for the participants (the leader will have to prepare though); and the discussion material (the film) will be fresh in the minds of the
group. The film discussion may be more lively and more
spontaneous for those reasons, although the leader will have
to allow the group time to gather its thoughts after viewing
the film. Printed material, on the other hand, allows reflection prior to the meeting. It also lets you consult the
text during the discussion, which is often helpful and even
necessary, and further, it allows the participant to read the
text again after he has had the benefit of the discussion.
The choice of film or book will depend on the availability
of materials, the subject to be discussed (some subjects are
better served by film and others by print), and the kind of
audience you aim for (some young people, for example, may
prefer a film to a book). One thing to consider with any use
of film is that they add technical complications (the details
will be described later).

Films for discussion should not be too long, since
there must be time left to talk. More than thirty minutes
seems undesirable, although some absorbing and provocative
films that were much longer have been successfully used.
Fortunately, there are a lot of good, short films that are
packed with stimulating ideas. The Hand, a 19-minute
Czechoslovakian film from CRM/McGraw-Hill, could lead
to a discussion of dissent, privacy, rebellion, and a whole
range of problems involving citizens and the government.
Chemical Feast (Benchmark) is a humorous, 11-minute film
about food additives and Marguerite (American Educational
Films) presents something about the relationship between
women and men in four minutes. (We hope most relationships last longer.)

Film discussion groups have been held with all kinds
of people. They are useful for people who are nonreaders
or those who are highly visually oriented. They can be used
with any age or any group. A branch of The New York Public

Library held a film discussion group for teenagers. It was
entitled "Talking About Sex." They used the film About Sex
(Texture Films) and staff members of a youth services organization were on hand to act as resource persons. A library in New Jersey held a film discussion group for senior
citizens. They showed films like Norman Rockwell's World,
Helen Keller, Fun Factory (about the Keystone Cops, Charlie
Chaplin and others), and some of the films of W. C. Fields.
The elderly people discussed their experiences and life in the
past. That library purposely avoided films dealing with the
problems of the elderly, feeling that that was not what they
wanted to talk about. At another program in the same library, the elderly people watched Televisionland (Pyramid)
a film of short clips from television programs, and they were
shown some videotape equipment by the audiovisual specialist.
They then discussed modern means of communications, in
the light of their experiences.

In New Carrollton, Maryland, the County library ran
a film discussion series for teenagers that dealt with some
of the problems teenagers face. The flyer describing the
series gives the following description:

> Brian at Seventeen Some times in the life of a typical
> teenage boy.
> Claude, and Ivan and His Father A funny and serious
> look at the generation gap.
> Changing A young family changes its lifestyle.
> Bunny, Tom, Guy and Teddy The youth culture from
> four different viewpoints.
> Nobody Waved Goodbye At odds with his family, Peter
> strikes out on his own.

Film discussion series have been held on the black
experience in the United States. One of these covered such
subjects as slavery, the black soldier, the generation gap, a
film about a black teenager who is torn between her black
and white friends, and a film about teaching the problems of
prejudice. Other intergroup relations can be the subjects for
film discussion groups. There are many films about the
American Indian experience, such as Ballad of Crowfoot
(National Film Board of Canada), Charley Squash Goes to
Town (Learning Corporation) and The Pride and the Shame
(Time-Life), that present the problems and provide material
for discussion. Films about labor problems, such as Decision at Delano (Q-Ed Films) and Harlan County U.S.A.
(Cinema 5, Ltd.), present another intergroup conflict. The

destruction of the environment is very filmable and very discussable. There are films on every aspect of the subject and some of them can evoke very strong feelings--feelings that can be channeled by a discussion leader into enlightening discussion.

Violence is another subject that is a film discussion natural. Violence, in its outward manifestations, can easily be presented by visual means. Violence takes many forms, and it seems to be pandemic. There is much debate, among experts, about the nature of human violence and there is a lot of good material available. For these reasons, violence seems to be an ideal subject for film discussion. Toys (CRM/McGraw-Hill) is a seven-minute color film in which children's toys become alive; they conduct a full-scale war, which is inter-cut with the faces of children. This short, powerful film provides much discussion material. Culloden (Time-Life) recreates the battle of that name and shows war, and the effects of war, in all their horror. Other aspects of violence--in the family, in the street--can be brought into the picture.

Another discussion group wrinkle could be used for this subject (and for others). Since much has been written on the various theories of violence, readings could be used along with the films. This method would allow you to bring together those aspects of the subject that are best presented visually, and those that are best presented verbally. As in book discussion groups, participants could be assigned a reading beforehand, and, at the session, they could watch a complementary film.

A librarian who has led a discussion group of this kind said she thought the amount of material contained in a film plus a book was too much to discuss at one session. She suggested the possibility of alternating films and books. Shorter readings might be another answer. (This librarian wanted to try, but never had, another variation; participants would each be given a reading on a different aspect of the subject; they would then become, for purposes of the discussion, experts, and would be used as resource persons; the film would be shown to the group as a whole.)

Many other subjects are usable for film discussion groups. Banks and the Poor (Indiana University) presents a variety of viewpoints on banking practices. The Woman's Film (Newsreel) and Women on the March (CRM/McGraw-

Hill) present aspects of women's liberation. The National
Endowment for the Humanities and the City University of
New York have put together several film discussion programs.
"The Identity Crisis" uses The Hand (CRM/McGraw-Hill),
A to B (Time-Life), and such feature films as Loneliness of
the Long Distance Runner, The Overcoat and Member of the
Wedding. "The Uses of the Past" uses Black History: Lost,
Stolen or Strayed (BFA), The Island Called Ellis (McGraw-
Hill), All the King's Men and others. "Freedom and Re-
sponsibility" uses films about Socrates, Galileo, and the
Nuremberg trials, and one about an important case in law
in which a ship was abandoned. One difficulty with many of
these films is that they are very long. They have, however,
been successfully used in library discussion groups.

Recordings and Books

The use of recordings with books in discussion groups
presents several interesting possibilities. Since poetry should
be heard as well as seen, the use of recordings in a poetry
discussion group is highly desirable. There are many excellent recordings of poetry on the market; the poems are
often read by the poets themselves, or they are read by some
of the best actors, and these readings bring the poetry to
life--completing the poetic process.

A music discussion group would obviously need to use
recordings. One group used LeRoi Jones's book Black Music.
There were four sessions: "New Wave in Jazz," "John Col-
trane," "Black Mysticism," and "Rhythm and Blues and the
New Black Music." Participants borrowed a copy of the
book and a variety of recordings for each subject. Twenty-
five enthusiastic adults and teenagers attended.

Another music discussion group ran for several years
at the same library. It was entitled "Music, History and
Ideas," and it followed the same pattern--a book, or books,
was available for each member, and they could also borrow
recordings related to the subject under discussion. (Records
were also played during the sessions.) Some of the books
used were Music, History and Ideas by Hugo Leichentritt,
Beethoven; His Spiritual Development by John W. Sullivan,
French Music; From the Death of Berlioz to the Death of
Faure by Maring Cooper, Schumann and the Romantic Age by
Marcel Brion, and the essays of Romain Rolland. Each
session was devoted to either a musical period, or to a

major composer such as Bach or Beethoven. The discussion leader had to be musically knowledgeable; in both these cases, librarians were the leaders, but potential leaders could probably be found in the community.

There are other possibilities for music discussion groups. The development of American music, for example, could be covered, tying in the literature and art of each period with the music. The development of rock music alone would make material for a series of discussions. All kinds of folk music could be used as bases for discussion; it could be tied in with the historical events, personalities, or customs that it celebrates.

Other media that could be the bases for discussions are painting, drawing and sculpture. One would probably have to either use slides or obtain very good reproductions. An artist or other knowledgeable person might be wanted as a resource person. The works of an artist, a school of artists, a period in art history, or a theme could be the basis for a discussion. The historical and social backgrounds could be explored as well as the artists' techniques. Such a discussion could be very beneficial, since most people don't explore a work of art in any depth or for any length of time. Supplementary readings might be used in place of, or in addition to, a resource person.

In the East Meadow (N.Y.) Public Library there is a discussion group that is not tied to any medium or group of media; they use records, tapes and "whatever else is relevant" to stimulate discussion. It is a morning group entitled "Mental Encounters," and they talk about films, the theatre, contemporary problems and other things that interest them.

Another variant at Port Washington was to use no materials at all. "Youth Speaks Out" was the title of the series, and it was devoted to the problems teenagers had in that community. Representatives of the police, the schools, and various youth agencies met with the group to talk about these problems.

Discussion Groups: A Summary and
Checklist of Preparations

KINDS (media)
Print media--can use books, pamphlets, magazines,

newspapers or any combination
Film
Film and one or more print media
Recordings
Recordings and one or more print media
Paintings, drawings, sculpture, etc. and one or more
   print media
Other--any combination of above

MATERIALS
   Print media--readings for each participant and for
      leaders
   Film--films to be shown to group at the session
   Recordings--to be played for group at session, and to
      be borrowed
   Paintings, drawings, sculpture, etc.--reproductions and
      slides to be viewed at session, readings for each
      participant

EQUIPMENT
   Chairs
   Tables--desirable but not essential
   Ash trays--if smoking allowed
   Pencils and paper
   Projector(s)
   Record player

STAFF
   One or two trained leaders--allow several hours of
      preparation time for each session, as well as time
      at session (staff can often be supplemented with out-
      side leaders, from, e. g. , schools and colleges, li-
      brary users)
   Projectionist--unless leaders are experienced, probably
      desirable to have projectionist separate
   Clerk--to charge out materials, if large group and only
      one leader

AUDIENCE
   Best for ten to twenty participants, but groups work
      with five to twenty-five or thirty
   Adults and teenagers

SESSIONS
   Number--one, or a series of three or four, or longer
      series up to fifteen or sixteen (some groups continue
      year after year)

Spacing--one or two weeks apart
Length--from one to two hours

SPACE
Size--400 sq. ft. adequate for most groups (even a film
can be shown in a small space to a small group)
Location--quiet and away from public use area, or in
such an area when not used by public

SUBJECTS (Examples)
Economic, social and political problems--foreign affairs,
women's rights, destruction of the environment, urban
problems, mental health, drugs, sex, capital punishment, war, intellectual freedom, democracy, privacy,
minority groups, violence
Philosophical problems--free will and determinism, il-
lusion and reality, beauty, truth, morality
Poetry--modern American, English, Black, American
Indian, Romantic, war, individual poets
Drama--Greek, modern, American, tragedy, comedy,
theatre of the absurd, individual dramatists
Fiction--modern, great, American, European, science
fiction, women novelists, protest novels, experimental
Music--Romantic, rock, American, Black, European,
individual composers, avant garde
Art--modern, European, American, great art of all ages,
primitive, avant garde, individual artists
General series--Great Books, Significant Modern Books,
American Idea, Black Experience, Oriental Thought

NOTES

1. Sigler, Ronald F. "A Study in Censorship: The Los
Angeles 19," Film Library Quarterly, Spring 1971,
p. 37.
2. Elsmo, Nancy. "Junior High Book Discussions," Wisconsin Library Bulletin, Sept. 1966, pp. 279-80.

2 ★ FILM SHOWINGS

Films are useful in many kinds of programs. They appeal to all ages, and have been successfully used in programs with preschool and elementary school children, teenagers, the middle-aged and the elderly. Films can be used by themselves, or in combination with music, dance, drama, poetry readings and lectures. They can be the basis for a discussion group, or the subject of a workshop. In this chapter, we are dealing with film showings of interest to teenagers and adults only. Film programs for children are discussed in the chapter on children's programs. Other uses of film are mentioned elsewhere.

Popularity of Film Programs

Film showings are the most usual kind of library program. One reason is that films are widely available, many thousands having been produced in the last fifteen years. Furthermore, the art of the film has become tremendously popular, especially with the young. There are some indications that now films are being thought of as old hat--certainly live performers are often more popular--but film programs continue, and will continue, to be very popular.

Another reason for the popularity of film programs is that they seem to be an easy kind of program to produce. They can be simple and successful, if one is careful--or they can be disasters. The reason for this proclivity to disaster is that, with films, attention must be paid to many details that are not present in other programs.

The Projectionist

First, one must have an experienced projectionist-- one who is thoroughly familiar with the projector and who

will know what to do in an emergency. In spite of all precautions things can go wrong. They usually don't, if one
has prepared well, but they can. Films break. They jam
in the projector. Bulbs burn out. So the more knowledgeable the projectionist is, the better.

If possible, the projectionist should be a separate
staff member. He should have no other duties while films
are running, so he can watch for developing problems. He
must watch the focus and the sound, loss of the film loops,
trouble developing in the projector, etc. These things can
happen very quickly, and they must be quickly attended to
or both film and projector can be badly damaged. It is also
wise to have a backup projectionist, in case of sickness,
death or any other adversity. One library that was presenting many film programs trained every staff member to
run a projector. Fortunately, it is easy to learn.

The Projector

If the library doesn't own a projector, there are
several possibilities. For a few showings--if, for example,
one wanted to test the potential popularity of film showings--
a projector could be borrowed. Other libraries, museums,
schools and colleges are some possible sources of 16mm projectors. Individuals often own 8mm projectors. However, if
film showings are to become part of a library's permanent
programming schedule, it should own two or more 16mm projectors. Consult various issues of Previews and EPIE publications for ratings and discussion of makes and models, along
with queries to your AV technician and repairman.

It is possible to buy a used projector, but as a recent
article on the subject says, "The rule is a definite buyer
beware."[1] The article gives some rules for testing the projector. Listen to the projector and see if it squeaks,
whistles, clatters or jerks through the motions. Take 100
feet of unused black leader (from a processing laboratory)
and run it through. If there are scratches on the film, don't
buy. Look at the film gate for rough spots. Be sure the
projector can take the strain of running the length of films
you want to show. Check the focus and look for cracked
condensers in front of the projector lamp. Check the sprockets
for missing points and the pull-down claw movement for
missing pins. Run a sound film through without picture and
listen to sound. Run the picture without the sound. Adjust
the framer so the frame line shows on the screen; it should

be steady.   The article ends with a final caveat: "Get a good
guarantee and check it out before you finally accept any piece
of equipment and part with your money."

Whether one is purchasing a new or a used projector
the newer models of the name brands are preferable, because
parts and servicing are more readily available.

Other Equipment

An extra projection lamp is essential.   The newer
lamp designs can yield up to 200 hours of use as opposed to
the older 25 hour models.   The electrical outlet may be some
distance from where the projector must be placed so an extension cord is necessary.   A set of take-up reels of the right
size is important.   Otherwise the films may have to be re-
wound during the program, causing delays and annoyance. [2]

There are two types of screens--the standing screen
and the wall-hung lenticular roll-up screen which is perma-
nently attached and therefore the safest.

Acquisition of Films

The next thing a film showing needs is films.   They
can be acquired in several ways: they can be purchased,
leased, rented, or borrowed free of charge.   If films are
being bought, one would naturally want to be sure they are
going to be used fairly frequently over a long period of time.
Most films can be previewed by would-be purchasers.   When
films are going to be used for a lot of programs, but it appears that they might date or that interest in the subject
will wane, they can be leased.   One company leases films
for one year for a third of the purchase price. After three
years, you have bought the film.

Rental Films.   Many films will be shown only once
or twice; these can be rented.   Experience has shown that
the companies that rent films are usually efficient; that is,
the films come a day or two ahead of the program, and they
are the right films.   That doesn't mean that one shouldn't
be watchful, however.   When films are rented, there are
rules about their showing.   Some companies are fussy about
these rules, and some are not.   Often, for instance, one is
not allowed to advertise rental films.   Sometimes, each

showing must be paid for, so if the film is going to be shown
twice in one day, additional fees would be paid. Sometimes
the rental is for a day, or for two or three days. Usually
the film must be shown at a specified place and time. The
library pays the return postage, and should insure the film
even if it is not required. Fortunately postal insurance
rates are cheap, as are mailing rates for library materials.
The package can be marked, Library Rate--16mm Films, or
Special Fourth Class Rate--16mm Films. Library rate is
cheaper and can be used by specified organizations only.
They should also be sent special delivery. The company's
catalog will give its rules and will often provide an order
form. Most libraries will probably not want to rent a lot of
films as that would be very expensive. But many films are
available for from $15 to $25 and when a film that costs
$300 can be rented for $15, rentals are worth a look.

Free-Loan Films. The category of most interest to
many libraries is that of the free-loan film. As with most
free things, there are some drawbacks, but if the "emptor
caveats," there are many good free films to be found. The
first thing to know is that free films are not always entirely
free. Usually, one must pay the postage--sometimes both
ways--and sometimes a deposit is required. Then, those
lending the films are often inefficient. Some will send substitute films that you won't want. Sometimes the films are
late. Sometimes the wrong film is sent by mistake. Occasionally a film won't come at all. And whenever films are
used, one must be sure they are not on the reels backward
or upside down. So when using films, alertness is a pre-
requisite; check in plenty of time to be sure the right film,
on the reel the right way, arrives at the right time. If the
distributor is close enough, some of these problems can be
avoided by picking up and returning the film in person.

There may be other problems with free films. Sometimes films from commercial sources have, not unnaturally,
commercials included. If the commercials are at the beginning or end of a film, one can avoid showing them. Sometimes they are not so blatant or objectionable that it would
matter anyway. Even if there are no commercials, a film
from a commercial source (or any source) may be propaganda
for a particular point of view. Whether or not it is shown
depends on the objective of the program. The program may be
designed to show different points of view, or to show examples of propaganda.

The availability of the films is important. Rental

films, possibly because the renting agency has more than one copy, usually seem to be available. With free-loan films it varies. If the film is a popular one, or the subject is of seasonal interest, it is best to book a couple of months in advance. With rental films, they can sometimes be booked as little as two weeks ahead. All distributors, even of free-loan films, will confirm bookings. As far as the efficiency of the distributor is concerned, it is best to experiment and find the efficient ones.

Sources of Free Films

The sources of free films are many. State and regional libraries may have circuit collections of films and they will be the first places to check for free films. Professional baseball, basketball, football and hockey leagues and teams offer free films. They may cover a team's highlights for a season or cover a World Series, Super Bowl or Stanley Cup playoff. Or they may be how-to-play films, with one or two players showing how to shoot baskets or play the infield. These films tend to be slightly chauvinistic but they have a lot of action. The consulates, information bureaus or airlines of some countries may provide free films--and sometimes speakers--for programs. Large corporations (IBM, Exxon and others) and some smaller companies produce and loan films to groups and organizations. These films may be well-produced and have some useful information, in spite of their obvious propaganda purpose.

The United States Government is a big producer of films. More than 1500 films are available free from 47 different federal agencies. Colleges and universities use films and libraries may be able to borrow from them. Museums, scientific and historical associations sometimes have films they will lend. Religious organizations, labor unions and organizations, such as environmental groups, that are promoting a cause may have films to lend. National health organizations such as the American Cancer Society and the National Multiple Sclerosis Society have free films. Films dealing with social and economic problems may be available from such organizations as Planned Parenthood and similar groups, agencies concerned with drug abuse and prevention, organizations working with the elderly, and consumer agencies. Youth organizations like the Boy Scouts and Girl Scouts have films available.

Film clubs and individual collectors are an important source of free films. These are usually 8mm or super 8mm films, and often include such unfailingly popular films as those of Charlie Chaplin and Laurel and Hardy. Sometimes the collectors will come along with the films, and they are often very knowledgeable. One student of films, who also collected them, not only provided his films free, but also provided an enriching commentary.

Then there are the individuals who make their own films. Sometimes they are in college or high-school film courses. Often they are experimenting on their own or they have formed clubs. They produce animated films, documentaries and films with actors; many of them are imaginative, funny, thoughtful and well-photographed. To find them one should contact the teachers of film or photography in the schools and colleges, contact youth centers, talk to library users (particularly those borrowing books on film making), watch local newspapers, and talk to the proprietors of stores that sell the necessary equipment.

Getting the Room Ready

The room must be made dark. During the day, one may have to fasten some opaque materials, such as construction paper or heavy cloth, over the windows. Chairs must be arranged so the audience will have a clear, full view of the screen. Avoid putting chairs in front of the projector. The screen should be raised or lowered as far as it will go, and it should be places so that an opening door won't cast light on it.

The placing of the projector speaker is important. Check the acoustics when the film is running. Most projectors are designed with a classroom in mind. For a larger room, a large external speaker is preferable. Often the speaker is best placed in front of and at the center of the screen, and raised off the floor. But experimentation might show it is better raised high and off to one side of the screen. Put it on something solid and steady such as a stool or table. If power lines must be placed so the audience will have to step over them, tape them to the floor to avoid accidents. The projector should be placed so that the picture exactly fills the screen. If this cannot be achieved, changing to a lens with a longer or a shorter focal length might do it. A zoom lens with its variable focal lengths can solve such problems.

times there is no alternative, and it might be better to show
a film under less-than-ideal conditions than not show it at
all. Except that if you can't get a sharp picture, or clear
sound, don't show films; that will send audiences away, never
to return. If the audience is small, one can show a film in
a very small space. During a high school "career night,"
the authors showed a film to small groups of teenagers, in
a space of not more than 100 sq. ft. They just sat up close
to the small clear picture, and enjoyed it. (There is a more
detailed discussion of seating at the end of this chapter.)

Projecting

The projectionist should clean the film gate on the projector with a soft lintless cloth or soft bristle brush before running each film. When threading the film, the end should not be
allowed to fall on the floor where it will collect dust. Pinched
reels should not be used as they can damage the film. Avoid as
much as possible, stopping and reversing the film, as the
film can be torn in that way. Never put the films on a
radiator. Films and take-up reels should be put in the
order in which they will be shown so time won't be lost between films. Have the first film threaded and focused before the audience arrives. Help the projectionist adjust the
sound. Long, narrow rooms are a problem, since the sound
is often too loud near the front and too soft at tne back. Using
one speaker at the front and one at the back will solve this problem. Be alert to changes in focus and tell the projectionist.
Silent films made before 1920 should be run at "silent speed."
Silent films made after 1920 are usually run at "sound speed,"
in which case the amplifier should be turned off.

When running sound films, be sure the sound switch
is on. If the voice is not synchronized with lip movements,
the lower loop of the film may be too big. If the sound is
indistinct, one can try adjusting the treble dial; spoken words
are often more distinct if the treble is fairly high. If there
is a manual with the projector, it will pay to study it. If
there isn't one, try to get it from the company directly.

All these technical details should be checked in plenty
of time before the program so that any deficiencies can be
corrected. One might need to borrow another projector, to
buy an extension cord, or to get more room-darkening materials. Know in advance where you can get those things
you might need, and allow time to get them. The foregoing
might seem formidable to the uninitiated, but if a little care

is exercised, film programs usually run very smoothly, and with a little practice it will all seem routine.

Previewing Films

Something else needs to be done before one has a film program, and it is very important: if it is at all possible, the film should be previewed. One can not and should not depend on reviews, although there may be some exceptions to this rule. A well-known film like Man of Aran, for example, about which much has been written, might not have to be previewed. But even then, it would be helpful for the person introducing the program to see it himself.

There are several excellent reasons for previewing. First, one needs to check the technical qualities: color, sound, focus. Then, the effectiveness of the film in presenting its subject should be considered. Is it original? Does it raise questions? Does the filmmaker show a bias? Will it be offensive to anyone? These are all questions that the previewer might ask, depending on the film and the purpose of the program. Having a bias, or being offensive, doesn't necessarily exclude the film from the program, but at least one will want to be aware of these qualities, and either prepare the audience for what is coming, or be ready for audience reaction.

The authors had an experience that emphasizes the importance of previewing. They were showing what they thought to be a perfectly harmless Pearl White film. It was being shown to a racially mixed audience, and, to the authors' horror, some of the characters in that film displayed all the worst stereotypes that have been associated with black people. If the film had been seen first, they would have either substituted another film, or carefully introduced the Pearl White film.

Introducing the Film

One of the main reasons for previewing is to prepare to introduce it. All films should be introduced, but some should be introduced more than others. A brief, well-prepared introduction can add to the audience's appreciation and understanding of the film. At the same time, one can mention, or describe, library materials that will also add to their understanding or enjoyment. Furthermore, these things will make them feel more at home in the library, and make them more conscious that this is a library program. If the audience just comes, watches the film, and then leaves, the program has not achieved its full potential. Of course, if one can get a guest expert to introduce the films, that would be great. But by viewing the film first, and possibly doing some background reading, one can make a satisfactory introduction. It might also be useful to consult experts on the subject of the film, or filmmakers, or film librarians. Sometimes members of the audience can make enlightening comments and they should be encouraged. Sometimes they can make boring, pointless or too long comments (so can experts and librarians) but it is worth giving them a chance.

Experimental and avant-garde films need to be introduced--even more than other films--because audiences will often not feel at home with newer techniques or with different styles of filmmaking. One can give some background on the film, describe the filmmaker's techniques, or tell what he is trying to achieve. Renaissance (Pyramid Films) is an example of fascinating special effects--a room explodes and puts itself back together again. The audience will certainly want to know how those effects were achieved. Moon, 1969 (Scott Bartlett) is a poetic interpretation of a trip through space, using videographic techniques. The sound and images are purposely garbled and indistinct. The audience should be warned and the techniques described. Many such films are also so short they will be over almost before the audience is settled, or realizes what the filmmaker is about. For instance, Viewmaster (Serious Business) only lasts three minutes. In it, forms of different shapes and colors run around a circular treadmill, in order to demonstrate different styles of animation. A slightly longer (8 min.) film is Evolution of the Red Star (Serious Business). It is also an abstract, animated film, and uses a star motif in all its permutations. There are bright, pulsating colors and an electronic soundtrack. Cubits and Shorelines (Al Jarnow) are two films that last a total of seven minutes. The first is a musical presentation of rotating geometric forms, and the second is a montage of objects found at the shore. We might mention two more of the many films of this kind. Frank Film (Pyramid, 9 min.) is an autobiographical film in which a flood of visual images accompany each phase of the film-maker's growing up in America. Organism (Hilary Harris, 20 min.) uses time-lapse photography in a marvelous way to develop the idea of New York City as a living organism.

Of course, films can be over-introduced, and you wouldn't want to predispose the minds of the audience. Comments should be carefully chosen--and short.

Films that are important in film history and films dealing with early filmmakers, such as La Fantasie de Méliès (Blackhawk) or A Corner in Wheat (Blackhawk) by D. W. Griffith, are enhanced by some background on the techniques used, and on the filmmaker's place in film history. Controversial films may also need an introduction, and one should assess the potential audience. It may be useful to put the film in some kind of context, or to explain why you are showing it. This can be done without labeling the film or prejudging it in any way, and maybe you can stimulate a worthwhile discussion of the issue.

Many films are, of course, technically good, have no special qualities that need introduction, and are not controversial. But they still should be previewed. They may be moving, thought-provoking, sad, funny or beautiful and still not fit into the program. They need to be examined with an eye to style, content, mood, up-to-dateness, age level, background needed by the audience and other factors to see if they are exactly what is wanted for a particular program, and for a particular audience. One of the authors needed a film in a hurry for a program for a woman's club. Clouds (New Line Cinema) was recommended as a beautiful film. It is a film about Crow Indians; they talk about their heritage, and they are seen at work and at an all-Indian rodeo. It is a beautiful film, but it was a ho-hum film for that group, and if it had been previewed, that fact would have been recognized.

Where to Show Films

As with other programs, the where and when of a film program is important. In spite of needing projectors and an electrical power source, film showings can be given in many places. Libraries have had film programs in vacant lots, playgrounds, parks, parking lots, on sidewalks, in hospitals, nursing homes, drug rehabilitation centers, churches and in many other places, as well as in libraries. The Iowa State Traveling Library has taken films to county fairs; they have devised a simple, efficient set of equipment, and they have spread film showings, and news of the library, far and wide. [3] They would get permission to use a small

space--as small as 10' x 20'--in a dark corner of one of
the tents. They carried ten to fifteen folding chairs, a six-
foot collapsible aluminum table for the projector, a collapsible typewriter table for the screen which was made from a
cardboard box two feet square with a black interior and a
white poster board. One staff member at a time was needed
for the program, which ran from noon to 9 p.m.[4] each day of
the fair. Silent comedies, horror films, films about war
and natural history were among those shown. They attracted
people of all ages and occupations. The librarian talked
about the library's services, and there were discussions,
eagerly participated in, of the films.

When to Show Films

        Just as film programs have been produced in every
imaginable place, they have been run at most imaginable
times. Libraries have shown films during mornings, afternoons and evenings, in every day of the week, and in every
season of the year. Some libraries, in business areas, have
had success with noontime programs. Others, in residential
areas, have attracted large audiences of housewives to
morning programs. Late afternoon programs have drawn
both teenagers and adults, in some places. Sometime Saturday or Sunday afternoon is a good time. So one can be
flexible in planning, and, considering the audience and other
factors, pick the best potential site and time.

        The length of the program, the number of films used,
and the order in which they are to be shown are all factors
to be considered in deciding when to show them. The length
of the program will vary somewhat with the age of the audience. The very young, the elderly, and the sick may not
want to sit as long as the rest of us. The subject and the
nature of the films will also have a bearing on the length of
the program. Only the most devoted filmaniac would want to
sit through two hours of computer-made films, but a four-
and-a-half-hour film like The Sorrow and the Pity does not
seem long. On the average, from one to one and a half
hours seems like a good length for a film program.

Number of Films on Program

        Film showings will usually be comprised of from one
to no more than four films. (There are exceptions.) With

more than four films, one would be using more time changing
the films than showing them, unless more than one projector
is available. Of course, if somebody is commenting on the
film, that time could be put to good use. Again, the number
of films depends on the kinds of films and on the kind of
audience. One fairly long film such as Robert Flaherty's
Man of Aran (CRM/ McGraw-Hill) makes a good program by itself at 70 minutes. A three-film program on New York City
might include Summer Days (Scott Morris, 20 min.), a portrait of two teenagers at liberty during the summer in New
York City; La Dolce Festa (Cecropia Films, 28 min.), about
the San Gennaro Festival in the city's "Little Italy"; and
Harlem Wednesday (Audio-Brandon, 10 min.), which evokes
the mood and activities of a Wednesday in Harlem. Or one
might want one long film and a short opener. For a program
on art, The Louvre (EBEC), a 45-minute film, could be
used, and the program could be opened with Dwellings (Museum at Large), a short film that follows an artist from one
demolition site to another as he constructs miniature cities
in areas laid waste by the wrecker.

Order of Showing

The order in which films are shown is important.
Pace, style, and length should be varied so that rigor mor-
tis doesn't start in the audience. With a short film and a
long one, the short one would probably be used as a curtain
raiser. A fast-moving film, or a light film, might be shown
after one that was more serious or slow-moving. On the
other hand, if a particularly impressive, thought-provoking
film is being shown, that could be the finale so that the audience would go out thinking about it. Think about the audience
and the purpose of the program. One might not want to
show several animated films together, unless one was trying
to compare styles of animation. Or one might show different
kinds of films together for ironic contrast. The point is that
the order should be thought out. A haphazard arrangement
may work, but why not make the program better?

Selection of Films

But before films can be arranged in a particular
order, they must be selected. They are, of course, selected
with an eye to that order, as well as to the length of the
films, the length of the program and the technical qualities

of the films. Other bases for selection might be age, educational level, race, religion, national origin and sex. These
factors are clues to the interests of the potential audience.
But they are not conclusive. Interests cut across all these
lines, and interest, after all, is of paramount importance
in the selection. Methods of determining interests are discussed in another section.

Known interest is not the only criterion for selection,
however. Sometimes people don't know they will like something until they see it, and, in fact, they often don't know
that that thing exists. Even with television, colleges, film
societies, film festivals and individual collectors showing
more and more films, there are still many films that one
might never see. And in many parts of the country--except
for television--even these outlets do not exist. Film programs are, therefore, a chance for libraries to provide useful, interesting, stimulating, humorous and moving filmic
experiences to persons that would not otherwise have been
aware of them. Of course, getting the public to attend these
films may be difficult, but that's where canny selection comes
in.

If one is showing the films of Charlie Chaplin or
Laurel and Hardy (both very popular with all ages) one might,
at the same time, show such silent film stars as Harry Lang-
don, Charlie Chase or Snub Pollard; these comedians are
little-known to the general public, but would be enjoyed.
For a program of traditional films, one can slip in one unusual or experimental film. Not everybody will like it, but
if it is a short film, they will tolerate it, and some will be
surprised. If the program deals with the United States, An
American Time Capsule (Pyramid) can be shown as a change
of pace. This film covers all of American history by showing 1300 pictures in less than three minutes. If the program
is on dance, Dance Squared (National Film Board of Canada)
could be shown; it is a four-minute film using animated geometric shapes.

Variety Programs

The possible subjects for a film showing are almost
limitless. At least, there are enough to fill any librarian's
programming lifetime. One possible subject is no subject.
If the library is in an area where people will readily attend
film programs, or the time is right, or the program can be

made attractive enough, imaginative, variety film showings
can be very successful. This is often true when people have
a lot of spare time, such as vacationers, retired persons,
people wanting to fill up lunch hours, Saturdays and Sundays,
some housewives, the unemployed and the ill or disabled.
This kind of programming allows for flexibility of choice.
If one is not confined to a subject, the most imaginative,
humorous, beautiful or moving films available can be chosen.
It also allows more freedom if last minute substitutions must
be made, or if one wants to respond quickly to an event by
getting a film on the subject.

There are innumerable combinations. A silent comedy,
an animated film, a computer-made film, and a documentary
might make a program. Or a showing could include a nature
film, a travel film, and a film about some historical event
or period. One actual program included: People Soup (Learning Corporation), a 13-minute film in which two boys, in a
kitchen, mix some odd ingredients into their food, which
turns them into animals; Rock in the Road (BFA), a 10-
minute, animated film on the need for tolerance; K-9000
(Creative Film Society) an 11-minute, animated spoof of
2001; Barber Shop (Blackhawk), a 23-minute W. C. Fields
film. Another program included: Charley Squash Goes to
Town (Learning Corporation), a 5-minute, animated film about
an Indian who tries to follow everybody's advice; Minestrone
with Music (Grove Press), a 6-minute animated film that
touches various aspects of modern life; The National Flower
of Brooklyn (out of print), a 12-minute evocation of the history of the Brooklyn Bridge through the use of old pictures,
newsreels and radio broadcasts; The Ride (CRM/McGraw-
Hill), an 8-minute slap-stick comedy.

Subjects for Showings

Usually, film showings are built around a particular
subject. Often, a library will present a series of showings,
with each showing devoted to a different subject. That kind
of program will draw both those people with special interests,
and those with a variety of interests who just want to see
some films. For film showings built around subjects, there
are many kinds of possibilities. Programs of topical interest
are useful. Films on such subjects as China, American
Indians, women's liberation, consumerism, the destruction
of the environment or impeachment can be shown when interest in the subject arises. Films on art do well in some

places, and there are many kinds of arts and many excellent films to choose from. Music, dance, theatre, poetry, painting, sculpture, and printmaking are some subjects.

A poetry series could include films on William Butler Yeats, Robert Frost, Dylan Thomas, James Dickey, Gwendolyn Brooks, Allen Ginsberg and Lawrence Ferlinghetti. For sculpture, there are films available on Michelangelo, Giacometti, Barbara Hepworth, Henry Moore, Jose de Creeft and others. There are many fine films on painters and painting, including Rembrandt, Picasso, Frans Hals, Jackson Pollock, Marc Chagall and Paul Klee. There are films dealing with popular, classical and folk music, such as It Ain't City Music (Tom Davenport Films) and Andrés Segovia (Irving Lesser), as well as such narrower categories as blues and jazz.

Dance is a subject that lends itself naturally to filmic treatment and there are many films on classical, modern and folk dancing. A program on modern dance might include such imaginative films as Capriccio (James Seawright), which is a special effects film made with television equipment that produces multiple exposures of two modern dancers, and Nine Variations on a Dance Theme (Radim), which explores the movements of a modern dancer. A ballet program could include Beginnings (Lightworks), which is about training young dancers at the School of the American Ballet Theatre; Dance: New York City Ballet (Indiana University); and Galina Ulanova (Audio/Brandon), a film about a Russian ballerina. A program on folk dancing could include Norwegian, African, Scottish and Spanish dances.

Natural history films make beautiful and fascinating programs and although many are now being show on television, many are not. They are also much better when seen on a big screen. There are fine films about white-throated sparrows, monarch butterflies, animals of the Arctic and life in sand dunes among other more usual nature films.

Films about places are often popular, and showings can be organized in a number of ways. One might do a series about cities, and again there are many films in this category. Rome, London, Paris, Venice, and Kuala Lumpur can all be brought into the library, and they have been filmically treated in many ways. A good program could be produced about Paris alone. 1848 (Radim), a 22-minute film

about the uprising of that year in Paris, could start the
program. Eugene Atget (CRM/McGraw-Hill), a 10-minute
poetic evocation of a Paris morning at the turn of the century, could follow. Then would come In Paris Parks (CRM/
McGraw-Hill), a 13½-minute, 1955 film about the day of
some children in a Parisian park. And the pièce de résis-
tance would be The Louvre (EBEC), a 45-minute film in
color, that presents the evolution of that museum and some
of the magnificent works of art it contains. So many films
have been made about New York City that several series
could be done on that subject. (For example, The New York
Public Library's film catalog lists 35 films on New York
City.) Showings can be given about countries, groups of
countries and continents. Many films are available on Brazil,
Great Britain, Africa and South America, to name a few.
One library had a program about places of the past, with
films about Pompeii, ancient Peru and Angkor Wat. Another
library showed films of island life, including Pitcairn Island,
Easter Island, Trinidad and the Queen Elizabeth Islands of
the Arctic.

Biographical films suggest some ideas. For instance,
there are a number of films on women; they include such
diverse people as Margaret Mead, Lorraine Hansberry,
Eleanor Roosevelt, Grandma Moses, Frances Flaherty (the
wife of Robert), Madalyn Murray O'Hair (the advocate of
atheism) and Imogen Cummingham (a photographer). There
is a wide range of other biographical films from Gandhi to
Ulysses S. Grant, and including Dr. Martin Luther King,
Jr. , Bertrand Russell, Dr. Ernest Jones and Wilfrid The-
siger. From the available biographical films one could make
a number of interesting combinations.

Religion is a possible subject for a series of showings.
There are films on Buddhism, Hinduism, atheism, Judaism,
various forms of Christianity and others. There are a number of films about child care, mathematics, railroads, and
migrant workers, indicating the diversity of available films.

Another possibility is to group films by form. One
could have showings on abstract, animated or avant-garde
films. And, in fact, these categories often contain the most
interesting films, but they are not usually classifiable by
subject. They are also not widely shown, and that makes
them ideal for library programs. A librarian in Atlanta,
Georgia, for example, was told by a film critic that, "Atlanta movie theaters simply do not offer the more complica-

ted and sophisticated films at their theaters because the
general public is not educated in film language and has no
appreciation for the cinema as an art form. "[5]

One example of this kind of program was given at the
Boulder (Colorado) Public Library. [6] It was a Norman
McLaren festival. Sixteen films of this indefatigable ani-
mator were shown. The films were arranged chronologically
to give a feel for his developing techniques. The program
was shown on three consecutive days and drew two hundred
people--a respectable number for any library film program.
This program also, incidentally, indicated another idea for a
film showing: the works of one filmmaker or director. Or,
one could have programs devoted to an actor, such as Buster
Keaton or Charlie Chaplin (who was his own director--and
producer and scriptwriter). For filmmakers, one could
show the work of such greats as Robert Flaherty, modern
documentary filmmakers like Julien Bryan, avant-garde
filmmakers like Stan Brakhage, or young filmmakers like
Scott Morris.

Films Popular with Teenagers

There are several kinds of films that teenagers like.
"Sports above all," says one librarian who works with teenagers. And what they like most are those films that show
action; films that are borrowed from the professional basket-
fall, baseball, football and hockey leagues and teams, and
those that show those teams in actual games; and films of
action from other sources, such as Sports Action Profiles;
Calvin Murphy (Paramount Communications), The Professionals:
Basketball (Warner Brothers/Seven Arts), that show Wilt Cham-
berlain and Jerry West in action, Rosey Greer (Churchill): a biographical film about the former football star that contains
actual footage of him in action on the playing field would
also go over well with teenagers. Films that teach one how
to play a game are not, says this librarian, as popular as
the action films, although teenagers do attend them. A film
of this kind, such as Willis Reed: Center Play (Schloat Productions), might be included on a program with an action
film.

With the growing interest, in recent years, in the
Olympics, there has been increased interest in films on
this subject--especially on gymnastics. There are some
fine films in this area. Games of the XXIst Olympiad

(Macmillan) documents key events and personalities of the contenders. Nellie Kim (Macmillan) covers the training and personality of that Russian gymnast.

Aikido, judo and karate are subjects that have become very popular in recent years and one might have a program including Aikido (Japan Publications Trading Co.), a demonstration of the techniques of that sport, and San Nukas (Black Horizon Films), a film that shows students learning judo and karate, and the instructor of a school in Harlem discussing the importance to black people of learning these sports as a means of developing pride, dignity and self-discipline. Here again, one can include the unusual or avant-garde film with the more popular, to develop an appreciation of films. If Tokyo Olympiad (Jan-Or) were being shown, the short, beautiful diving sequence from Leni Riefenstahl's poetic documentary of the 1936 Olympic Games could be slipped in.

Science fiction and horror films are attended by teenagers in large numbers. Many of these are feature films and must, usually, be rented. But there are shorter, often humorous, films, many made by young filmmakers, that teenagers like. Invasion of the Teacher Creatures shows ghoulish teachers rampaging through a school. Curse of the House of Horrors is about the investigation of a creepy old house which results in a series of murders, and it is a spoof on old horror movies. And Flash is about a boy from another planet who saves the earth from an invader from outer space. All three films are made by teenagers and distributed by Young Filmmakers Foundation (for purchase only).

Also available are clips of many of the famous horror movies. A librarian in the tiny town of Joice, Iowa, used these to put on film programs for the horror film addicts of that community. 7 She found that the younger teenagers were engrossed in horror comics, movies and models of the characters. So she decided to try some programs that would show the history of the horror film and would encourage discussion of the techniques used in making those films. She collected books on filmmaking and some of the classic horror stories for the teenagers to borrow. Some of the films were The Mummy, The Mummy's Tomb, The Bride of Frankenstein, Dracula, Dr. Jekyll and Mr. Hyde, Tarantula, My Son the Vampire and The Curse of Frankenstein. The audiences entered fully into the spirit of the programs; they played games and did pantomimes (sometimes on their own) related to the films, and they discussed the films.

Films on crafts, such as Macrame (ACI), and films
about their special interests, such as oceanography and archeology, will draw some teenagers. Films about their
problems are also of interest. About Sex (Texture Films)
is such a film; it is also a good example of a film that
should be previewed, because of the language used by the
teenagers and because of one explicit scene; one could then
be ready for any reactions to the film. Venereal Disease:
Why Do We Still Have It? (Perennial Education, Inc.) and
Phoebe (CRM/McGraw-Hill), about the problems of a pregnant
teenager, are other films in this category. Films of this
kind are best used with a guest expert, to clear up any
questions the films may provoke and to lead further discussion of the subjects.

One librarian had an especially interesting experience
with teenagers in a New York State reformatory.[8] This
reformatory held many black and Puerto Rican teenagers,
aged 14 to 17. Their usual film fare, in the reformatory,
had been the sappy, harmless television-type movies, which
finally caused a near-riot. The librarian, finally, was able
to bring in other kinds of films, and made the immediate
discovery that what they liked were the best and most sophisticated films. Among those they particularly liked were
Un Chien Andalou, Potemkin, Two Men and a Wardrobe,
Neighbors, The Hand, The General, The Gold Rush and
Nanook of the North. They found none of the drug films
good, except a couple made by teenagers. If nothing else,
this shows the folly of generalization, and the folly of under-
estimating anybody.

Not a few teenagers are interested in the art of filmmaking. One could have programs of films like The Sound-
men (Universal Education and Visual Arts), The Stuntman
(Pyramid), and Special Effects (Pyramid) which show how the
professionals do those things, and include films made by
other teenagers to show them what their peers have accomplished.

Teenagers and children, as well as most adults, like
the films of the old-time comedians. The people in rural
Iowa mentioned earlier, the black and Puerto Rican teenagers
in the reformatory, and middle-class suburbanites all like
the films of such favorites as Buster Keaton, Charlie Chaplin, Laurel and Hardy and W. C. Fields. Many of these
films are short and are available to libraries at reasonable
prices, both to buy and to rent. If a sure-fire program is
wanted to bring the crowds into the library, this is it.

Aside from the subjects of the films, there are several ways to have a film showing. One could have a single showing for a special purpose, such as celebrating a holiday or an occasion, or because a special film is available, or because the filmmaker or other person is available. One library, for example, every year during the Christmas season, shows The Nutcracker (Macmillan Films). This is a 60-minute film of Tchaikovsky's ballet featuring famous dancers from around the world, and it makes a fine holiday program, drawing a family audience. Libraries often present a series of film showings. These can all be on one general subject such as the arts, or each showing can be devoted to a different subject. A series can be designed to appeal to a particular group such as mothers of pre-school children, businessmen, teenagers, the elderly or others. They could be seasonal programs designed to take advantage of good weather or leisure time. One might have a spring series or a summer series, or a Saturday afternoon series.

Film showings can also be unplanned or unstructured, to take advantage of special situations. One library showed films, during the summer, to any group that appeared in the library and asked for them. Another library had continuous film showings during a school strike.

Guest Experts

Having an expert present to comment on the films and to answer questions is another variation from the straight showing. This can either be an expert on filmmaking, or a subject expert, depending on the program. The authors found a film editor who was persuaded to talk about the work of an editor at a showing of some avant-garde films, and who also, incidentally, answered the questions of some teenagers about opportunities in the film industry. At another program, a film historian showed some of the milestones of film history and commented on their significance. Used in this series were The Great Train Robbery (Film Classic Exchange), one of the first films to tell a story; Abel Gance, Yesterday and Tomorrow (CRM/McGraw-Hill), about the innovative French director; and The Great Director (Killiam Shows, Inc.), about the work of D. W. Griffith. In the Oak Park (Illinois) Public Library, an independent filmmaker showed some of his films, and talked about the use of the camera. He then moved among the audience and made a film of them, which they returned a week later to see. [9]

Showcase for the Young and Unknown

      As with other media, libraries have an admirable op-
portunity to show the work of young or unknown filmmakers.
This can be in the form of a festival or contest, or it can
be a series of straight film showings. The authors have
several times presented programs of films made by local
college students, always to overflow crowds. The Randallstown (Md.) Public Library has, for several years, been presenting programs of films made by teenagers, and it has become a regular feature of their programming. A file of
about forty young filmmakers has been built up, through the
years. [10]

Contests

      The Los Angeles Public Library has had several suc-
cessful contests for teenage filmmakers, and they have a
number of suggestions for those who wish to try one. [11] They
had some difficulty in finding films at first. They contacted
film organizations, recreation centers, high schools (teachers
and students), and they asked around among the teenagers
they saw; gradually they built a list of films and contacts.
Once one has the contacts succeeding festivals become easier.
They needed judges and they found the colleges a good source.
Entry blanks were found to be useful. They provide material for publicity, and they can give such information as the
age and experience of the filmmaker if one wants to divide
the entries into categories. In Los Angeles, they showed
the films in the order of the ages of the participants. This
was found to be helpful when there were many participants.

      Equipment presented some problems. They had
several projectors lined up so they could show the films one
after another. This was also useful since the projectors
were getting long hard use, and several broke down during
the festival. Most beginning filmmakers don't use sound
films and to supply sound, use records, cassettes, and reel-
to-reel tape of different sizes and speeds. It was therefore
desirable to ask the entrants to bring their own sound equipment. It was felt that the library should supply, at least,
a three-speed record player. Shears and splicing tape (8mm,
super-8, and 16mm) were needed, as was an adapter so that
super-8 film could be threaded on an 8mm projector. Since
many of the teenagers were knowledgeable about films, they
could be used as projectionists. Teenagers also helped with

the publicity, handing out flyers and writing articles for
school newspapers. They found that the room needed to be
especially dark, since some of the films were under-exposed
or were less sharp than professional films.

Prizes added greatly to the interest. The prizes
were contributed by a music store, a book store, a camera
shop and a gift shop; they were records, paperbacks, reels
of film and posters of horror movies. There was no con-
sensus about the value of the prizes and it was thought best
to display them all and let the winners choose the prize they
wanted in the order that they won. One festival was attended
by two hundred people. Thirty-eight films were collected
but only 21 could be shown because of projector breakdowns.
Twenty-one films were shown at another festival, and although it lasted four hours, seventy people stayed to the
end. Clearly both were successes.

The Providence Public Library is also sponsoring a
film competition.[12] This contest was open to filmmakers of
all ages and levels of experience and the films were to focus
on community problems and their solutions. Prizes were to
be awarded in the following categories: eighth grade and
under, ninth through twelfth grades, college, hobbyist and professional. The winning entries would then be shown to the public.

The Room

For film showings, the subject of space deserved some
extra discussion. This is so because of the equipment involved.
Factors that must be considered are the size and type of the
screen, the size of the film, and the focal length of the lens.
(The type and wattage of the projection lamp are not a major consideration any longer with the new lamp designs and switches
that can be set to Lo/Med/Hi.) These things are considered in
relation to the size and shape of the room, and the size of the
audience.

There are two main problems: where to place the
audience in relation to the screen; and where to place the
projector in relation to the screen. One film librarian suggests that experimentation is the best way. Simply move a
chair around to determine how close to the screen, how far
back from the screen, and how far to the sides the audience should sit. The same can be done for projection distance. Move the projector or screen back and forth to
determine the best distances. But there are some guide-

lines. A rule-of-thumb is that the minimum viewing distance is twice the height of the picture, and the maximum
viewing distance is eight times its height. The size of the
audience determines the width of the picture. And the width
of the picture is determined by its distance from the projector, and the focal length of the lens. The tables shown
on pages 48-53 are guides. But remember they are only
guides. College and high school students have crammed
themselves into every available space at some film showings
--breaking all the rules of audience seating but enjoying the
films. And with projection distances, they may be factors,
such as light leaking into the room, that make the rules
invalid. "In the final analysis," says the film librarian we
consulted, "you have to depend on your eyes." And, of
course, libraries--not commonly having a lot of money--may
not be able to buy all the lenses, projection lamps, screens
and projectors necessary for excellent viewing in every situation. In some cases, it may be better to show the films
under less than ideal conditions than not show them. If the
words con't be heard or the picture is too dark, naturally you
won't show the film. But for some kinds of films and some
audiences, perfect viewing conditions are secondary.

Screens

If a library is lucky enough to have a choice of
screens, a screen can be chosen to fit the shape of the
room, thus enhancing the viewing and in some cases allowing a larger audience to view the film. One film periodical
gives the following advice:

> If you have a wide viewing area the matte
> screen is probably the best for bright projection
> because it reflects light evenly in all directions
> providing an adequate image when viewed from an
> oblique angle.
> If you have a narrower room you can use a
> lenticular screen, which is made up of a series of
> tiny cylindrical lenses that are embossed on the
> screen itself. It is quite bright over a fairly
> broad angle of viewing.
> If the audience sits directly in front of the
> screen, a beaded screen reflects light in a nar-
> rower angle, about 30 degrees. For a very nar-
> row room, the best screen to use is the silver
> screen, coated with metallic aluminum, for it has

(cont'd on p. 54)

SEATING GUIDE

THEATER-STYLE SEATING FOR DIFFERENT ROOM SIZES

(For conference-style seating, use one-half seating capacity shown)

Room Ratio 1:1				Room Ratio 4:3				Room Ratio 3:2				Room Ratio 2:1				Room Ratio 3:1			
Room Size— ft L x W	Viewing Angle* 50°	60°	90°	Room Size— ft L x W	Viewing Angle* 50°	60°	90°	Room Size— ft L x W	Viewing Angle* 50°	60°	90°	Room Size— ft L x W	Viewing Angle* 50°	60°	90°	Room Size— ft L x W	Viewing Angle* 50°	60°	90°
	Seating Capacity				Seating Capacity				Seating Capacity				Seating Capacity				Seating Capacity		
16x16	10	11	13	16x12	8	8	8	16x11	6	6	6	16x8	—	—	—	16x5	—	—	—
20x20	18	21	25	20x15	15	16	17	20x13	13	13	13	20x10	7	7	7	20x7	—	—	—
24x24	28	33	41	24x18	24	26	28	24x16	22	23	23	24x12	14	14	14	24x8	5	5	5
28x28	41	48	60	28x21	36	39	43	28x19	33	34	36	28x14	22	23	23	28x9	9	9	9
32x32	56	66	83	32x24	50	55	60	32x21	46	48	51	32x16	33	33	33	32x11	16	16	16
36x36	73	87	109	36x27	66	73	80	36x24	61	65	69	36x18	45	46	46	36x12	23	23	23
40x40	93	111	139	40x30	85	93	104	40x27	78	84	90	40x20	59	60	61	40x13	32	32	32
44x44	115	137	173	44x33	106	116	130	44x29	98	105	113	44x22	74	77	77	44x15	42	42	42
48x48	139	167	210	48x36	129	141	159	48x32	119	128	139	48x24	92	95	96	48x16	53	53	53
52x52	166	199	252	52x39	154	169	191	52x35	143	154	167	52x26	111	115	117	52x17	66	66	66
56x56	195	234	296	56x42	181	200	226	56x37	169	182	198	56x28	132	137	139	56x19	80	80	80
60x60	226	272	345	60x45	211	233	264	60x40	197	212	232	60x30	155	161	164	60x20	96	96	96
64x64	259	313	397	64x48	243	269	305	64x43	227	245	268	64x32	180	187	191	64x21	112	112	112
68x68	295	356	453	68x51	277	307	348	68x45	259	280	307	68x34	206	214	219	68x23	131	131	131
72x72	334	402	512	72x54	313	347	395	72x48	293	318	349	72x36	234	244	250	72x24	150	150	150
76x76	374	452	576	76x57	352	390	445	76x51	330	357	393	76x38	264	275	283	76x25	171	171	171
80x80	417	504	642	80x60	393	436	497	80x53	368	399	440	80x40	296	309	317	80x27	193	193	193
84x84	462	558	713	84x63	436	484	552	84x56	409	444	489	84x42	330	344	354	84x28	216	216	216

*The 90-degree figures should be used only with screens capable of producing good brightness characteristics in that range, and only when the maximum seating capacity is necessary. This chart and the explanation on the facing page are from Kodak Publication No. S-16, copyright © 1979 by Eastman Kodak Company, and are reproduced with their permission.

The diagram below illustrates the room arrangement used to calculate the seating capacities shown in the seating guide. The screen is positioned to cover the maximum seating area for the room.

The capacity figures shown in the table are based on the use of two side aisles (each 3-feet wide), and a rear aisle (4-feet deep). Six square feet of space is allowed per person, with provision for a 42-inch aisle, front to back, after every fourteenth seat.

For maximum legibility, seat the members of the audience within the specified angles for the screen material you choose; do not seat them closer to the screen than two times (2 H), nor farther than eight times (8 H) the height of the projected image unless the quality or size of the visuals dictates otherwise. You can determine minimum image height for legibility by dividing the distance from the screen to the rear of the back row of seats by eight. For visual effect, you may want to project an image somewhat larger than legibility standards specify. To avoid obstruction of the screen by the seated audience and establish a minimum ceiling height, add 4 feet to the minimum image height. In addition, you may need to add extra height at the top to allow for the positioning of the screen to clear overhead obstructions.

Determining the maximum viewing area depends on the screen material you use. The *KODAK EKTALITE* Projection Screen has excellent brightness characteristics within a viewing area of 60 degrees. Most matte and a few lenticular front-projection screen materials can provide good brightness levels for viewing areas up to 90 degrees wide. Beaded front-screen projection materials and the most commonly used rear-projection screen materials can give good brightness in a viewing area of up to 50 degrees. Examples follow:

1. **Given:**
   a. Screen material—matte (60-degree viewing area).
   b. Room size—28 x 21 feet.
   Find:
   a. Seating capacity for theater-style and conference-style seating.
   b. Minimum image height.
   c. Minimum ceiling height.

The room has a 4:3 ratio. Using a 60-degree viewing area, you find in the table that the theater-style capacity is 39. Conference-style capacity, half that of theater-style, is 19. Allowing 4 feet for the rear aisle, the distance to the rear of the last row of seats is 24 feet. Dividing this distance by eight gives you a minimum image height of 3 feet. Adding 4 feet to the image height gives you a minimum ceiling height of 7 feet.

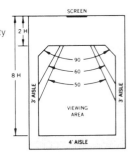

2. **Given:**
   a. You plan to build a meeting room with theater-style seating for 90 people.
   b. Screen material—beaded.
   Find:
   Suitable room dimension.

Fifty degrees is the recommended maximum viewing angle for beaded screens. In the table, under the 50-degree columns, you find that a 40 x 40-foot room will accommodate 93 seats, a 48 x 24-foot room will seat 92, and a 60 x 20-foot room—96. Your ultimate choice will depend on such factors as the dimensions of available rooms or space, the ceiling height required, etc.

Seating Arrangements

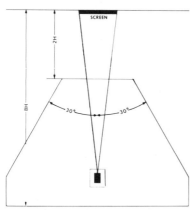

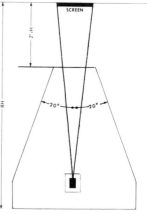

Matte, Lenticular, or KODAK EKTALITE Projection Screen, Model 3*

The diagram directly above shows the best viewing area for matte, lenticular, and KODAK EKTALITE Screens.

The seats nearest the screen should not be closer than twice the height of the picture (2H); the rear seats should not be farther than 8 times the height of the picture (8H).

Beaded Screen*

The diagram above shows the best viewing area for beaded screens.

The seats nearest the screen should not be closer than 2½ times the height of the picture (2½H); the rear seats should not be farther than 8 times the height of the picture (8H).

---

*For additional information about projection screens, refer to Kodak Pamphlet No. S-18, *Reflection Characteristics of Front-Projection Screen Materials.*

These diagrams and the chart with text on the facing page are from "Kodak Pageant 250E Sound Projector" and are reproduced with the permission of the Eastman Kodak Company.

Screen • Lamp • Lens Combinations

Proper selection of screen, lamp, and lens for your particular setup is important. The screen image should be of adequate size and brilliance for comfortable viewing. With the wide variety of lenses available for your PAGEANT Projector, you can tailor your equipment to meet this requirement.

The chart below shows the relation between projection distances and screen sizes for each of the currently available lenses. It is best to use a lens that provides a screen image of a height that is not less than one-eighth of the distance from the screen to the back row of seats. If the image is smaller than this, the viewers in the back rows will not be able to see the fine detail in the pictures.

Make sure that the screen image is neither too bright nor too dark. If it is too bright, flicker may become objectionable; if too dark, detail will be lost in the shadow areas of the pictures.

Shown in the table below are the maximum image widths or heights for adequate illumination on matte screens and on lenticular or beaded screens with lamp set on HI. These maximum widths or heights are for good projection conditions in a darkened room; they will have to be somewhat less if there is much stray light in the room.

Projection Lamp Setting	Maximum Image Width or Height in Inches (Meters) in a Darkened Room*			
	Matte Screen		Lenticular or Beaded Screen	
	W	H	W	H
LO	70 (1.8)	53 (1.3)	100 (2.5)	75 (1.9)
MED	80 (2.0)	60 (1.5)	120 (3.0)	90 (2.3)
HI	90 (2.3)	68 (1.7)	130 (3.3)	98 (2.5)

°Using 2-inch lens alone or combined with CINE-KODAK Bifocal Converter.

Three-Position Lamp-Brightness Control Switch: You can select one of the three available lamp brightness settings: LO, MED, or HI. Use a screwdriver or similar tool to rotate the lamp control switch to the desired position.

Be sure to turn off the lamp and motor during this procedure. The switch is accessible when the lamp is removed. See the next section for a lamp removal procedure.

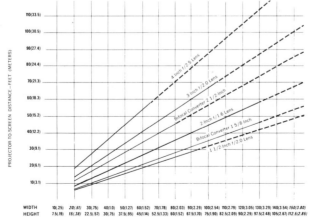

Solid lines equal or exceed recommended brightness (with HI lamp setting).
SCREEN IMAGE—INCHES (METERS)

Projection Distance Tables for KODAK Motion Picture Projectors

(Projection distances are approximate and are measured from projector gate to screen.)

KODAK Pageant Projectors (16 mm) — Lens Focal Length (in inches); Projection Distances (in feet)

KODAK Super 8 Projectors — Lens Focal Length (in millimeters); Projection Distances (in feet). (Columns 20–32 are the Zoom range.)

½	1	1½	1⅝	2	2½	3	4	Screen-Image Dimensions (inches)	15	17½	20	22	25	28	32
1½	2¾	4¼	4½	5½	7	8½	11	9 x 12	3	3½	4	4½	5	5½	6½
1¾	3¾	5½	6	7½	9¼	11	15	12 x 16	4	4½	5¼	5½	6½	7½	8½
2¼	4½	6¾	7½	9	11	14	18	15 x 20	5	5¾	6½	7¼	8¼	9¼	10½
3½	6¾	10	11	14	17	20	27	22½ x 30	7½	8½	9¾	11	12	14	16
4½	9	13	15	18	22	27	36	30 x 40	9¾	11	13	14	16	18	21
5½	11	17	18	22	28	33	45	37½ x 50	12	14	16	18	20	23	26
6¾	13	20	22	27	33	40	53	45 x 60	15	17	20	21	24	27	31
8	16	24	26	32	40	48	64	54 x 72	18	20	23	26	29	33	37
11	21	32	35	42	53	64	85	72 x 96	23	27	31	34	39	44	50
13	27	40	43	53	66	79	106	96 x 120	29	34	39	43	49	54	62
16	32	48	52	64	79	95	127	108 x 144	35	41	47	51	58	65	75

Projection Distance Tables for KODAK EKTAGRAPHIC and CAROUSEL Slide Projectors
(Projection distances are approximate and are measured from projector gate to screen.)

1.4	Lens Focal Length (in inches)							4 to 6 (Zoom)	Screen-Image Dimensions (in inches)			
	2	3	4	5	7	9	11		135–35mm	126	Super-Slide	Single-Frame Filmstrip
	Projection Distances (in feet)											
2	3	4	$5\frac{1}{2}$	7	10	$12\frac{1}{2}$	$15\frac{1}{2}$	$5\frac{1}{2}$ to $8\frac{1}{2}$	$13\frac{1}{2}$ x 20	$15\frac{1}{2}$ sq	22 sq	10 x $13\frac{1}{2}$
3	4	6	8	10	14	18	$22\frac{1}{2}$	8 to 12	20 x 30	23 sq	$33\frac{1}{2}$ sq	15 x 20
$3\frac{1}{2}$	$5\frac{1}{2}$	8	$10\frac{1}{2}$	13	$18\frac{1}{2}$	24	29	$10\frac{1}{2}$ to 16	27 x 40	31 sq	$44\frac{1}{2}$ sq	20 x 27
$4\frac{1}{2}$	$6\frac{1}{2}$	10	13	$16\frac{1}{2}$	23	$29\frac{1}{2}$	36	13 to $19\frac{1}{2}$	$33\frac{1}{2}$ x 50	39 sq	$55\frac{1}{2}$ sq	26 x $33\frac{1}{2}$
$5\frac{1}{2}$	8	$11\frac{1}{2}$	$15\frac{1}{2}$	$19\frac{1}{2}$	27	35	$42\frac{1}{2}$	$15\frac{1}{2}$ to $23\frac{1}{2}$	40 x 60	45 sq	60 sq	30 x 40
$6\frac{1}{2}$	9	$14\frac{1}{2}$	18	23	$32\frac{1}{2}$	$41\frac{1}{2}$	51	$18\frac{1}{2}$ to $27\frac{1}{2}$	48 x 72	56 sq	80 sq	36 x 48
$8\frac{1}{2}$	12	$18\frac{1}{2}$	$24\frac{1}{2}$	$30\frac{1}{2}$	$42\frac{1}{2}$	55	67	$24\frac{1}{2}$ to $36\frac{1}{2}$	64 x 96	75 sq	87 sq	48 x 64
$10\frac{1}{2}$	15	23	$30\frac{1}{2}$	38	53	69	84	$30\frac{1}{2}$ to $45\frac{1}{2}$	80 x 120	93 sq	132 sq	60 x 81
$12\frac{1}{2}$	18	27	$36\frac{1}{2}$	$45\frac{1}{2}$	64	82	100	$36\frac{1}{2}$ to 55	96 x 144	112 sq	160 sq	72 x 96

This table and the one on the preceding page are from Kodak Publication No. S-49 and are reproduced with the permission of the Eastman Kodak Company.

a very narrow brightness reflection angle. It is also good for stereo projection with polarizing filters for its narrow angle of view will not result in double images.

If you cannot darken the room properly for ideal projection conditions, there is the Kodak Ektalight Screen which gives good brightness for narrow angle viewing. [13]

The safest and best screen is a wall hung lenticular roll-up.

Videotape Showings

A program of videotape showings is clearly similar to a film showing. There are, however, a number of differences, some not immediately apparent. Where film is shown in a darkened area and with a large screen, videotape is usually seen on a small screen in a lighted room. The size of the television screen makes for intimate viewing, and the video artist must work with that in mind, using material requiring narrower scope and smaller actions. This is, doubtless, one of the reasons many movies don't work well on television. The lighted room, as opposed to the darkened film screening room, probably helps to create a different experience, too. Watching a television screen, one is much more part of a group, whereas at a film showing (when the lights are out), one is alone--or at best with one other person. The resolution of the images is also much finer on film than on a television screen, again indicating a different response from the video artist. All of these differences mean that translation from one medium to another isn't as successful as a work done originally for a particular medium. As Robert Frost has pointed out, poetry is what is lost in translation. That doesn't mean that a translated poem--or film--doesn't have value. But, if one is showing videotapes, the main usefulness would seem to be in showing works created for that medium.

A lot of events might, of course, have been better shot on film, but only are available on videotape. This usually applies to local events, such as meetings, library programs, a tape about a neighborhood and so forth. Whether these events would be better on film or on videotape is a matter of judgment, but the question is often immaterial, since a videotape is so much less expensive and easier to make. In any case, one should be aware of the differences in the two media. A program can then be more intelligently chosen.

The small size of the television screen can create a more mundane problem. Some of the audience simply might not be able to see, or to see well. So some forethought will be necessary--as always. One nineteen-inch monitor is adequate for about 60 people, in six rows. Two or more monitors, then, might be required as the audience size is increased. Clearly, one has to judge the potential size of the audience and be prepared. There are large television screens that are capable of handling audiences of 300 or perhaps more. No doubt libraries should look into such screens if they are going into video showings in a big way, but whether or not large screens change the nature of the medium is open to question.

Another problem with video showings might be finding enough tapes of high quality. Many tapes, for example, are films transferred to videotape, and aside from the fact that they are different media--the image is likely to be washed out. There are, however, a number of people working in video, and libraries can have some fine programs. Nam June Paik, Tomiyo Sasaki, Barbara Buckner, William Wegman, Gary Hill, Earnest Gusella, Christa Maiwald, and Kit Fitzgerald and John Sanborn are some names that come to mind. Sometimes one can get a group of videotapes to show which is part of a circuit. The Ithaca (N.Y.) Video Festival, for example, tours the country annually. Since these tapes have been considered the best of the entries, one gets good quality programs. It is always best, however, if you can make your own selection.

Videotapes can be purchased or rented. Possibly their producers can be persuaded to give library showings for nothing; this can often be done if the video artist is local, or if he is trying to establish himself. While no one wants to take food from the mouths of the artist's children, libraries have less money than they ever did (they never had much) and such savings may be essential. You might be doing the artist a favor by giving him a showcase.

If you want to buy tapes, there are a number of distributors, most of whom will also rent. However, you may have to buy directly from the maker of the tape. (Some sample distributors are listed in Appendix E.) The subjects of the tapes (if tapes transferred from films are included) are practically endless. Public Television Library, for example, sells and rents many of the tapes that have been shown on PBS stations, and the subjects covered by other producers are also many. A sampling taken from the Video

Catalogue of The New York Public Library indicates the
range. There are tapes on election night coverage, a New
York City ethnic festival, the last run of a rural train, the
troubles in Northern Ireland, rape, battered wives, parole,
street musicians, the techniques of some potters, an albino
gorilla in a zoo, and former mental patients protesting the
loss of civil liberties in institutions--and this doesn't include
the various kinds of video art.

Since showings can be held in lighted areas, they may
well be in parts of the library devoted primarily to other
activities, such as a browsing room, a record and/or film
room, a teenage room, and so forth. Thus, it is often possible to have continuous showings--sort of a drop-in program
--where viewers come to see a particular tape, or engage
in impulse viewing. This is useful if one is renting a group
of tapes and wants to get the maximum use out of them.

There are other possibilities in addition to straight
showing. Many videotapes would obviously make good discussion material. They also can be used by lecturers on
various subjects as demonstrations, in lieu of actually having
the materials present. The maker of the videotape might
be present to discuss the tape and to discuss video techniques.
Has this been done anywhere? Have a film and video showing, with the filmmaker and the producer of the videotape
present. One might have an interesting and stimulating discussion about the differences and similarities in the two
media.

Film Showings (Adults and Teenagers): A Summary and
Checklist of Preparations

KINDS
    Straight showing
    Showing with commentary--by a director, editor, et al.
      or by a subject expert
    Contest or festival--of locally made films
    Showing as part of a larger celebration--e. g. , an open
      house or a group of activities celebrating the culture
      of a country

MATERIALS
    Films--8mm, super 8mm, or 16mm
    Books, pamphlets, periodicals, recordings on the sub-
      ject, or on film making--for display, for use in in-

troduction or by commentator, or to be borrowed by
audience

EQUIPMENT
Projector(s)--appropriate to film size (8mm projector
has adapter for super 8 film); an extra projector is
always desirable
Reels--a set of all sizes for taking up film
Extension cord
Screen-get the library to install a built-in screen, if
possible; but everything from window shades to poster
board has been used; weigh the alternatives of show-
ing or not
Projection lamp--at least one extra
Chairs--some librarians have found that teenagers like
to sit on the floor, and you can get more in that way
Lectern--for speaker or commentator
Flashlight--it's dark in there
Record player--one might wish to play appropriate music
before program, during intermissions, or as part of
program

STAFF
Projectionist--the more experienced the better, and have
a backup
Librarian--to introduce the program and films, and to
relate films and program to the library's other
services
Clerk(s)--to charge out materials being borrowed; could
be same as projectionist
Ushers, ticket takers--as needed (the projectionist should
have no other duties while films are running)

AUDIENCE
Age--any; some programs are for one age group only,
some for combinations, some for all ages
Size--from twenty to capacity, ordinarily; for some purposes, might show to smaller groups; audience size
also depends on size of film (8mm, 16mm), size of
screen and other factors

SESSIONS
Number--one, a short or long series, or a regular part
of library's programming continuing each year
Spacing--one or two weeks apart, once a month, several
in a year (if major programs), many in a short space

of time (a day or a week) for special purposes, such
as open house, festival, etc.

Length--one to two hours, unless film or reason is unusual

SPACE

Must be able to be made dark, have electrical outlets
within reach of extension cord, and away from public
use area so readers won't be disturbed; a minimum
of outside noises is desirable, but films have been
shown under all conditions; again, the alternatives
should be weighed

SUBJECTS (Examples; see Appendix C for sample film
programs)

The film as an art form--animation, abstract, avant
garde, documentaries, silents, films without narration, film history, films of a director, films of an
actor, horror, Westerns, science fiction, works of
local filmmakers

The arts--architecture, painting, printmaking, sculpture,
crafts, dance (ballet, folk, modern), music (popular,
folk, black, classical), mime, theatre, poets, novelists, photography

Travel--cities, countries, continents, islands, ancient
places, groups of people

Science--archeology, astronomy, mathematics, medicine,
biology

Natural history--birds, mammals, ocean life, insects,
life of a region (Africa, Australia, the Arctic)

Sports--archery, automobile racing, fishing, judo,
karate, track and field, gymnastics, baseball, basketball, boxing, football, hockey, golf, tennis, the
Olympics

Social problems--abortion, sex, venereal disease, homo-
sexuality, destruction of the environment, population,
poverty and unemployment, minority groups, city
problems, consumer education, housing, the handicapped, mental health, the elderly, prisons, protest,
crime, war, disease, work (migrants, assembly line),
alternative energy

Other--biography, religion, railroads, cowboys, humor
and satire, family life (in various parts of the world),
history, youth, films from books

SOURCES (of films; see Appendix E for names and addresses
of sources)
  Libraries (state and regional), sports leagues and teams,
    agencies of foreign countries (consulates, airlines,
    information bureaus), colleges and universities, mu-
    seums, scientific associations, historical associations,
    labor unions, U.S. government, national health or-
    ganizations, businesses (particularly large corpora-
    tions), religious groups, organizations that are pro-
    moting a cause (environmental groups, etc.), con-
    sumer agencies and organizations, youth organizations
    (Boy Scouts, Girl Scouts), individual collectors, inde-
    pendent filmmakers
  How to find the sources--visit film libraries, attend
    film festivals, get on mailing lists of distributors,
    watch newspapers for reports of films available to
    groups, look at film magazines, explore the telephone
    directory's Yellow Pages for some of the organiza-
    tions listed above, talk to library users, contact
    youth centers, contact teachers of film or photography
    in schools

PLANNING AND PRODUCING
  Select target audience (general public or special group)
  Decide where to show films (in library or elsewhere in
    community)
  Be sure space can be darkened, has electrical outlets,
    outside noise won't spoil films, won't disturb library
    users
  Check projector, and be sure you have necessary equip-
    ment (see above)
  Find a projectionist, and learn to run projector yourself
  Make preliminary list of possible subjects for showing
  Survey potential sources of films
  Preview films, if at all possible
  Select dates and times for showings (if outdoors, it must
    be dark enough and not too cold); consider the occu-
    pations of potential audience, other community activi-
    ties
  Plan introduction
  Plan related displays
  Checkup--in plenty of time before showing (several hours
    to several days), be sure right films have arrived,
    projectionist is available, equipment is working, chairs
    and other furniture in place, and visiting speaker has
    been reminded

PUBLICITY

Use flyers and posters (with film annotations, color, running time), announcements in newspapers, on radio and television, in community calendars

Distribute to schools and colleges, other libraries, film societies, groups interested in subjects of films (ethnic, religious, literary, artistic, scientific organizations), centers for age groups (elderly, teenagers)

Use mailing list to individuals

NOTES

1. Hoelcl, Gisela. "Projection," University Film Study Center (Box 275, Cambridge, Mass.) Newsletter, Suppl. vol 3, no. 4, p. 4.
2. If the sequential order of the film showing is not important, use the "leap-frog" method. Start with the longest film and when it is finished, use the reel it came on as the take up for the next longest film. That way you don't end up with too long a film and too small a take up reel.
3. Vaughn, Susan Beach. "8mm at the County Fair," Film Library Quarterly, Spring 1970, pp. 33-6.
4. Rear projection screens give an image bright enough for daylight viewing and get the projector out of the area where the audience will be sitting.
5. Le Clercq, Anne. "Featuring Films: A Children's Librarian's Programmatic View," Library Journal, May 15, 1972, p. 1510.
6. Heckel, James. "McLaren Film Festival," American Libraries, Dec. 1971, pp. 1195-7.
7. Vaughn, Susan. "Monster Movies," Library Journal, Oct. 15, 1971, p. 231.
8. Halleck, DeeDee. "Films in the Joint," Film Library Quarterly, Spring 1972, p. 34-5.
9. American Libraries, Oct. 1973, p. 542.
10. Library Journal, March 15, 1972, p. 1120.
11. Campbell, Patty and Jane Brooks. "The Media Novice Plans a Young Film-makers' Festival," Wilson Library Bulletin, Jan. 1973, pp. 440-5.
12. Library Journal, May 1, 1974, p. 1263.
13. Hoelcl, op. cit.; reprinted by permission of the University Film Study Center.

POETRY READINGS

Poetry may always be a minority interest. Nevertheless, a significant number of people read it and perhaps even more write it. Poetry workshops for teenagers are growing in number and becoming more and more successful. Workshops for the elderly--even those in nursing homes-- have achieved considerable success. One of the authors, who has been a librarian for thirty years, is getting more requests for poetry from library users than ever before. None of this is to say the demand is great. It isn't. And unless you can get a big name poet for a reading, such a program is not likely to be wildly popular.

But one can build an audience. Furthermore, the size of the audience is not necessarily indicative of its success. One of the authors recently conducted a poetry reading by Pedro Pietri, a Puerto Rican poet. Fifteen people, mostly teenagers, attended, but he knew it was a good program. A programmer knows when a program goes well. It went well--and this is important--because of the personality of Mr. Pietri. He mixed the reading of his own poems with talking to the young people about poetry and encouraging them to read their own. It was an entertaining afternoon, and-- without doubt--inspiring for those embryonic poets who attended.

But back to the audience. It does take some intensive work, usually, to get that audience. Selective mailing lists to groups and individuals are useful. Talking it up is even more so; mention the subject each time you are asked for poetry. Since many young people are interested in poetry, visiting the schools may help. Quotations from the poet's work on the publicity are useful. So is a picture of the poet. Try to get it into the newspaper before the event, and use it on other publicity.

As we indicated with Pedro Pietri, the selection of the poet is important, the force of his personality being a large factor in the success of that program. Some poets do not read well, even though they are highly regarded as poets. So it will be important--if at all possible--to hear him read beforehand, or at least to find out from someone who has heard him. The age, race, and ethnic background of the poet may be important factors in selection. So are the educational levels and sophistication of the potential audience. It is, therefore, helpful to not only hear the poet, but also read some of his poems and gain a feeling for his style and content.

While it is good to have published poets with established reputations come to a library reading, we can serve another function by providing space and an audience for the new and the unknown. This function seems especially important for poets who are likely to have small audiences for their work in any case. If that is the purpose, one can't be overly concerned with the quality of the poems. And sometimes good things are discovered. Who knows. Maybe you'll find the grail in your own castle.

If the poet merely reads his poetry and leaves, that may be enough. The program can be much more varied, interesting and meaningful, however, if he will also talk about his poetry and himself, or if he answers questions, or carries on a dialogue with the audience. In a library program entitled a "Poetry Jam Session," three young friends --who were published, but not established poets--read their poems, played some music and talked about themselves and their poetry.

Much poetry is difficult to grasp on first hearing it. If the poet will tell you in advance what he is going to read, it may be desirable to have copies made for distribution to the audience prior to the program. This was done when Hugh MacDiarmid read in New York City a few years ago, and even with the Scottish dialect words (a glossary was included) he was readily understood. In many cases the poems are obscure, or they have qualities that need to be both seen and heard.

There are other kinds of poetry programs, in addition to having a poet read his own works. Sometimes a poet (Dylan Thomas used to do it) will read the works of a group of poets. Or you may be able to get an actor, or someone

else who reads well, to present a reading.   There are many
possibilities, depending on your potential audience, current
interests, and who is available to read.   A program centered
around a form or style of poetry might be possible.   Love
poems, light verse, or the works of a group of poets that
are somehow linked are a few possibilities.

A group of actors in New York City who call themselves the "Sunday Brunch Company" have presented programs at libraries, and the range of their programs offers
some ideas.   "Eliot Among the Nightingales" was one of
these.   The program follows:

Counterpoint--Lines for Cuscuscaraway and Mirza Murad
    Ali Beg/ The Love Song of J. Alfred Prufrock
The Fire Sermon (from The Wasteland)
Burbank with a Baedeker: Bleistein with a Cigar
A Game of Chess (from The Wasteland)
The Letters between T. S. Eliot and Groucho Marx

Intermission

Old Possum's Book of Practical Cats (five selections were
    read)

Intermission

Sweeney Agonistes--Fragments of an Aristophanic Melo-
    drama
Sweeney Erect
Sweeney Among the Nightingales
Sweeney Agonistes--Fragment of a Prologue

To paraphrase Eliot's own words, how pleasant it
must have been to meet Mr. Eliot under such circumstances.
Another program on a single poet presented the songs of
Sappho.   A variation which took cognizance of a current interest was presented as the works of "Three Women."   Sylvia
Plath, Dorothy Parker and Edna St. Vincent Millay were the
writers chosen.   Gertrude Stein and E. E. Cummings, two
poets with obvious affinities, were chosen for another program entitled "Playing with Words."   Holidays are frequently
used as pegs on which to hang programs, and in this case
it was the Christmas season.   The Company brought together
writers as diverse as Dylan Thomas, Truman Capote, S. J.
Perelman, A. A. Milne, Jimmy Cannon, T. S. Eliot, William Carlos Williams, Shakespeare, Boris Pasternak, and
the author of Isaiah.   The title was "When Icicles Hang."

"Contemporary Poetry" was the title given to a program at the Springfield (Mass.) City Library, and a wide range of poets were read and discussed. Among the poets were Black Elk, Gwendolyn Brooks, Dudley Randall, Frank O'Hara, James Tate, Jim Morrison, Nicanor Parra, Allen Ginsberg, Jack Kerouac, and Gregory Corso.

The poetry of a country or a culture can make a fine program. A great program of Chilean poetry could be gathered together, for example. Consider that Gabriela Mistral, Pablo Neruda and Nicanor Parra were, or are, Chilean. Even "Anonymous" has been resident in that country, and produced fine work there! Scotland has a rich poetic tradition and much of it is practically unknown in this country. Poets from the age of Dunbar and Henryson to the present one of MacDiarmid and McCaig might be successfully presented. One of the authors produced two programs of ethnic poetry which included poets from Italian, Greek, Puerto Rican, Polish and Russian backgrounds reading and talking about their works.

A library in Flushing, New York has had some very successful ethnic poetry programs. Each session is devoted to the poetry of one or more groups. The reader for that session starts out by giving some information about the poet --biographical details, poetic style and the themes he uses. Then a poem is read in English, followed by a reading in the original language. Eleven or twelve poems are the normal number for a program and it may last from forty-five minutes to an hour. The readers are local residents--poets, students, housewives, librarians--who know the language in question. Sometimes there is background music on a guitar. Readers frequently wear a costume of the country, and in some cases the food of that country is served. The walls are hung with works of art that are appropriate. The small costs have been met by fine money and by donations of material by librarians. Programs were attended by both teenagers and adults. A sample list of programs follows:

Hebrew and Yiddish Poetry--read by the wife of a local poet.
Seven Centuries of Italian Poetry--read by an Italian-American poet residing in the neighborhood.
World Poetry Reading--Pakistani poems read by a 12 year old student; Spanish and Italian poems read by a high school Spanish teacher
Black Poetry Reading--works of Nikki Giovanni, Imamu

Amiri Baraka, Don L. Lee, Langston Hughes, Countee
Cullen, Claude McKay, Linda and Dennis Robinson
read by a library trainee.
Chinese Poetry Reading--read by a librarian
Federico García Lorca, El Poeta en Nueva York--read
by a community resident and college Spanish major
who had visited South America.

The lesson to be learned here is that many libraries could
present similar programs, even though they might not have
much in the way of resources.

Poetry workshops for people of all ages have--as we
said earlier--been successful as library programs. The
results are frequently put together by the library in magazine
formats of varying quality--depending on how much is available to spend. Workshops also frequently lead to programs
of readings, and although these readings may be largely
attended by relatives and friends of the participants, they
serve a good purpose in providing a chance for the poets to
be heard, and to hear themselves.

Workshops are usually run by poets, or by teachers.
The poets need not be established themselves. In fact, some
of the most successful workshops have been run by poets
whose main strengths lay in eliciting poetry from others.
The leaders often do not so much criticize as encourage,
possibly suggesting themes or points of departure. Of course,
some participants may want a lot of criticism. People who
write poems often do not know how to go about submitting
their work for publication and such information might use-
fully be part of a workshop too.

One variation was a bilingual workshop. Poems were
written in English and in Spanish, and sometimes in both.
Such workshops could be presented in any number of languages
(if the appropriate leader were available) and they could be
very interesting and instructive for all concerned.

DRAMA

Libraries have had a long connection with the theatre,
dating at least from the nineteen thirties and the establishment of the Rose McClendon Workshop Theatre in the auditorium of a Harlem library. (Many prominent actors

came from that workshop, among them, Canada Lee and
Dooley ["Play it Again, Sam"] Wilson.) Since plays and
books about the theatre form a significant part of the collection in most libraries, the liaison seems natural. Dramatic presentations also seem to draw well everywhere,
which is not a bad reason to have a program.

There are many possibilities. Full-length plays have
been presented in libraries, but they are often too long for
most library occasions. But there are a lot of short plays.
Since many are seldom seen, there is good reason to do
them. Eugene O'Neill, John Millington Synge, Anton Chekhov, and Tennessee Williams have all written one-act plays,
and what better company could we be in. A number of poets,
such as Robert Frost, Wallace Stevens, and William Butler
Yeats, have written short plays that are rarely performed.
What about an evening or a series of plays by poets? Presenting such works is--or should be--one of the functions
of a public library, just as is buying some books that only
a few people will read.

Another library function is the presenting of new artists, including playwrights and actors. A word of caution
is necessary here. As with any library program, it is important to be familiar with the content and the quality of the
performance. It's not usually desirable to present a botched
performance or a poor play. If the actors or the playwright
are local people, or particularly if they are young, lesser
quality can be tolerated. In any case, try to see a performance first, or at least know what's coming.

Presenting plays from the culture of ethnic groups in
the community is another good thing for a public library to
do. The South Bronx Project of The New York Public Library, for example, has presented numerous plays and dramatizations of authors from a wide variety of Spanish-speaking
countries, and covering several centuries. Among these
have been the fourteenth-century Spanish author, Juan Manuel,
Cervantes, Horacio Quiroga, García Lorca, Gabriela Mistral,
and Pura Belpré. Other ethnic groups might be equally well
served.

Full scale dramatic presentations often require a lot
of props, and all kinds of other items that are not available
to most libraries. Also a theatrical company, used to such
things, can eat a librarian alive with what seem to be un-
ending requests. In some cases, it may be better to go to

another form, since the props won't be available anyway.
Program space is also often inadequate in libraries. Dramatic readings will do very nicely, in such cases. The
works of George Bernard Shaw have lent themselves well
to this form, as do the plays of such poets as Gertrude Stein,
E. E. Cummings and Dylan Thomas. Spoon River Anthology
is a standard piece that is done in this way. Such performances need not be confined to plays, or parts of plays.
Poems, letters, short stories and other prose passages are
often used. This is a good way to present the works of an
author who works in a variety of forms, and a program of
this kind is often done by one actor. The method allows the
range of an author's work to be presented as well as showing
something of his life.

The program needn't be confined to one author. A
common theme could be used and there are almost endless
possibilities. Love, Christmas, spring, fathers and sons,
and freedom are a few that come to mind. A program of
this kind can be elaborate, or it can be simple--a single
actor with one prop, or none at all. Sometimes the simplest
presentations are the most effective, as has been demonstrated
with programs about Mark Twain, Samuel Beckett, Dylan
Thomas and others. One program of Beckett's works lasted
about an hour, a good length for a library program. It included two humorous short stories ("First Love" and "The
End"), a romantic poem ("Cascando") and excerpts from a
play (Krapps' Last Tape). A program on Gertrude Stein included "Pigeons on the Grass Alas," "Susie Asado," excerpts
from "Tender Buttons," and three plays: What Happened,
I Like It to Be a Play, and Three Sisters Who Are Not Sisters. For a more elaborate program on Margaret Fuller,
an actress used lights, props, slides and sounds, and she
dressed in costume, while presenting selections from Fuller's letters and articles.

Most theatre groups will have prepared certain programs and you accept those, which is often fine. If you
have some imaginative suggestions, on the other hand, a
company may be interested. The authors did that with the
Paul Zindel program described at the end of this book, working closely with the theatrical director and Mr. Zindel. And
one of the authors has put together a Robert Burns program,
but he is still looking for four (in this case) characters to
perform it.

Sometimes there isn't a satisfactory theatrical group

around, and librarians have assembled one of their own.
It has been done most frequently with children, but also with
teenagers and with the elderly. Perhaps there are staff
members who can act, direct, or perform other theatrical
chores. A group of this kind can follow several paths--play
readings, workshops, performances of full plays--and the
available time and talent will dictate the road. Usually the
simpler method will be the best. One librarian, who formed
teenagers into a play-reading group, gives some general
rules. Fifteen members, she says, is about the most you
will want, as plays with larger casts are hard to find. It
is also important that everyone should perform each time.
This group tried all kinds of plays: tragedies, comedies,
histories, and musicals. With the musicals, they found it
useful to play recordings of the songs at the appropriate
times. 1

The Salt Lake City (Utah) Public Library formed forty-
five teenagers from junior and senior high schools into a
theatre company. The teenagers not only act, but also design costumes, make-up, lighting and scenery. A staff
member with theatrical experience directs them. The enthusiastic response to this venture has led the young adult
department to sponsor a playwriting contest for teenagers,
with the best plays to be performed by the company. 2

Another such group has been running for several years
now in the Countee Cullen branch of The New York Public
Library. It is led by a staff member who majored in theatre
in college. The workshop is called The Book/Theater Club
and its members are mostly children and teenagers. They
are encouraged to read works of various poets and playwrights that are in the Library's collection. In this way
the workshop very effectively incorporates the use of the
library and its materials. They have staged plays in celebration of Christmas and Kwanza, dramatizations of African
folk tales and the Spanish folk tale Oté by Pura Belpré, excerpts from the play Raisin in the Sun, by Lorraine Hansberry, and dramatizations of poems by Langston Hughes,
using dance and movement, as well as works by other poets
and playwrights. In addition, adults in the arts are invited
to the workshops to interact with the young people.

The group has performed in the geriatric ward of a
local hospital, in churches and in other libraries. The aims
of the workshop are, in the words of the staff member conducting it, "(1) to develop self confidence in the young people,

(2) to improve their reading ability, and (3) to provide a setting where young people can come together and in the spirit of cooperation work towards a common goal." Another important aspect of this workshop that should be noted is that it involves the parents who contribute time and advice to their children's activities.

MUSIC

Music has wide appeal, and many libraries have had successful programs for the devotees of St. Cecilia. An advantage of musical programs is that they usually come pre-packaged; an existing group has a program and the library presents it. On the other hand, there are many permutations and combinations in this field, and--given the time and the energy--some very imaginative programs can be dreamed up.

The size, acoustics, and location of the playing space are important. Library meeting spaces are often small, rarely seating more than 200, and often many fewer. They may have low ceilings and bare walls which will bounce the sound around too much for comfort and they may be in places that will disturb the readers. But there are possibilities everywhere. Some libraries have concerts when the library is closed. In Plainfield, New Jersey they have Sunday after-noon concerts, which have been regular library features for a number of years, and a large, steady audience has been built up. Other libraries have had concerts in the evening after the library closed. Or the program can be held out-side the library, although the weather would have to be watched rather carefully. In Salt Lake City, Utah they have a plaza they use for concerts, and in Oyster Bay, New York they use a back yard. Some libraries in cities have used adjoining sidewalks and alleys. Perhaps there is an appro-priate space in the building that can be used when the li-brary is open. One library was able to have fully amplified hard rock concerts, because the auditorium was several levels and some distance removed from the public service area. And, although rock would be regrettable in the refer-ence room, some kinds of music can be played near a public area: the clientele, the time of day, and even the season of the year might be factors to consider.

The season and the time of day are important consid-

erations in any case, as is the potential audience. In Salt
Lake City, there are "Brown Bag Concerts" at noon. It's
a pleasant way to spend a lunch hour, and if the library is
in a business area, it is a good programming bet--particularly
if there is a good outdoor space, and if the weather is likely
to be clement. Summer evenings are also popular times for
outdoor concerts. In the Bronx, New York there have been
--as in many other places--afternoon concerts to catch the
coming-home-from-school-crowd. Outdoors is good for this
kind of concert too, and little publicity is required--the
sound of music being ample. That leaves midnight and morning. Most librarians don't care to work at midnight, and
concerts don't seem to be given in the morning. Maybe it's
worth a try, in the right place.

Single concerts are fine, and serve their purpose.
Many libraries, though, have been successful with a series.
And if such a series is held every year, people get to expect it and look forward to it--if it's good. A series can
be devoted to a type of music, or related types, or the concerts can be discrete. (Sometimes indiscreet, especially in
the street). One might, for example, trace American music,
having programs of blues, jazz, ragtime, rock and so forth.
Or a series of ethnic music might be given, as the Brooklyn
(N. Y.) Public Library has done with its "Voices of Brooklyn"
series. There was Afro-American music, Gaelic ballads,
songs from Norway, songs in Greek, Arabic, Yiddish and
Hebrew. Salt Lake City, on the other hand, varied its fare
completely, presenting chamber music, Dixieland, Renaissance music, and Spanish music among other kinds.

But there are many kinds of music, and innumerable
variations. Individual artists (pianists, flutists, guitarists,
etc.) can make good programs. So can small groups--string
quartets, jazz groups, and rock groups. Vocalists, individually or in a group, are a possibility. The music of any
period, country, or style might make for a successful program. The public library of Spring Valley, New York has
had musical programs ranging from a string quartet playing
Haydn, Brahms and Mendelssohn to an all day jazz program.
The latter program was different enough to be worth describing. It was divided into three sessions. The morning was
devoted to workshops and a seminar; there were also exhibits. Workshop performances were featured in the afternoon. And the evening was given over to a concert by existing jazz groups. Thus, there was something for every-
body--a public library ideal. That the program was held

in a facility on Viola Road may have been a coincidence.
Other libraries have had a "Festival of Puerto Rican Music,"
"The Rags of Scott Joplin," W. H. Auden's Christmas Ora-
torio, "For the Time Being," and programs of American
folk music. Opera has been taken to libraries in small
towns and rural areas around Seattle, Washington, which
shows that even the smallest libraries can try something
different. In that program, arias were sung--accompanied
by commentary on the background and the story--and they
were followed by an informal discussion with the audience.

Having some kind of commentary with the music,
makes for one of the most useful and interesting kinds of
programs. This is particularly true with opera--where the
words are often in a language other than English, and the
form may not be so familiar--but it is also true with many
musical programs. In a program of American folk music,
for example, the two singers displayed and played on various
types of instruments, and they talked about the background
of the songs--thus, deepening the listeners' pleasure in the
music. A pianist, who played for silent films, showed film
clips, played the appropriate music, and discussed his technique. Sometimes the musicians merely make informal remarks before the piece they are playing. At a program in
which a group played pieces representing various stages of
modern music, the leader commented on each piece and related it to the other styles. This kind of program could be
applied to styles of music (ragtime, blues), a particular
instrument (lute, sitar), the music of a period (Elizabethan),
or the music of a culture or country (American Indian, African, Chinese).

A music-with-commentary program could also focus
on the works of a composer (Mozart, Stockhausen) or the
works of a group (The Beatles). Live musicians aren't
even necessary with this type of program, given the availability of recordings. All that's needed is a knowledgeable
commentator. The library can compile lists of appropriate
books and recordings. Scores and libretti can be displayed.
Musical instruments can be on hand for people to examine
or for demonstrations, and pictures or slides can show opera
settings, costumes, and other paraphernalia related to the
music.

One function of a public library is to present material.
An annual program of the Dallas Public Library fulfills that
obligation. In a "Composer's Conference," composers submit

scores of new compositions. This music is played by professional musicians and then discussed by the audience and
a panel of music critics. The composers are given a chance
to hear their works performed--and picked apart. And the
audience has a chance to act as critics, to agree or disagree
with the panel, and possibly to be in on an exciting discovery.
Programs of this kind could be done with performers, too,
and they might be especially good with teenage musicians.

DANCE

Dance, as an art form, has achieved major popularity
in this country in recent years, rivaling music and drama,
and there is even a National Dance Week. (Perhaps that
doesn't mean much; pickles have had their own week for
years, not to mention libraries.) Nevertheless, there is
much more interest in ballet, modern dance, etc. than
there was a few years ago. Ballroom dancing, on the other
hand, has always been popular.

Library programs have gone in both directions.
Dances have been held as fund-raisers, and as parts of open
houses. Sometimes a program demonstrating dances will
end with the audience being urged to participate. And dances
are held in libraries just to have a dance. That most frequently happens with young adult programs, and it seems to
be worldwide. A library in Sweden held a dance as part of
a Sunday evening youth program. A German library had
"dancing among the bookshelves." And a Danish library had
an evening of jazz with dancing.[3] The Plainfield (N. J.)
Public Library held a square dance for children and their
parents, and a library in New York City presented a "Funky
House Review," at which the audience was invited to dance
to the music of a number of local groups with names like
"Intensive Heat," "Delmystics," and "Supreme Experience."
Local youth groups are often willing to play free for such
affairs.

Demonstrations and workshops for all kinds of dances
have been held in libraries. Belly dancing demonstrations
have been big in recent years. At this writing, disco dancing is the "thing" and libraries are having workshops on the
subject. Other programs have ranged from tap dancing to
the hula. When a Puerto Rican group performed in a library,
the leader prefaced each dance with a demonstration of the

steps, and comments on the symbolism and historical background. A choreographer, who had worked with Pearl Primus
and her company, gave a lecture entitled "Black Dance U. S. A."
at which he traced its development from its African roots
through minstrel shows, revues of the twenties, Black music
of recent years and modern Black ballet. He gave a slide
show, exhibited memorabilia, and demonstrated steps, as
he talked.

The director of one dance company gave a lecture and
demonstration during which he covered a variety of subjects.
Among these were African dance; the folk dances of early
Europe; ballet; the contributions of immigrants to American
dance; the influence of slaves; comedy in dance; tai chi; the
samba; the influence of Isadora Duncan, Katherine Dunham,
Ruth St. Denis, and others; and American jazz. He supplemented his program with a film, and he used recordings.
The program was designed to appeal to all ages.

A different kind of program has been given by speakers
from the American Dance Therapy Association who demonstrate how dance and body movement are used for a range
of disorders including schizophrenia, retardation, autism,
learning disabilities, and neurosis. A film or a videotape
supplements the program.

Folk dances offer one of the most obvious possibilities,
and they are, for all practical program purposes, endless
in their variety. There might be a program demonstrating
the dances of the ethnic groups in the community or the
dances of the ethnic groups not in the community could be
shown. Either of these ideas could be a series, or one program, depending on the performers available, and the potential interest. Ethnic dances are often used as one facet of a
program about a particular culture, along with poetry, drama
and music. The authors have done this with programs on
Chinese and Puerto Rican culture, and the dance segments
are often very popular. Although folk dances are usually
innocuous, we might give one suggestion. They are sometimes erotic, as well as being exotic, so it's just as well to
see them ahead of time, and to be prepared to explain this
feature, in the context of the culture.

Poetry Reading: A Summary and Checklist of Preparations

KINDS
    Reading of poems in English
    Reading with commentary and/or questions
    Reading of poems in one or more foreign languages ac-
        companied by English translations
    Reading to music
    Reading to dance
    Reading in combination with music, dance, drama
    Film or slides with some of above

MATERIALS
    Books, periodicals, pamphlets, recordings for use in
        program, for display and for borrowing

EQUIPMENT (as required by poet/performers)
    Lectern
    Chairs or stools
    Microphone
    Pitcher of water and glasses
    Record Player
    Projector(s) and related equipment

STAFF
    One to introduce program and to relate it to library's
        services
    Ushers, ticket takers as needed

AUDIENCE
    All ages--often popular with older teenagers and young
        adults, but don't discount any age
    From twenty persons to capacity

SESSIONS
    Number--one, a series of several programs, or several
        times a year as a regular feature of library programs
    Length--one to one and a half hours

SPACE
    Can be held in small space, from 400 sq. ft. up
    Away from public use area
    Think freely--library yard or front steps, basement,
        story hour room, work area

SUBJECTS
    Poetry of a culture, country or group (Italian, Hispanic,

Zuni Indian)
Work of one poet
Poetry of a historical period
Work of a school of poets (New York School)
Poetry on a theme (love, war)
Humorous poetry
Dramatic monologues
Narrative poems
Parodies
Poems in memory of a person or event
Unpublished poetry

SOURCES
Schools and colleges; unaffiliated poets (especially un-known or unpublished); actors; others who read well, or who have a special knowledge of poetry or the ability to read in a particular language

PLANNING AND PRODUCING
Hear reader first--for content and reading ability
Contact poet/reader and discuss fee (if any), length of performance and his role, library's role, kind of audience, contents of program
Arrange date
Decide on location
Gather library materials appropriate to subject for dis-play or borrowing
Gather materials and equipment needed by performer
Checkup--microphones, record player, projector, lights to read by
Print tickets (if wanted)

PUBLICITY
Get biographical details, poem quotes, picture of poet
Read some of poems in order to better write publicity and make introduction
Publicize in schools and colleges, literary organizations, organizations of college graduates, appropriate ethnic groups, selected individuals

Drama: A Summary and Checklist of Preparations

KINDS
Complete play
Scenes from play/plays--on similar theme
Reading of complete play, or scenes from plays

Dramatizations of stories
Dramatic reading of other than play (story, poem)
Combination of some of the above (useful when presenting
the work of an author, or when program is built
around a theme)
Presentation of the works of new or unknown playwrights
Pantomime

MATERIALS
Copies of plays or readings for actors. Books and recordings for display and for borrowing

EQUIPMENT (can run the gamut from one chair or lectern
to a full range of theatrical props; much can be im-
provised)
Lectern
Chairs (a few)
Table(s)
Screens--one or two for entrances, exits, and quick
changes
Other--many small props, household items, etc., can
be borrowed

STAFF (if outside group performing)
One to make introductions and relate library materials
to program
Possible needs--someone to control lights, ushers,
ticket takers

STAFF (if group formed by library)
For directing, costuming, staging, etc.

AUDIENCE
All ages--everybody loves the theatre; library programs
have been successful with children aged three to five
on up
Size--probably not practical for less than twenty, but up
to capacity

SESSIONS
Number--one, several performances of same program,
or short series; if resident company is formed, have
potential for continuity over a period of years.
Spacing--if same program, repeated because of popularity, have performances close together; otherwise
could be a month apart, or several times a year.
Length--one to two hours, but might be longer

SPACE
> 600 sq. ft. up. A theatre in the library is desirable,
> but not likely. Next best is a stage or raised plat-
> form with side entrances (screens can be substituted
> for entrances). At worst, an empty space on the
> floor can be used, or even library yard. Pantomine
> could be done in public use area.
> Audience can be facing the performers, around them, or
> on either side
> Dressing room, curtain, spotlights are sometimes useful

SOURCES
> Schools and colleges; local theatrical groups; library
> users; aspiring, unemployed or retired actors

SUBJECTS
> Popular plays, little-used plays, short plays, short
> stories, dramatic poems, original plays

PLANNING AND PRODUCING
> See performance before contacting any group (if possible)
> Contact performers and discuss fee (if any), contents
> of program, kind of audience expected, length of pro-
> gram, library's role
> Arrange for performers to examine performing space
> and discuss lighting, dressing rooms, props
> Arrange date(s)
> Arrange for rehearsals with performers and library
> staff; plan for delivery and storing of props
> Gather library materials for display and borrowing
> Check any audiovisual equipment to be used and be sure
> it is in place and working on day of program

PUBLICITY
> Get biographical details and pictures of previous per-
> formances
> Possibly use quotes from plays on publicity
> Publicize in schools and colleges, among drama groups,
> and everywhere, via playbills/oral announcement

Music: A Summary and Checklist of Preparations

KINDS
> Concert by small group, or by individual
> Group or individual performing and describing or com-
> menting on instruments, style of music, historical
> background, etc.

Performers and audience are one--group singing, each
one playing
Performance followed by discussion of music
Presentation of compositions by new or unknown composers

MATERIALS
Scores, song lyrics, books about music, recordings--
for use in program, and for display and borrowing

EQUIPMENT
Piano is highly desirable, because it is useful in many kinds
of programs (if regular musical events are planned, li-
brary should consider buying a secondhand piano)
Chairs or stools (as needed)
Music stands (as needed)
Microphones (as needed)

STAFF
One to introduce program, and to relate it to library's
services and materials; can also handle discussion,
question period
Ushers, ticket takers as necessary

AUDIENCE
All ages--from preschool children to the end
Size--from twenty to capacity

SESSIONS
Number--one, a short series, several times a year, or
part of library's regular programming every year
Length--one to two hours

SPACE
600 sq. ft. up; must be removed from public use area,
or when public use area is closed; stage or platform
desirable
Area should be tested for acoustical properties beforehand

SOURCES
Schools and colleges; local, unaffiliated, musical groups;
individual performers, professional or amateur

SUBJECTS
Rock; jazz; chamber music; folk music; blues; gospel;
opera; avant garde; electronic; movie music; individual instruments; music of countries, cultures or
groups; music of a historical period

PLANNING AND PRODUCING
> Listen to performers beforehand--for quality and content
> Contact performers--discuss fee (if any), length of performance, their part in program, library's role
> Have performers examine performing space
> Arrange date
> Gather printed materials and equipment
> Checkup--have piano tuned, check microphones, see that everything is in place

PUBLICITY
> Get biographical information and details of program; also pictures of performers with instruments
> Learn something about the music to be played for publicity and introduction
> Publicize among library record borrowers, schools and colleges, music stores, music clubs, teachers of music, and on radio stations playing appropriate kind of music.

Dance: A Summary and Checklist of Preparations

KINDS
> Straight performance
> Performance interspersed with commentary or explanation
> Performers involving audience
> Performers and audience are one--"a dance"
> Dance used with other media--dancing to recitation of poetry; dance and film; dance integrated into program with music, drama, poetry
> Dance contest

MATERIALS
> Books, periodicals, recordings for display or borrowing

EQUIPMENT
> As required by dancers (probably little or nothing)

STAFF
> One to introduce program and relate it to library's services
> Ushers, ticket takers, someone to operate lights, play records

AUDIENCE
> All ages
> From twenty persons to capacity

SESSIONS
>One, a series of related programs, or a regular feature of library's programs
>Length--one to one and a half hours

SPACE
>400-500 sq. ft. if a single dancer and a small audience (much depends on kind of dancing)
>Floor should be clean, smooth and free from splinters
>Location depends on decibels; could even be in public use area if one or two dancers demonstrating without music

SUBJECTS
>Ballet; folk; ballroom; modern; square; dance of a country, culture or group; original dances

SOURCES
>Schools and colleges; aspiring and unaffiliated dancers members of ethnic and racial groups, local groups concerned with theatrical arts

PLANNING AND PRODUCING
>See a performance by prospective dancer(s) first
>Contact performers and discuss any fee, length of performance, their part in program, library's role, content
>Have dancers examine space, discuss lighting and other requirements
>Arrange date
>Arrange for rehearsals with dancers and library staff
>Checkup--see that audiovisual equipment is working and everything in place

PUBLICITY
>Get biographical details, pictures of dancers dancing, and contents of program
>Learn something about the dances for writing publicity and for introduction
>Publicize in schools and colleges, local cultural organizations, among appropriate ethnic groups, in music stores and stores selling dance equipment.

NOTES

1. Fogleson, Marilee. "Between Librarian and Teenager,"

Wisconsin Library Bulletin, March-April, 1971, p. 86.
2. American Libraries, April, 1974, p. 178.
3. Renborg, Greta. "Pop in the Library," Top of the News, April, 1968, p. 291.

A program in which a talk is the main feature can take many forms. Speakers--sometimes there are several together--can just talk, with no props. They can show objects. They can use slides, films, filmstrips and recordings. Sometimes they demonstrate aspects of their subjects. Often there is room for a question and answer period, or an informal discussion. There are many varieties of talk programs that involve more than one speaker. In a panel discussion, a few (three, four, or five) persons discuss a subject informally and a moderator leads the discussion; this kind of program is useful for controversial subjects. Symposia also involve several speakers; they each give a short talk on some facet or side of a topic; these talks are usually followed by some form of audience participation, and again, there must be a leader. A dialogue is a discussion between two persons, and an interview is an interview is an interview. Dialogues and interviews are useful for some subjects, kinds of people, or forms of programs. They are often used on radio and television, and they are useful if you have secured an author or other celebrity for your program.

Question Period

If questions are to be asked of the speaker, they can either be written questions that are handed in to be read by the speaker or moderator; or they can be asked verbally from the floor. Written questions have several advantages; they avoid long speeches from people who are supposed to be asking questions; they can be put into a sequence that is more useful than random questioning; they avoid repetition (people often ask repetitious questions); rambling questions can be shortened or rephrased; and, if necessary, you can leave, until it is too late, a question that is irrelevant or in bad taste.

Written questions do involve handing out paper and pencils, and collecting them again. Such things can be disrupting, but they needn't be. The materials can be handed out before the program, and they can be quickly collected by ushers if this detail has been well-planned. Verbal questions are also useful in some situations; they create an air of informality, and even excitement, that written questions can kill; they are probably best used with small audiences.

Librarians Talk (About Books and the Library)

Librarians have traditionally given talks both in and out of the library. Adult librarians have given book talks on radio and television, and to women's clubs, men's clubs, garden clubs, parent-teacher associations, church groups, ethnic and racial groups, and many other kinds of groups and organizations. For these talks, they frequently go to the group's meeting place and talk about three or four books of interest to that group. It is often hoped that members of that group will then rush to the library. They rarely do. What many groups want is a program--something to fill the available time. However, if you can follow Ezra Pound's advice and "make it new," maybe you can interest them. Talks of this kind are a lot of work; they are less work if you give a lot of them, however, since you can repeat them, or rework them for different groups. In spite of the drawbacks, they can be useful. They are good publicity; they build good community relations; and they may draw people to the library indirectly.

It is probably best to talk about books for which there are several copies available, in case they do come. Most talks of this kind are chatty and informal; you are probably not there to give a detailed critical analysis of a book. Just tell something of the plot or the contents. Throw in an anecdote or two about the author. Relate it to other books and, possibly, read a passage or two. This is also an opportunity to mention the library's many services and resources; one doesn't do this in great detail, giving the audience a lot to remember, but merely mentions, or briefly describes, the salient points.

Adult Education (Literacy) Classes

Adult classes are good groups to give talks to. It is

most useful if these groups can come to the library, and the
teachers usually agree that it is worthwhile.   These classes
will usually be in English for the foreign-born, or for the
semi-literate native-born.   Sometimes citizenship classes
are combined with English.   The students are often eager to
learn, which is a big plus.   One difficulty is that there may
be many different educational levels, ranging from the semi-
literate to the highly educated (in any language); that makes
giving a book talk a problem.   There will also be different
languages represented within the group.   But, their eagerness to learn will overcome most of these obstacles.   For
such classes, particularly if the group isn't too large, a
tour of the library, talking as you go, is most desirable.
They can then be registered and handled like any reader.
Tours of the library can be made interesting by showing
them things which they may never have been aware of; things
like your audiovisual gadgetry, your treasured books, or a
hundred-year-old newspaper on microfilm.

Book Talks to High School Classes

Many young adult librarians feel that the most effective way of reaching the largest number of teenagers at one
time is by talking to classes of students, either in the school
or public library, about books and the library.   In this way
the librarian is able to get across information on the library's materials, resources and services (many of which
teenagers often are not aware exist), as well as tell them
about books on a variety of subjects that are of interest to
them.   The latter is done in the format of a "book talk."
This consists of telling about an incident in the book, usually
one that comes near the beginning of the book, and telling it
so effectively that the students want to read the whole book.

The librarian may work out his own book talk and/or
--as is true in some libraries--draw from a pool of book
talks that he and his fellow workers have contributed to.   He
talks about books that he himself enjoyed reading so that he
can communicate his enthusiasm to his audience.   First and
foremost, he talks about books that he knows will be of
interest to the majority of his audience.   (Later when doing
"floor work" in the library he will get to know the teenagers individually and will help find the right books for
those who have more unusual or specialized interests.)
Emphasis is put on recreational reading and not on curricu-
lum-related materials, since the latter are felt to be the

special province of the school library. If this program is
well done, the librarian communicates both the pleasure that
reading can give and the fact that teenagers are welcome at
the library--that librarians are interested in serving them.
The following very persuasive justification for classes is
given by the Coordinator of Young Adult Services for the
King County Library System, Seattle (Washington).

> It keeps me in contact with kids and that's vital.
> For my library system it means increased circu-
> lation, community goodwill, and exposure to an
> underserved population. For the school librarian
> and faculty, it means at least one period with some-
> one else handling the class, exposure to new views
> and increased awareness of public libraries and
> YA materials. For the kids, it's storytelling at
> their level, with a lot of interesting materials
> and resources to discover.

The book talk program also gives the library an opportunity to extend amnesty, either complete or partial, to
the many teenagers who have kept books out for a long time
or who owe fines, often from early childhood, and who,
thinking that they now owe a fortune, have stayed away from
the library ever since. It is a chance for these teenagers
to clear up any such problems with the library; this encourages those who might otherwise never return to start
using the library again. For all these reasons, many young
adult librarians feel that this program is one of the most
valuable the library has to offer. It is also an experience
that most of them find enjoyable and even exhilarating.

It is the feeling among many librarians that this program has more successful results if classes go to the library (rather than librarians to the school) because the materials and services they talk about are right there, and the
teenagers can take out the books they hear about, or others,
immediately, clear up their overdue problems on the spot
and register for adult cards. The chances of their coming
to the library on their own are greater if they establish or
reestablish contact with the library through a class visit.

In The New York Public Library, many eighth grades
still come on class visits to their neighborhood branch library. These visits are arranged ahead between the librarian and the teacher or principal. They usually last an
hour; if they are any longer, the students, even the brighter

ones, begin to get restless. The activities during the visit proceed generally as follows:

For the talk, the class congregates in the library's meeting room. Hopefully this is not in the children's room; teenagers will often resent it. However, if that is the only place available, the librarian explains this fact apologetically. The talk itself is then given, lasting approximately twenty minutes, about books and the library, during which time the students have a chance to ask questions and make comments. The librarian gives book talks for about ten minutes on three or four books, spending about four or five minutes on the first or main book, two or three minutes on a second and one minute on the other one or two. There is at least one copy of each title he talks about available for circulation. It sometimes happens, however, that some of them may not appeal to anyone in one class, while in another class, half the students want the same book. It is a good idea, therefore, to have other books displayed on a table and a word or two said about them.

The remaining time is devoted to registering or re-registering for adult borrower's cards, clearing up overdue records, possibly a tour of the library, pointing out the reference area, and browsing and checking out books, magazines and recordings. It is a chance for the librarian to help the teenagers find what they want and also to establish contact with the teacher if it is the first time they have met.

However, because of transportation problems, discipline problems and tight class period scheduling, schools in New York City (as well as in other parts of the country) often prefer to have librarians give book talk programs in the schools. Such a program requires more experience and a larger repertory of book talks, because the librarian talks for most of the forty-minute class period on as many as ten books. They always bring either the book itself or the book jacket, although students are often disappointed if they cannot see the book itself. Librarians prefer to speak to individual classes in their English period (or in the school library if there are no distractions) rather than to large numbers in an assembly, because the former allows for better rapport between the librarian and the students. Also, in a classroom the students are able to look at the books; some librarians leave five or ten minutes at the end of the period for this activity. Another advantage is that it gives the students a chance to make comments and for the librarian to find out more about their reading interests. However, the librarian still does most of the talking for the whole period, and this can be quite demanding. Therefore, most of them schedule no more than three classes each visit.

Some things to remember when scheduling book talks in the school are: (1) Make the arrangements with the school librarian whenever possible. In some schools the principal perfers this be done by him, the assistant principal, or the English chairman. It is best to visit the school rather than do it by telephone. (2) If a teacher contacts you directly for book talks, make sure the school librarian knows why and when you are coming. Stop by and see him and let him know ahead of time, if possible, what books you are going to talk about. It is important to get across to the school librarian that you are not trying to usurp any of his province and that you are both working towards a common goal: to get young people to read. (3) Stop by the school office and introduce yourself to the principal. They are usually glad to hear of any outside services being rendered their school, and it will help establish good relations between the school and the public library.

The New York Public's Young Adult Services does high school classes to a certain extent. However, its main emphasis is on working with the eighth and ninth grades because of the feeling that these young people need the help of the young adult librarian the most, now that they are in that transitional stage of going from the children's into the adult department.

Sample List of Books

The following are some of the books which young adult librarians of The New York Public Library have used successfully in book talks. You will notice that some titles, such as Best Wishes, Amen by Lillian Morrison, Breakout by Ron LeFlore, Guinness Sports Record Book by Norris and Ross McWhirter, The Telltale Line by Peggy Mann, and Jay Bennett's mystery novels may be used with classes on more than one grade and reading level.

8th grade--on grade reading level

Bennett, Jay. The Birthday Murderer
Bethancourt, T. Ernesto. Dr. Doom: Superstar

Bethancourt, T. Ernesto. The Dog Days of Arthur Cane
Blassinghame, Wyatt. Science Catches the Criminal
Cohen, Daniel. Real Ghosts
Jackson, Reggie. Reggie Jackson's Scrapbook
Kerr, M. E. I'll Love You When You're More Like Me
Litowinsky, Olga. The Dream Book
McWhirter, Norris and Ross. Guinness Sports Record
   Book
Mann, Peggy. The Telltale Line
Mathis, Sharon Bell. A Teacup Full of Roses
Morrison, Lillian. Best Wishes, Amen.
Myers, Walter Dean. Mojo and the Russians
O'Brien, Robert C. Z for Zachariah
Pascal, Francine. Hanging Out with Cici
Peck, Richard. Ghosts I Have Been
Peck, Richard. Through a Brief Darkness
Seide, Diane. Looking Good
Severn, Bill. Bill Severn's Big Book of Close-Up Magic
Sherburne, Zoa. Why Have the Birds Stopped Singing?

<u>9th grade--on grade reading level</u>

Anderson, Dave. The Yankees
Bennett, Jay. The Dangling Witness
Bennett, Jay. Say Hello to the Hit Man
Guy, Rosa. The Disappearance
Keane, John. Sherlock Bones
LeFlore, Ron. Breakout
McWhirter, Norris and Ross. Guinness Sports Record
   Book
Mann, Peggy. The Telltale Line
Mathis, Sharon Bell. A Teacup Full of Roses
Pascal, Francine. My First Love and Other Disasters
Samuels, Gertrude. Run, Shelly, Run
Scoppettone, Sandra. The Late Great Me
Seide, Diane. Looking Good
Severn, Bill. Carnival of Sports
Zindel, Paul. The Pigman

<u>10th grade--on grade reading level</u>
or
<u>9th grade--above grade reading level</u>

Anderson, Dave. The Yankees
Boetung, Yaw M. The Return
Carew, Rod, and Ira Berkow. Carew
Elder, Lauren. And I Alone Survived

Guest, Judith. Ordinary People
LeFlore, Ron. Breakout
Leitner, Isabella. Fragments of Isabella
McWhirter, Norris and Ross. Guinness Sports Record Book
Nyad, Diane. Other Shores
Robertson, Dougal. Survive the Savage Sea
Rushing, Jane Gilmore. Mary Dove
Thompson, Estelle. Hunter in the Dark
Wilhelm, Kate. When Late the Sweet Birds Sang

8th to 10th grades--on 1st to 3rd grade reading level

Carlson, Dale. The Plant People
Carlson, Dale. A Wild Heart
Jameson, Jon. The Picture Life of O. J. Simpson
Madison, Arnold. Great Unsolved Cases
Platt, Kin. Run for Your Life
Rabinowich, Ellen. Toni's Crowd
Sarason, Martin. A Federal Case
Shea, George. Nightmare Nina
Sprague, Jane. That New Girl
Sullivan, George. Picture Story of Catfish Hunter

8th to 10th grades--on 4th to 6th grade reading level

Aylesworth, Thomas G. Movie Monsters
Brisco, Pat. Campus Mystery
Cohen, Daniel. The World's Most Famous Ghosts
Cohen, Joel H. Steve Garvey, Storybook Star
Cook, Fred. City Cop
Edwards, Audrey, and Gary Wohl. The Picture Life of Muhammad Ali
Edwards, Audrey, and Gary Wohl. The Picture Life of Stevie Wonder
Evans, Larry. How to Draw Monsters
Gutman, Bill. Modern Women Superstars
Gutman, Bill. More Modern Baseball Superstars
Haskins, James. From Lew Alcindor to Kareem Abdul-Jabbar
Garden, Nancy. Vampires
Garden, Nancy. Werewolves
McWhirter, Norris and Ross. Guinness Book of Amazing Achievements
Morrison, Lillian. Best Wishes, Amen

Morrison, Lillian. Touch Blue
Robinson, Nancy. Department Store Model
Wood, Phyllis Anderson. Win Me and You Lose

10th grade--Vocational High Schools

The following books have been used successfully by a librarian who works primarily with vocational high schools in New York City in which young people are learning a trade. The titles range from fairly easy reading books published as juveniles but with teenage characters to some fairly difficult adult titles.

Anderson, Peggy. Nurse
Angelou, Maya. I Know Why the Caged Bird Sings
Arundel, Honor. The Terrible Temptation
Baldwin, James. If Beale Street Could Talk
Bennett, Jay. The Long Black Coat
Columbu, Franco. Coming on Strong
Duncan, Lois. I Know What You Did Last Summer
Duncan, Lois. Summer of Fear
Elder, Lauren. And I Alone Survived.
Grillone, Lisa, and Joseph Gennaro. Small Worlds
    Close Up
Gilfond, Henry. Genealogy
Holman, Felice. Slake's Limbo
Lawson, Donna. Mother Nature's Beauty Cupboard
LeFlore, Ron. Breakout
McCormick, Donald. The Master Book of Escapes
McWhirter, Norris and Ross. Guinness Sports Record
    Book
Murphy, Barbara Beasley. No Place to Run
Nyad, Diane. Other Shores
Scholefield, Alan. Venom
Walker, Samuel. Sneakers

Tips for Success

One young adult librarian in The New York Public Library offers the following tips on how to do successful book talks:

(1) When choosing a book for a talk before teen-agers, select one that you have enjoyed reading and you feel will be of sure-fire interest. It should lend itself easily to a book talk; many do not. Sometimes it is neces-

sary to go through a half dozen books or more to find one that will make a good book talk.

(2)   Select books appropriate to the grade and reading level.   Find out in advance from the teacher if the class is below, on, or above grade in their reading.

(3)   Prepare by the method that suits you best. Write the whole thing out, write a few notes, or just keep going over it in your mind.   Practice is important.   When the class appears, all notes should disappear.

(4)   If the class is coed, start out with a book that will appeal to the boys such as sports or adventure.   Girls are more willing to listen to a book for boys than vice-versa.   Once you have the boys' attention, you can then use a book addressed primarily to the girls.

(5)   Do not spend more than five minutes on any book, and keep within the time.   Your opening statement can be related to the weather, something you have read in the paper, a school happening or even a background comment on the book itself, the time period or the setting.   It should not be, "Here's a book you will like," or "This is the funniest book I've ever read."   The audience will decide that when they hear the talk.

(6)   The closing statement should be prepared; then you won't ramble.   You will want to come to a nice, neat end but not too dramatically.   Avoid cliff hangers ("Will Pete get out of the cave?   Read this and find out")   Your audience will groan.   But do give them a little promise of what they can expect beyond what you have told them.

(7)   Give the author and title at the beginning and end.

(8)   Choose an episode that occurs early in the book. You don't want to give the story away.   Don't tell the whole story unless it is a short story in a collection.   Don't tell the only exciting incident in an otherwise unexciting book. They will just feel cheated when they do read the book.

(9)   Use a few of the author's own words if you can do it casually, to give the flavor of the book.

(10)   It's usually not a good idea to read unless it's a poem or questions and answers such as those in Ask Beth, You Can't Ask Your Mother.   Reading from a book tends to separate you from the audience.

(11)   Don't gesture wildly or be too theatrical.   Your audience will feel uncomfortable and embarrassed for you. Don't tell in the first person.

(12)   Be careful of suggestive words or scenes that will upset them.

(13)   Limit descriptions and introduce only one to three characters.   If they lose track of what you are talking about, they will become bored and stop listening.

(14) Define hard or unusual words by restating them in simpler words--but not in a pedagogical way, naturally. Do it casually. Make sure that they know what you're talking about.

(15) Be sure to get all information correct. Special terms and facts should be accurate.

(16) Keep your feelers out for responses to what you're saying and be responsive in turn.

(17) Ask the teacher to remain in the room. It is hard to be entertaining and play the authority figure at the same time.

(18) Wear attractive but not distracting clothes.

(19) Have a good time and the class will too!

At Prince George's County (Md.) Memorial Library System, the young adult librarians prefer to work as a book-talk team of two or more people who talk to no more than six classes a day. They, too, prefer giving talks to individual classes and do not do assemblies. The team works out a list of books that are popular with YA readers, titles that meet as many reading interests as possible and on several reading levels, and books that the librarians enjoy and feel comfortable in presenting. The number of titles varies on the lists, but they try to talk about as many as they can, usually twenty to twenty-five. Copies of this list are given out to the students who can then select the titles they want to hear about. Staff often take along additional books and try to match up titles on the list with those in the collection.

Basically they use the Enoch Pratt Free Library's technique of book talking which Margaret A. Edwards describes so well in her book, The Fair Garden and the Swarm of Beasts (Hawthorn). Their presentation is informal and chatty and they try to get reactions from the young people. They use mostly short talks of under one minute that would answer the question, "What's this book about," and it is not memorized. At least one long book talk is given in every class period; this one is memorized. There is a "pool" of long talks available for staff to use. The following is their "Book Talk Core List" for 1979-80.

Acorn People, by Ron Jones
Ammie, Come Home, by Barbara Michaels
Bad Seed, by W. March
Best Friends, by H. W. Stine
Birthday Murderer, by Jay Bennett
Blizzard, by G. Stone
But I'm Ready to Go, by Louise Albert
Child is Missing, by Charlotte Paul
Contender, by Robert Lipsyte

Deathwatch, by Robb White
Dragonsong, by Anne McCaffrey
Dropout, by N. Borisoff
Dueling Machine, by B. Bova
Fighting Back, by R. Bleier
Fire Came By, by John Baxter
Franco Harris, by Thomas Braun
Friends, by R. Guy
Gentlehands, by M. E. Kerr
Ghosts I Have Been, by Richard Peck
Hanging Out with Cici, by Francine Pascal
Heads You Win, Tails I Lose, by I. Holland
His Own Where, by J. Jordan
I Know What You Did Last Summer, by Lois Duncan
If I Love You, Am I Trapped Forever, by M. E. Kerr
Ironhead, by Mel Ellis
Jay J. Armes, Investigator, by J. J. Armes
Lost Summer, by J. Oppenheimer
Memoirs of a Tall Girl, by E. Ronayne
Missing Persons League, by F. Bonham
Mojo and the Russians, by Walter Myers
Mortal Instruments, by Ernesto T. Bethancourt
Mother, Where Are You?, by Dorothy Woolfolk
Mrs. Mike, by Benedict Freedman
Night Stalks the Mansion, by Constance Westbie
No-Return Trail by Sonia Levitin
Nun in the Closet, by Dorothy Gilman
One Fat Summer, by Robert Lipsyte
Out of Love, by Hilma Wolitzer
The Pack, by David Fisher
Pigman, by P. Zindel
Pistachio Prescription, by Paula Danziger
Prince of Central Park, by Evan Rhodes
Run, Shelley, Run, by Gertrude Samuels
Snow Bound, by Harry Mazer
Solid Gold Kid, by Norman Mazer
Story of Stevie Wonder, by J. Haskins
Summer to Die, by Lois Lowry
They Call Me the Big E, by E. Hayes
Thing at the Door, by Henry Sleasar
Weird Moments in Sports, by Bruce Weber
Weird Stories From Real Life, by Marjorie Burns
When Michael Calls, by John Farris
Wilma, by Wilma Rudolph
Winning, by R. Brancato
Witches Get Everything, by K. M. Teall
You Are the Rain, by R. R. Knudson
You Can't Eat Peanuts in Church, by Barbara Seuling

Z for Zachariah, by Robert O'Brien
Zoo Vet, by David Taylor

Prince George's County Memorial Library System also gives talks to 12th grade classes that will not be going on to college. In these talks they stress materials and services that can help in life "after graduation from school." The young adult librarians talk about non-fiction books on the following subjects and, in addition, give short book talks on five or six fiction titles (books to read for fun).

I. CAREERS, JOBS

Tests
Changing jobs
How to do a better job on the job
Job etiquette
Armed Forces

II. HOW TO

Get legal advice
Get medical advice
Help your family make a better move
Make car repairs
Buy antiques
Arrange flowers
Make over furniture
Cut hair at home
Use Consumer Reports
Figure out gambling secrets
Use handyman's book
Get a good night's sleep
Figure income tax
Make wills
Play the stock market

III. SINGLE STATE, MARRIAGE AND HOME

Living in the big city
Marriage etiquette
Entertaining
Cooking
Decorating
Sewing
Get along with in-laws
Buying a home, furniture, etc.
Having a baby--care & feeding

IV. TRAVEL

  Stress travelling in USA--car, plane, bus, rail
  Camping
  Parks
  Tours
  Hotels

V. RECREATION

  Sports, music, art, theater, movies, TV

The Coordinator of Young Adult Services of Seattle
Public Library has the following to say about her approach
to work with classes:

> We make arrangements with the school librarian
> to visit certain classes (or the arrangements might
> be made with the language arts head, too). Usually
> we remain in each class 10-20 minutes. Our book
> talks are teasers, not in depth. The idea is to
> promote library service in its variety. We each
> have our own style in how much we ask questions
> of the audience, etc. : I usually talk about some
> books that have been made into movies and so it's
> a natural to ask which the kids liked better. The
> answers are fascinating. In classes I've been in
> within the last year we've also had spontaneous
> discussions on the occult and on the nature of
> friendship. When that happens I'm so pleased, be-
> cause I'd love to be able to get the idea across
> that we have the books and that books have ideas
> in them. Our normal time in each class is short
> enough to allow us to visit two classes a period.
> I have done three classes rarely, but that really
> is no fun because it's so short that there's little
> chance for any interchange at all. Usually two of
> us try to go to a school together but we don't visit
> the same classes. Instead it is sometimes neces-
> sary to cover the classes in a given period, and
> if it isn't in some periods it is in others. It also
> gives us a chance to arrange our schedules so that
> a teacher who has four classes in a day only listens
> to the same person two times instead of all four.
> [from a letter to the authors].

What she does that is a departure from Prince George's

County Memorial Library System and Enoch Pratt Free Library is to advertise the record collection in the YA department. This is done by playing a cassette on which small sections of various popular records have been taped and then having the students try to guess the song and performer. In this case, however, it is necessary to bring a player along also.

The books that she and other young adult librarians have used successfully with junior high school classes include the following:

Adams, Richard. Watership Down
Bethancourt, T. Ernesto. Dog Days of Arthur Cane
Bosworth, J. Allen. All the Dark Places
Bradbury, Ray. Fahrenheit 451
Brancato, Robin F. Winning
Church, Ralph. Mork and Mindy
Duncan, Lois. Summer of Fear
Elder, Lauren. And I Alone Survived
Fleischer, Leonore. Ice Castles
Foster, Alan D. Black Hole
Hall, Lynn. Flowers of Anger
Horwitz, Elinor. Soothsayer's Handbook--A Guide to
    Bad Signs and Good Vibrations
Invasion of the Body Snatchers (Fotonovel)
Kerr, M. E. Gentlehands
LeGuin, Ursula. Wizard of Earthsea
McWhirter, Norris. Guinness Book of World Records
Mowat, Farley. Never Cry Wolf
Offit, Sidney. What Kind of a Guy Do You Think I Am?
Panshin, Alexei. Rite of Passage
Peck, Richard. Ghosts I Have Been
Roddenbury, Gene. Star Trek
Sleator, William. House of Stairs
Sobol, Donald J. Two-Minute Mysteries
Wersba, Barbara. Tunes for a Small Harmonica
White, Robb. Deathwatch.
Zindel, Paul. The Undertaker's Gone Bananas

All three libraries mentioned above concentrate on the book in their presentations. On occasion they have used short films. At The New York Public Library young adult librarians sometimes use filmstrips with bilingual classes, very slow classes and with the physically and mentally handicapped. Also, they have played records while the class is settling down in the library. However, the feeling in all three libraries is that books can stand on their own.

Non-librarians Talk (About a Lot of Things)

Absorbing and even exciting programs can come from talks by experts on various subjects. And the possible subjects are almost as varied as the subjects in your book collection. Such talks can be combined with displays of books and other library materials that relate to the subject. Objects relevant to the talk can also be displayed. This is also a good opportunity to describe library resources in the subject area, and to distribute booklists on that subject.

The sources of the talks are varied. Authors--whether creative writers or subject experts--often make good programs. (They may not be good speakers, however, so beware.) Local authors particularly are often willing to talk at the library. One library invited a herpetologist to speak when his first book was published. They displayed copies of the book, the manuscript, galley proofs, photographs and snake collecting equipment. The author arrived complete with a boa constrictor, which crawled around his neck as he talked, and with a rattlesnake which did not. The large audience of all ages was charmed. Another author of a book about caring for hurt, wild birds has described her experiences to library audiences in a number of successful programs. Other subject experts come from businesses, schools and colleges, the library staff, government agencies, hobbyists, and, indeed, almost everywhere you look.

Libraries have had talk programs at many different times of the day. The Manhasset (N.Y.) Public Library had a "Books and Breakfast" talk on a Sunday at 10 a.m. Coffee, coffee cake, croissants, jam, and orange juice were served. Lunchtime talks are not uncommon in libraries. One familiar format is for the audience to bring their lunches while the library provides coffee. Natrona County (Wyo.) Public Library calls theirs "The Brown Bagger." This is an annual series that covers a variety of subjects each year. "Malpractice Insurance," "Participation in Party Politics," "How to Write and Publish," "The First White Man in Casper," "1978 Wyoming Legislative Review," and "Wills and Estate Planning" are some of their titles, indicating the breadth of subject. This kind of regularly scheduled series is useful since a potential audience is built up that comes to expect the programs, and (one hopes) to look forward to them.

What is now commonly called parenting for want of a better word is one category of possible library talks. Within that category there are many subjects. The New York

Public Library's Early Childhood Resource and Information Center, for example, listed the following possible program topics:

Exploring the Creative Arts

Consumerism--Getting the most for your money

International Year of the Child
    A multi-cultural world

The Learning Environment
    Museums
    Television: using TV constructively; developing a
       critical child viewer
    Free and inexpensive material
    Parent interaction with professionals
    Music for toddlers

Caring and Responsibility
    Child abuse/child advocacy
    Alternate family styles
    Fathering
    Pets

Books and Children
    Decisions in publishing
    Books for parents
    Storytelling
    Books you can make
    Reading

Health, Nutrition & Physical Fitness
    Sex education
    Toilet training
    Teaching infants to swim

Special Children
    How are handicapped children shown on TV
    Relating to special children
    Invisible handicaps: emotional disturbances
    Deafness
    Blindness
    Mental retardation

Development of Values
    Transferring moral and social values to children

Sources for these programs include doctors, psychologists, psychoanalysts, various special teachers and librarians. An educational consultant, for instance, lectured on "Choosing Toys That Extend Your Child's Creativity"; a librarian talked about "Books and Toddlers"; a director of social services discussed "Sexuality in the Young Child"; an agency head talked about "Child Abuse and Neglect"; and a teacher told parents how not to chase their children away when they are cooking in a talk entitled "Cooking with Young Children." "Art from Scraps," "What to Do with Kids in the City in the Summer," "British Infant Schools," "Magic, Fantasy, Lies and Dreams" are the titles of a few more of the many programs held at this center. Such programs, moreover, do not only benefit parents. Grandparents, foster parents, the staffs of day care centers, baby sitters and students of education all find them useful.

A Potpourri of Programs

Food will be a popular subject as long as people must eat and libraries have presented a number of lecture/demonstrations of interest to the inner man (person?). At the Bethpage (N.Y.) Public Library, the food editor of a newspaper told the audience "How to Build a Good Home Cookbook Library." Hot and cold hors d'oeuvres were the subject of a talk and demonstration at the North Merrick (N.Y.) Public Library. Copies of all the recipes were distributed to the audience. The growing popularity of natural foods stimulated a program at the Wantagh (N.Y.) Public Library. The speaker described the benefits of growing sprouts, and told her hearers how to do it--both summer and winter. She also talked about medicinal herbs and homemade bread. The dangers of eating unnatural foods (and some natural ones as well) were described in a talk entitled "You Are What You Eat," given at a branch of The New York Public Library. In addition to the talk, several short films were shown. They were Brand Names and Labeling Games (Benchmark, 9 min.); Chemical Feast (Benchmark, 11 min.); and Look Before You Eat (Churchill, 22 min.).

Appearance is another perennially popular subject and it has a number of facets. After all that food, you might have wanted to attend a talk entitled "Permanent Weight Control Through Behavior Therapy" that was given by a psychologist at another library. Having become slim, you could have gone on to another library for two talks about your face.

One dealt with cosmetics--their purchase, dangers, and uses--and at the other program facial exercises were described and demonstrated.

Summer subjects should be the next step, now that you are well-fed and looking good. A forest ranger gave a talk on "New Angles for Anglers" at one library, and a naturalist talked about "Summer Wild Flowers and Where to Find Them," at another. Boating safety, swimming safety, tips on playing golf and tennis, and canoeing and backpacking techniques are among the possible subjects in this category.

Winter, on the other hand, calls for different subjects, and at the Finkelstein Memorial Library in Spring Valley, New York, their different subjects include astrology, Jewish mysticism, and hypnotism. At this last program, the audience was told what hypnosis can and can't do, and some volunteered as subjects for the hypnotist. (No doubt, many a librarian would like to learn the technique.) "How to Watch a Flying Saucer" was the title of a talk given by an astronomer at another library, during which he described --and showed--slides--of objects often mistaken for UFO's. The "Big Band Era" and "Black Music" were subjects of two other library lecture/demonstrations. Any of these subjects would, of course, be appropriate for any season. However, hurling, hockey, skiing, snowshoeing and ice boating might--although we don't know that they have been--be the subjects of library programs.

Money is of necessity, interesting to almost everybody, and libraries have dealt with the subject. In one library, a stockbroker talked on the "Movement of Money." Among the subjects he touched on were a history of paper currency, inflation, bank accounts, stocks, bonds, and the purchasing of valuable commodities. Another stockbroker told his audience "How to Purchase Stock Without Paying Commission Charges." Everything else to do with money has been discussed in library programs. If investing in gold and silver hasn't been talked about yet, surely it will be.

Arts and Crafts are obvious subjects for talks. Many such library programs are described in the chapter on workshops, but there are always others, and for many subjects a talk and/or demonstration is all you can hope for. "How to Build and Collect Miniatures" was the subject of one such talk. Dollhouses and miniature furniture were the objects emphasized. A program called "Attic Treasures" was a demonstration of the ways of using and refurbishing old things you might find in your attic or basement. The art of wood-carving was demonstrated at another program, and the art of stone sculpture at another. Cartoonists, egg decorators, furniture finishers and gardeners might all be prevailed upon to talk at their local library.

Sex may be an art or craft and it is certainly of general interest, but not many years ago libraries would not have had programs on the subject. They do now. One library even had a program called "How to Make Good Sex Great Sex." Such programs are aimed at audiences ranging from teenagers to the elderly, although they are most commonly for the teenager. This is undoubtedly because thoughts about sex, dating, love and marriage are often uppermost in the minds of teenagers, and because they will benefit the most from these programs. The speaker should be carefully selected: he should know what he is talking about and he should be able to relate well to teenagers and make them feel comfortable. They are sometimes still embarrassed when talking to adults about these subjects. Responsible, up-to-date and appealing films can also contribute to the success of such programs.

One branch of The New York Public Library did a series of three programs: "Sex and Dating," "Sex and VD," and "Contraception." Doctors from the local hospital's Division of Adolescent Medicine spoke. A male doctor was the guest speaker at the first program and a woman doctor at the other two. Three films were used: About Sex (Texture Films), an explicit and frank discussion of birth control, abortion and other sexual information by teenagers in New York City and a group leader from Planned Parenthood; The Date (Little Red Filmhouse), an exploration of the emotional pressures encountered by two high school students on a date; Are You Ready for Sex? (Perennial), a candid film that focuses on clarifying personal values and making responsible sexual decisions. It uses dramatizations and student discussions in which teenagers represent varied points of view.

Another branch library also held a three-session series on sex called "Straight Talk--for Teens Only." Discussion leaders came from a Center for Population and Family Health which is attached to a large hospital. The five subjects discussed were: Sexual Development, Sex Myths, Reproduction, On Being a Woman, and Moving Towards Manhood.

Talks: A Summary and Checklist of Preparation

KINDS
> Panel--several speakers and moderator informally discussing subject
> Symposium--several speakers and moderator; short speeches; audience takes part
> Single speaker
> Speaker using audiovisual aids (films, slides, charts, blackboard)
> Speaker giving demonstration (of an art or craft)
> Speaker displaying objects connected with subject (snakes, antiques, a horse)
> Dialogue
> Interview
> Ambulatory talk (tour of library; historical, architectural or literary walk in community)

MATERIALS
> Books, pamphlets, periodicals, recordings on subject are very desirable for display or for borrowing by public; library may supply films or slides for speaker

EQUIPMENT (as needed by speaker)
> Lectern
> Microphone(s)
> Pitcher of water and glasses
> Chair(s)
> Table(s)--for speakers to sit at, for demonstration, for display of objects
> Blackboard, pointer and chalk
> Flashlight
> Record player
> Projector(s) and related equipment

EQUIPMENT (as needed by audience)
> Chairs--have extras to bring out, in case audience larger than anticipated
> Microphone(s)--if large room
> Paper and pencils--for submitting written questions

STAFF
> One to introduce speaker, talk about library's services and materials related to subject, and to close program
> Projectionist--may be same as introducer
> Ushers, ticket takers, clerk to charge out books--depends on size of audience

AUDIENCE
>All ages; any number (small audience of twenty or thirty is best for demonstration)

SESSIONS
>Number--one, a series of several, a series for a season, or a continuing part of library's programming
>Spacing--if related subjects, a week or two apart; if long, unrelated series, once a month or several times a year.
>Length--each session from one to one and a half hours

SPACE
>Size--can range from about 400 sq. ft. up
>Location--depending on subject, can utilize public use area (for demonstration), auditorium, story hour room, library yard, work room, or parking lot

SUBJECTS
>Almost any subject is suitable; for example: acupuncture, astrology, Africa, the aged, aquariums, architecture, astronomy, automobile repair, basketball, Buddhism, birth control, cats, chess, China, cinematography, conservation, consumer protection, death, dogs, existentialism, geology, gift making, glaucoma, golf, investments, law, mental health, motorcycle repair, painting, plant diseases, pollution, pottery, religion, sculpture, sewing, snakes, taste, tea ceremony, venereal disease, vocational guidance, wills, Xosa literature, Yaqui Indians, zoning laws, Zuni poetry

SOURCES (of speakers)
>Schools and colleges (both faculties and students), museums, aquariums, zoos, scientific associations, businesses, athletic organizations, religious organizations, health agencies and organizations, consumer protection agencies, conservation organizations, clubs, artists, representatives of foreign governments, lawyers, ethnic groups, hobbyists, other individuals with special skills or backgrounds

PLANNING AND PRODUCING
>Select subject and find speaker (sometimes one finds a speaker first)
>Contact speaker--discuss fee, purpose of program, equipment he or she needs, kind of audience expected, length of speech and other parts of program, question

period, role of library in program; arrange date

Publicity--get biographical details and possibly a picture of speaker (also useful for introduction); learn something about the subject for writing publicity and for introduction; think of potential audience and places they will gather, for distributing publicity

Checking up--make sure microphones and audiovisual equipment are working at least several hours before program (in time to replace); see that enough chairs are in place or are available and that the room is well ventilated (important for large crowds); check off list of other equipment; remind speaker a day or two before program

Before the program--be there in plenty of time to greet speaker, offer him coffee, the use of a rest room, and a place to store his equipment and hang his coat; arrange with speaker and staff the handling of questions; discuss with ushers the seating of latecomers and other problems

5 ★ WORKSHOPS

Workshops are distinguished from talks and demonstrations in that the participants do or make something instead of merely receiving information. (We believe the word workshop is frequently misused, although sometimes there is a fine line separating them from demonstrations.) Workshops, to be beneficial, must cater to small groups, since the leader must pay attention to each person. From five to fifteen members seems to be the range for most workshops. Some workshops also need a lot of space, and some need expensive equipment. They require at least one expert to instruct the participants. They can range in length from one brief session to many sessions. Some can be held in any unused space in the library while others require field trips. For some workshops, a lot of staff help is needed, and others will require little more than an introduction by a staff member.

Obviously then, workshops tend to be expensive, if not in actual cash outlays and staff time, at least in terms of the size of audience. They can, nevertheless, be of great value. They can benefit the participants to a much greater degree than a lecture, and sometimes they greatly benefit the library. Film and videotape workshops, for example, have turned trouble-making teenagers into interested library users. Writing workshops have resulted in other programs where the writings have been read, and in a number of cases have led to some of the writing being published. The products of crafts workshops are often displayed in the library. So, "mighty oaks," etc. etc.... At least you may get a shrub.

There are many possible kinds of workshops, with cost, space and the availability of the instructor being the main limiting factors. In recent years, what might be termed survival workshops have flourished, reflecting--as library programs so often do--changes in needs and interests.

Job-related Workshops

One group of workshops in this category is job-related.
These programs show both the tightened economic situation
and changing attitudes. Writing a résumé is a preliminary
to getting many kinds of jobs, and a number of libraries
have held workshops on this subject. The Port Washington
(N. Y.) Public Library, for instance, had a two-session workshop, and for two hours in each session the participants
learned how to gather the necessary information, present it
effectively, and write the accompanying letter. Each participant prepared a résumé which was then criticized by a gui-
dance counselor.

Other aspects of the job hunt were explored in a series
of workshops in Hempstead, N. Y. These included "How to
Identify and Use Your Skills," "Will Returning to School Help
You?" "How to Do Well at an Interview," and "Assertiveness
for Job Hunters. " Part-time employment, career-changing,
and career exploration for women have been the subjects of
other library workshops. The latter subject, in one two-
session library program, included résumés, self-assessment,
trends, and the job search.

With job-scarcity comes higher and higher unemployment rates for teenagers, especially among minorities.
Summer job workshops have, therefore, become increasingly
popular around the country. The Osterhout Free Library of
Wilkes-Barre, Pennsylvania presented such a program. A
panel consisted of the manager of a local department store,
the manager of a McDonald's restaurant, a staff member
from a YWCA, and a representative of the Youth Employment
Service. Information on filling out applications, handling
interviews, possible job opportunities, and relating summer
jobs to career goals was provided. The 48 teenagers who
attended were later surveyed and they apparently had found
the workshop useful.

Babysitting is one job that has long been available to
teenagers but even that opportunity is drying up and more
skills are required. Prince George's County (Md.) Memorial
Library is one of many libraries to cover this subject. Their
workshops run three to four sessions and include child care,
emergency procedures, and entertaining the child. Past
speakers have included fireman and/or policeman, a nurse,
a librarian, and sometimes a panel of parents and/or ex-

perienced babysitters. At a similar workshop in another library, diapers were changed, minor first aid was demonstrated, meal times were discussed, and the participants were told about dangers to avoid. A children's librarian instructed the group in story-telling techniques, and in various crafts and other entertainment. Certificates were awarded to those completing the workshop.

Another way for teenagers, and others, to find employment is to create it. A library workshop in Maryland also explored that avenue. Participants were told to look around their neighborhoods and ascertain what people needed, such as having their windows washed, or getting things delivered. Representatives of the Board of Trade and the Chamber of Commerce participated in the program.

Education and Reading

Education is becoming more and more necessary for survival and library workshops have been right there. The Port Washington (N. Y.) Public Library ran a six-session review workshop in January for students planning to take the Scholastic Aptitude Test in March. The course emphasized math and verbal skills and was conducted by qualified teachers.

Libraries around the country are conducting programs for people who want to learn to read, to improve their reading, and to learn speed reading. In some programs, librarians and others teach the participants directly, and other programs teach the teachers. The New York Public Library runs a typical program of the latter kind. It is an 18-hour workshop in which volunteers learn several techniques of reading, how to plan appropriate lessons, and how to select materials for the students. The volunteers commit themselves to a certain number of teaching hours. In Brooklyn, New York, librarians teach people how to improve their reading. There are 12 two-hour sessions covering vocabulary, speed, comprehension and study methods. There is a program related to all the above workshops that librarians can do better than anybody--teaching people how to use the library. Such a program is especially useful for literacy classes and for the foreign-born--although the majority of people would benefit--and librarians have been running them for many years.

Alternative Energy Sources

Another aspect of survival is the search for energy alternatives. One two-hour workshop on "Home Heating with Wood" covered kinds of wood-burning stoves, the burning qualities of different woods, and safety. A two-session workshop covered the design and building of a solar hot water heater. The construction of windmills and the design of energy-efficient shelters might be the subjects of other such workshops.

Retirement

The other side of looking for a job is the prospect of leaving one--that is, getting ready to retire. This again is a subject that is necessary for survival, at least the kind of survival that makes it all worth while. The Long Beach (N.Y.) Public Library ran a six-session workshop that included the psychology of adjusting to retirement, social security and income planning, wills and estate planning, housing alternatives, existing programs for senior citizens, and sex after 60. (We don't suppose the last subject was demonstrated.)

Health

Good health is essential to the survival of the elderly, as well as to the rest of us, and library workshops are covering this ground too. Some libraries have helped people stop smoking in three sessions, with prizes to those who succeeded. Nutrition, including food preparation and storage, might be another useful workshop in this area. Looks are related to health in several ways, and one library conducted a course in summer hair care and summer skin care that dealt with the effects of sun, salt, chlorine and excessive blow-drying. To survive it is necessary to continue living and a two-day library workshop showed participants what to do when they saw somebody drowning, choking or having a heart attack. The local volunteer ambulance corps gave instructions in cardio-pulmonary resuscitation.

Arts and Crafts (Including Writing and Filmmaking)

The arts and crafts are workshop naturals, both because something can be made and because the subjects are

practically numberless--as numberless as the hairs on the
heads of at least some of us. A look at one newsletter of
the "crafty" Plainedge (N. Y.) Public Library will illustrate
the range of possible subjects. You could have at that library personalized a t-shirt or made an apron in one session, or fashioned a pine cone wreath or learned cake decorating in two sessions. If the cake decorating sweetened
your taste, you could have made candy wreaths, strudles and
appetizers in three other workshops. On other days you
might have designed a scarecrow or learned something about
furniture refinishing or Swedish husk weaving. In longer
workshops of ten or twelve sessions, you could have made
doll house furniture or leaded stained glass, or studied
painting and calligraphy.

Also at the Port Washington (N. Y.) Public Library one
could learn the art of pressing flowers or rubbing grave-
stones (for that one they needed a field trip). Basketry,
bicycle repair, astrology, photography, the folk guitar, drawing and dancing were a few of the other subjects of workshops there. Crafts workshops can require a lot of expensive material, but they need not. A number of workshops
can be conducted using inexpensive or found material. The
teacher needn't cost anything either. Sometimes a staff
member has a hidden talent. The owners of crafts shops
will often be willing to conduct a workshop free and other
residents can be found in almost any community who will
be willing to teach whatever it is they know.

Writing is a craft that seems to go with libraries,
and libraries are having an increasing number of writing
workshops--some of which have been very successful. A
poetry workshop for the elderly has been described elsewhere in this book, but they are most common, and probably
most popular among the young. These workshops are often
conducted by librarians and/or local poets. If money can
be found to pay the poet, that is fine; they will need it. If
not, they will usually teach free, poets not being used to
much money. Sometimes college students can be found who
will fill the bill. In any case, the poet need not be famous,
only be a good teacher (the two don't necessarily go together).
Sometimes writing workshops are not successful, but others
have been known to continue for several years. Poems,
plays and short stories are the most usual kinds of writing.
Often the writings are published by the library in a magazine
at the end of the workshop. This may be no more than
mimeographed sheets stapled together, but sometimes they
are attractive, finished-looking products.

One unusual writing workshop has been held at one
of the branches of The New York Public Library. It is an
area with large Chinese and Hispanic populations. Among
the teenagers it attracted were a number of recent arrivals
from Hong Kong, Taiwan, Puerto Rico and the Dominican
Republic. Some of them were shy and uncomfortable with
their new language, and many had never before used language
in a creative way. They wrote of their first impressions
of the United States, specifically about Chinatown, and about
life in their native countries. The workshop gives them the
opportunity to meet other young people who are learning to
adjust to a new world, allows them to express themselves,
and helps them become more fluent in English. They also
have a chance to read their works aloud, and to receive
constructive criticism, without the pressure and formal atmosphere of school.

Another branch of The New York Public Library conducted a bi-lingual workshop in Spanish and English--the
writings being in both languages. And a branch of the Queens
Borough (N.Y.) Public Library, after conducting a workshop
in English, is planning--at this writing--to conduct one
wholly in Spanish. Both programs were for teenagers.

The making of films is another craft or art that a
number of libraries have been able to utilize. Film workshops can be very effective and useful programs. They are
of particular interest to the young, up through college age.
The Queens Borough (N.Y.) Public Library conducted a
three-session Saturday morning series. They obtained the
services of a professional filmmaker. Two sessions were
devoted to the theory and aesthetics of film and the third
was a practical hands-on demonstration. The filmmaker
used 8mm equipment, since it was felt that that was what
teenagers could most likely afford. There were about thirty
teenagers in the group, and they ranged in age from 11 to
20; most of them were high-school seniors. Some had made
films but most were beginners.

At the practical session, some of the films that had
already been made by members of the group were screened.
That was followed by a discussion and a critique of the
techniques. Then the filmmaker demonstrated the use of
the camera and light meter, and the process of editing, and
he described ways of achieving various effects. He then
gave individual instruction for those who had questions and
problems, and the group talked with him and with each other
about filmmaking problems.

A high-school class in Sandy, Utah, went further and made a complete movie from start to finish. [1] They selected a 32-page short story by John D. Swain and turned it into a 58-page, 105-scene scenario. This writing of the script took most of three six-week mini courses. An original musical score for a 14-piece orchestra was also produced. The students made the properties including a shrunken head and a sword to do the beheading. The scriptwriters did the casting. Since there was no money for sets, they shot on location around town. They had the cooperation of the police, the airport, a local mortuary and a church. Initial contacts were made by the teacher and the students did the rest. Technical assistance was provided by a group called Filmakers, Inc. Although this was a class project, it could well have been done by a library and libraries have several advantages over schools: they can be more flexible and they can provide a freer atmosphere for those to whom the structured school has become anathema.

This was the case in one area of Boston, Massachusetts, and a branch of the Boston Public Library conducted a successful film workshop, made a movie, and inspired some bored teenagers. [2] Because teenagers used the branch library very little, and because they showed little interest in the other formal organizations in the community (there were no informal organizations), it was decided to try a filmmaking project combined with a series of semimonthly film programs. The film showings, it was hoped, would enhance the young filmmakers' appreciation of film. The program was planned neither to increase circulation nor to turn nonreaders into readers. Stimulating the thinking and imagination of the teenagers was considered goal enough.

As with many library programs, the money came from a variety of sources. An anonymous donation started the project, and the library provided a $100 charge account at a photographic laboratory. A young, professional filmmaker loaned his equipment and provided technical assistance. The project was publicized through school announcements, posters and talking to teenagers. The last method was the most successful. About twenty teenagers participated and most of them had not been in the library for years. Meetings were held twice a week. Wednesday afternoons were for planning in the library, and Saturday afternoons for shooting the film out in the community. The teenagers wrote the script, acted, directed, shot and edited the film. At first, jobs were rotated but later each settled into the kind of job he preferred. Shooting on location incurred some suspicion

from local people but they became impressed by the hard
work and seriousness of the teenagers, which is an added
benefit.   16mm film was used, presumably because it was
available.   The film cost about $180.   As is usual in film-
making only about one-fifth of the film that was shot could
be used.   Some of the films shown in the other half of the
program were An Occurrence at Owl Creek Bridge, Two Men
and a Wardrobe, Neighbors, Night and Fog and On the Bow-
ery.

The results of the project were obvious and gratifying.
One 15-year-old boy spent every afternoon for a month
editing film at the height of the softball season.   An "un-
disciplined, bored" 14-year-old boy spent half of his weekends earning money to buy film so he could spend the other
half of the weekends shooting it.   And a usually inarticulate
school dropout was heard to talk excitedly about the technical
qualities of a shot.   No librarian could ask for more.

Another kind of program allows several arts and
crafts to be explored at the same time.   In this type, libraries and museums have conducted workshops that have
explored the culture of a country or an area.   An African
workshop was conducted for teenagers.   They learned African dances, made music with African instruments and tried
out hairstyles and clothes from Africa.   A similar program
was an "Arts Workshop in Puerto Rican Culture."   The participants danced, and engaged in painting, woodcarving and
various art forms in order to explore the cultural tradition
and heritage of Puerto Rico.   A third program of this type
was a piñata workshop, which was followed by a piñata party.
And a program on American Indians involved dances, cooking, the making of masks, and the learning of legends.

And Still More Workshops

What follows is a group of more or less unusual workshops that libraries have conducted.   Some of them we know
to have been successful.   About others we don't know what
happened, but they all sound interesing, and they indicate
the wide range of such programs.

One library held a summer music workshop for teenagers.   A musician, paid by the musician's union, taught
guitar and clarinet every Tuesday morning for two hours.
The local school was willing to loan the instruments, because

they were not in session. At the end of the workshop, the participants gave a concert that was much appreciated by families and friends.

Making scrimshaw was the subject of a workshop at the East Meadow (N. Y.) Public Library. A film, <u>Eskimo Artist Kenojuak</u>, was shown. Then everyone in the group, limited to thirty by ticket, was taught to make a scrimshaw plaque on plaster--since presumably whalebone is hard to come by. Tools and other materials were provided and original Eskimo tools were shown. The workshop lasted for two hours.

Holography was the subject of a Port Washington (N. Y.) Public Library workshop. There were two sessions of several hours each. At the first session, holograms were explained and there was a demonstration of one being made. The second session met in a studio where participants attempted to make a hologram.

Whether or not the results created competition for Fred Astaire, participants probably had fun at a tap dancing workshop that a library held one Friday evening. It was taught by a professional dancer from a local dance school. Registration was limited to 60 persons over 16, and they were advised to wear comfortable clothes and leather soled shoes.

The Salt Lake City (Utah) Public Library presented a backpacker's workshop called "The Wilderness Experience." There were three sessions. The first, conducted by a staff member, was "What to Take on a Backpacking Trip." An employee of the Utah Wild Life Association taught the group "How to Survive in the Wilderness" at the second session. As an added touch of color, he appeared in full mountain man regalia--buckskins, moccasins, raccoon hat, rifle, bow and hunting knife. The same library staff member presented the third session at which he talked about interesting and unusual places to go. He also showed slides from some of his own trips. An interesting sidelight was that the program was aimed at young adults but the audience consisted largely of entire families--the first time teenagers had attended a program with their families. The entire cost of the program was $25.00 for some very attractive publicity. Which shows that good and successful programs need not cost much.

Users of the Finkelstein Memorial Library in Spring

Valley, New York did some stargazing during an astronomy
workshop held there. There was an introductory lecture at
the library, and then the group adjourned to a nearby field
for some observations. An alternative program on recent
advances in astronomy was prepared in case the weather
proved to be uncooperative; this is always a wise procedure
when any element of the program might fail you.

Motorcycle repair was the subject of a workshop at
the Spotswood (N. J.) Public Library. Some local dealers
donated disabled motorcycles and a department store donated
the tools. The workshop was taught by the director of the
library. Thus there was no cost to the library--except, of
course, the time of the director.

Videotape workshops are not so unusual now and in
fact seem to be almost commonplace. Nevertheless, they
will continue to be important. The experience of the Plymouth (Mass.) Public Library is fairly typical. They sponsored a six-week summer workshop for teenagers. The
first day was devoted to instruction. Then the group was
split up into camera crews, and each group wrote and shot
a half hour tape. One tape was called "The Plymouth Public Library's Wide World of Weird Sports." The sport was
a library obstacle course in the form of lost reserves, overdue snags, misfiled cards and other events. The other was
a serious tape, "Plymouth: Sights and Sounds," showing
historical and picturesque scenes of Plymouth, and including
interviews with tourists. Librarians, teachers, and a college student assisted in the instruction, editing, etc.

Workshops: A Summary and Checklist of Preparations

KINDS
    Film
    Videotape
    Arts and crafts
    Poetry, short story, journalism
    Energy alternatives
    Jobs and careers
    Drama
    Dance
    Music
    Citizen action
    Culture of an area or group--usually combines some of
        above

MATERIALS
Books, pamphlets, periodicals, films, recordings on
subject--for consultation during workshop sessions,
for borrowing during workshop, and for follow-up by
those wishing to go further

EQUIPMENT
Leader/expert will designate equipment needed; varies
tremendously
Dance--music (i. e. record player, recordings)
Writing--paper, pencils and possibly some books and
records
Arts and crafts--often inexpensive materials, sometimes
supplied by library, sometimes by leader, sometimes
by participants
Film and videotape--expensive, delicate and intricate
equipment (see appropriate section)
General--work tables, chairs

STAFF
One, or sometimes two, to work with expert and with
group in conducting the workshop in accordance with
the library's policies and goals (staff member may
receive enough training to conduct future workshops);
many workshops conducted initially by librarian experts

AUDIENCE
All ages--most are of interest to teenagers, many to
adults and some to children depending on level;
suitable for small groups, five to ten for film or
videotape, and up to fifteen or twenty for others

SESSIONS
Number--one (for some crafts) to ten or twenty de-
pending on scope
Spacing--at regular intervals, once or twice a week
Length--from one hour (for some crafts) to several
hours for film or videotape (travel is often involved)

SPACE
Probably small (400 sq. ft.)
Might require--electrical outlets, sink, dressing room,
good lighting, dark room

SUBJECTS
Survival--résumés, solar heaters, stopping smoking,

summer jobs
Drama--could be as simple as play reading, or could
encompass the whole range of theatrical activities
Dance--square, folk, modern, etc.
Arts and crafts--macramé, photography, kite making,
sewing, clothing design, pottery, knitting, yoga, batik,
automobile repair, egg decorating, poodle clipping
Film and videotape--record library activities, community
events, create original film
Citizen action--learn how to protect environment, protect
tenant's rights, lobby effectively
Writing--produce book, pamphlet, newspaper
Culture of area or group--learn about, create, and
perform music, dance, drama, arts and crafts (Chinese, American Indian, Israeli, Mexican, etc.)

PURPOSES AND USES
Film and videotape--show library events, community
events, on television, in the library, or elsewhere
in the community; spread knowledge of the techniques
and uses of videotape
Drama, dance, music--groups can perform in library
Arts and crafts--objects can be displayed in library
Poetry--can result in further library programs
Culture of area or group--further library programs
(All these results can be used for further library
publicity)

SOURCES
Schools and colleges, independent artists and craftsmen,
poets, theatrical, musical and dance groups, newspapers, businesses

SELECTION
Since some of these workshops require large investments
in time and money for small groups, it is wise to
predetermine interest by formally or informally polling
the community; it would also be wise to register participants

PLANNING AND PRODUCING
Find the expert or technician
Be sure there is a suitable space
Obtain equipment--if it is one time only, or an experi-
ment, and expensive equipment is needed, rent it;
if workshops are to continue, it is cheaper to buy
Gather printed or recorded materials on subject--on the

advice of an expert

Schedule--arrange with leader/expert, and, if it is a small group meeting over long period of time, with participants

With leader/expert--plan workshop's goals, discuss what library can and cannot do, what money can be spent, and what is to be done with products of workshop

Before first session--be sure equipment arrives on time and is working; remind participants, if small group

PUBLICITY

Describe goals of workshop

Describe what, if anything, participants need to know beforehand

Indicate what they should bring to first session

Publicize in schools and colleges, stores selling related material or equipment, clubs and organizations likely to have interested members, selected individuals

NOTES

1. Boberg, Lowell. "One Head Well Done--It's the 'Reel' Thing," Top of the News, June 1973, pp. 351-6.
2. Brooks, Andrea. "Filmmaking with Young Adults," The Bookmark, Oct. 1969, pp. 14-5.

Perhaps because children are more flexible, mentally as well as physically, or because they are interested in more things than adults, programming for children tends to be more varied than programming for adults; it also seems to involve audience participation more. Whatever the reasons, there are some children's librarians who are leaving no programming avenue unexplored.

An article in Illinois Libraries about the Chicago Public Library, shows something of the range of programs being tried; it also expresses the idea that the library has no walls--it can go anywhere--and that any medium or device might be used to serve the library's purposes. Each center, the article says, carries on a "full program of creative drama, writing workshops, musical choruses, camera clubs, reading clubs, tutoring, and whatever else seems to be worth trying." They also have rock festivals, magic shows, puppet shows, games and crafts, not to mention the traditional activities of story hours and films. They work in the library or anywhere in the community and they use the full range of audiovisual equipment and other devices. [1]

Children's librarians in Wisconsin have had many unusual activities. The Grafton Public Library had a kite flying contest. Another Wisconsin library, working with retarded children, borrowed from a pet store some rabbits and a kinkajou, which they let the children handle. A librarian in New York City tried something that Wisconsin, with its wide open spaces, might not need; she got a local hardware store to give her one hundred packets of seeds; using a walled-in, unused roof area that abutted the children's room, she had a plant-in; now she and the children have a roof garden with boxes of tiny marigolds, long-legged sunflowers, and even some lettuce. A New York City librarian also had a kite program; the owner of a store that sold unusual kites demonstrated kite building; during the program the children made their own kites, and then went to Central Park to fly them.

In Brooklyn (N.Y.) they had a top spinning contest, and something called a footsie[2] contest, with prizes for the winners and consolation lollipops for the losers. A librarian in The New York Public Library's Central Children's Room conceived an unusual program, a tongue-twister contest. Using a book from the library's collection, and an overhead projector, she flashed the tongue twisters onto a screen. The children, who were all of approximately the same age, were divided into teams of boys and girls, and the contest was run like a spelling bee. (If the ages varied significantly, one could run several contests.) As an added bonus, the author of the book acted as judge.

Some libraries have had another kind of contest, a pet show. The children would probably be asked to register so that enough space could be allotted and so that any necessary arrangements could be made or problems foreseen. This would be a good kind of program for the library's yard, if there is one. Outdoor programs provide added publicity by attracting passers-by. Prizes are often given in this kind of program and it is usual to be sure there are prizes for everyone. There might be prizes for the biggest, smallest, most unusual, etc. Judges might be a librarian, somebody from a pet store or the zoo, a veterinarian, or a farmer.

Games were the focus of a different kind of program in one library. First a large exhibit of antique and modern games was arranged in the library, through the cooperation of the Toy Manufacturers of America. (An individual manufacturer or a toy store might serve this purpose.) Many kinds of games were used including Scrabble and Monopoly in five languages. Then the children, age seven and up, who had registered for the program, were shown the games and heard a discussion of them. Finally they designed their own games using cardboard, various kinds of paper and fabrics, and some miscellaneous items, all supplied by the library at a cost of about $20. About forty children attended the program which lasted four afternoons. Two afternoons were devoted to designing the games and two afternoons to teaching them to other children and to playing them.

Programs for pre-school children present great opportunities for imaginative programs. Since these children are

usually brought to the library by parents, programs for the
parents can be arranged at the same time.   One library
that regularly produces these doubleheaders considers them
to be one of their most effective programs.   For the parents,
they showed films on education and child development; among
these were Kindergarten (CRM/McGraw-Hill), a 22 minute film
that shows a kindergarten class in action and in which the
cinematographers become part of the classroom experience
of the children; and Four Families (CRM/McGraw-Hill), a 58-
minute film that looks at the child-raising customs of India,
Japan, France and Canada.   At another program, a librarian
and an educator spoke on the importance of reading to children.   To vary this fare, at other sessions, a librarian gave
a talk on some books of general interest to adults, and the
staff showed some films of Chaplin, Keaton and other silent
comedians.   A recent suggestion, as yet untried, is to talk
to mothers on dangerous toys.

       For the children, a wide variety of activities was of-
fered.   They even formed a band.   The children were asked
to bring in coffee cans, pie plates and cereal boxes.   The
library supplied some bells, string, rice (for rattles) and
other small materials.   They made some simple instruments
and played them.   At another time, the staff taped two
sheets of brown paper (the length of the room) to the floor.
Then they read Little Blue and Little Yellow by Leo Lionni
and Colors by John Reiss to the children.   The children
were then invited to color the strips of paper while the staff
played records with colors as themes.   During the program,
the children grew tired of coloring; they were urged to dance
to the records, and later they returned to their coloring.
During other mornings, the children fingerpainted, listened
to picture books being read, and watched films and filmstrips.
One session was devoted to an Easter party, complete with
baskets.   This library had a videotape workshop for teenagers going on during this period.   The teenagers taped the
last pre-school session and showed the tape to the parents
and the children.   The children's librarian also displayed,
for the following month, the long sheets of paper that the
children had colored.

       Another library had a party during Easter vacation.
It started with an Easter egg hunt on the front lawn, using
balloons for eggs.   An Easter egg piñata was made of papier
mâché by one of the staff members.   It was filled with candy,
balloons and confetti and then smashed amid much excitement.   Then films were shown, followed by refreshments.

A "Summer Reading Club" run by the public library
of Plainfield, N. J. , presented many kinds of activities for
children.   It was built around a theme: "See the U. S. A. "
During the summer, there were three film programs on
various aspects of life in the United States.   There was a
puppet show, a sing-in, and square dancing for the children
and their parents.   There were numerous craft activities;
the children could made candles, do knitting or crocheting,
and engage in several other crafts.   And there were discussion groups for various age levels.   The children were also
asked to read one book of fiction and two non-fiction books,
show how they used the library to get information for an
activity, and also engage in four activities.   They were then
awarded certificates.   In addition to the activities described
above, they could write annotations that would be kept on
file in the library; make a scrapbook of the places they
visited during the summer; read a story to a friend; choose
a folk hero from the folklore map and read a story about
him (her?).

Storytelling

Although another field of human endeavor is usually
said to be the oldest profession, storytelling may be the
oldest of the arts, and it is certainly the oldest kind of library program.   The Carnegie Library of Pittsburgh has had
storytelling as a regular part of programming since 1899
and The New York Public Library dates regular storytelling
from 1908.   Not only is it the oldest kind of library program, but it is undoubtedly the most widespread.   Storytelling is done in bare library basements and luxurious
story-hour pits, in parks and on the front steps of city
houses.   Stories are told in different languages, to all kinds
of children, in all parts of the country.

Storytelling is also one of the most rewarding of library activities, both to the children and to the teller.   The
New York Public Library in a policy statement says:

> Stories are one of the most effective methods of
> introducing children to their literature, and of
> building through the folklore of the world, a uni-
> versal basis of understanding between people.   The
> storyteller sees storytelling as an opportunity for
> boys and girls to hear the spoken word, develop
> their powers of listening, and share an experience

with a living personality. Storytelling has grown
out of the relationship between children and books
that has developed within the Library walls. Great
emphasis is placed on the use of the best literary
versions of stories. The story hour assumes a
dignity through the kind of stories told, and the
manner in which the story hour is conducted. [3]

Because it is not advisable to tell stories to children
of widely different ages, this activity usually divides into
three main categories: a pre-school group, kindergarten
through second grade (ages five to seven), and third grade
and up (age eight and up). Picture books are usually used
with the first two groups, so that children can see the pictures as they are hearing the story. With the older children,
the longer stories are told without the book.

The length of the program varies with the age group.
For the pre-school children, this may be their first social
encounter. In any case they, unlike the older children, are
not used to school with its more-or-less orderly ways. So
one must start slowly, gradually increasing the length and
complexity of the program. This is, of course, only possible if approximately the same group attends each time. The
first session might run from twenty to thirty minutes, with
succeeding sessions building up to about forty-five minutes.
Individual stories for this group usually range from three or
four minutes to about ten.

With the five-to-seven age group, a storytelling session might last about thirty minutes and each story run from
eight to ten minutes. For the older group (ages eight to
ten or eleven, usually) the program can last from thirty to
forty minutes, and the stories run up to twenty minutes in
length. These time limits are all, of course, approxima-
tions and will vary with the sophistication of the children,
the experience of the storyteller, and other factors.

The scheduling pattern is important. As indicated
above, it is useful if the same group of pre-school children
attend each time. Some libraries run a cycle of storytelling
sessions of from six to eight weeks for pre-school children.
One might have a series in the fall and another in the spring.
It is useful, in such programs, to have the children register.
Registration helps to insure regularity of attendance, and one
can find out their ages and bar children who are too young.
Young children have been known to ruin an otherwise good

program, and unfortunately some mothers will even lie about their children's ages to get them into a program. Name tags are also a good idea. The tags can be simply made by a staff member out of construction paper of two or three different colors--perhaps in a simplified animal outline-- with the child's first and last name lettered on them, and they are left in the library between sessions. Tags enable the librarian to call a disruptive child by name, and the children enjoy having them and picking them out each time they come to the library. Programs for parents can be scheduled at the same time as the pre-school story hours, and they have been discussed elsewhere. A regular schedule for the older children is also important. Such scheduling has publicity value; in time it will become known that the library has a story hour on Thursday afternoons at 4 or on Saturday mornings at 10, and the audience will be gradually built up. Story hours can be scheduled weekly, bi-weekly or monthly, depending on the number of storytellers available, the number of children likely to attend, and the space available. Storytelling can also be tied in with Black History Week, Puerto Rican Discovery Day, Christmas, Halloween and other holidays.

The first thing a storyteller must do is select the stories to be told or read. Variety is important, particularly with the younger children. Since a diet of straight stories would probably be too much for very young children, one might intersperse story books with game books, for example. Ellin Greene suggests the kinds of books to use with pre-school children. One should, she says, choose

"books that represent a variety of art styles and literary forms;

books that employ word play, sounds and rhythms;

books with pleasing repetition;

books that encourage imaginative play;

books that present a positive self-image;

books that recognize feelings and deal with them sympathetically."[4]

With the increasing age of the children, the stories chosen will become more complex: there will be more

characters, a more involved plot, etc. The most important
point, all storytellers agree, is to choose a story you like;
if you like it, you will communicate that feeling to the children. Eulalie Steinmetz Ross, in The Lost Half-Hour, [5]
mentions some other points to consider. It is often a good
idea, she says, to choose stories from one's own background.
She mentions several literary qualities to look for: straightforward story lines, brisk dialogue, economy of words with
emphasis on nouns and verbs, and characterization that
comes from action rather than description.

Ross says folk tales will often be the easiest for the
beginning storyteller because they usually contain these elements. When looking for folk tales to read, Ross suggests
reading them very slowly--and possibly aloud--to make yourself aware of the fine points, since such stories move very
rapidly and much happens in them. It is best, she says, to
choose versions of folk tales that have been told by other
storytellers, or by authors "with an instinct for oral interpretation." She particularly recommends versions of folk
tales by the following authors:

Joseph Jacobs	Howard Pyle
Wanda Gag	Richard Chase
Seumas MacManus	Walter de la Mare
Gudrun Thorne-Thomsen	Ruth Sawyer
Parker Fillmore	

No one should need to be told that in the decade
since Mrs. Ross's book was published, tremendous changes
have taken place. Among these has been an increased
awareness of different cultures and there has been a trend
in storytelling, at least in urban areas, to include folk tales
from the many ethnic collections now being published. Pura
Belpré White's Puerto Rican collections, the two volumes of
folk tales, of many countries, edited by Augusta Baker, and
the several collections of African folk tales by Harold Courlander and others are some that are being used. China,
Mexico, the American Indian and the Eskimos are among
the other cultures represented in this trend.

The second necessity for a storyteller is to learn the
story. Stories fall into two broad categories; original stories
by creative writers and folk and fairy tales. Stories by
creative writers (since style is important) must be learned
word for word. Some believe folk tales need not be learned
word for word, and, of course, it is in the nature of folk

tales that they have changed as they have been passed down
from generation to generation. Folk tales, however, that
have been retold by a creative writer should be told word
for word, since presumably they are stylistically better than
the storyteller can do. And Ross believes that, at least for
the beginner, all stories should be so learned; she says that
changes tend to lose the flavor of the story and may violate
its spirit. [6] In the end, the decision probably depends on the
taste, skill and experience of the storyteller.

Ross says that, in learning the story, one should
read it over and over again, preferably aloud, until one has
a feeling for the style. Then, she says, put the book aside
and get the story into your mind. She does that by seeing
the story as a series of "colored moving-picture frames."
Others make notes to refer to until they have the story memorized. When the story has been memorized, practice it by
telling it aloud to a mirror or to anybody who will listen.

After the story has been selected and learned, and
the time has come to tell it, the children must be prepared
for listening. As indicated earlier, stories are being told
in all kinds of places, and under all kinds of conditions. If
the program is to take place in the library, it should be
held in an area that is free from noise and interruptions,
and, as in all programs, the audience should be comfortable
and able to concentrate on the story. Ross, who likes
chairs better than stools, suggests placing them in short
rows, and the chairs of each row placed
as shown here so that the children and
the storyteller can see each other's faces.
She says, "In the children's responsive
faces the storyteller often finds the in-
spiration to reach new heights of excellence. "[7]

The children who have assembled for a storytelling
session have to be made quiet and must have their attention
focused on the storyteller. Various devices are used. If
they assemble in the children's room and must go to the
storytelling area, it seems to be a good idea to form them
into a line and have them process--this helps to quiet them.
Some libraries use a "wishing candle." The candle is lit
after the children have been seated, and the children are told
they cannot talk once this has been done. When the story is
over, the children make wishes and someone blows out the
candle; one may select a birthday child, or, if it is a small

group, they can all gather around to blow it out. At Halloween, a candle inside a jack-o-lantern serves the same purpose, and also, when the lights are out, provides the right atmosphere.

Ellin Greene suggests setting up a table with fresh or dried flowers, the books to be used in the program, and any objects that might complement the stories. One need not buy expensive flowers, for as Greene points out, "weeds are pretty, too!"[8] Many librarians could find some goldenrod, chicory or Queen Anne's Lace along a roadside, and every lawn has its dandelions (which last, however, only a short time once picked). Greene also suggests the possibility of using a puppet to introduce the stories.

The final thing the storyteller must do is tell the story; Ross gives some hints.[9] Start slowly, she says, and she gives several reasons; the ears of the audience can then adjust to your voice, you can raise the volume if your voice is not carrying to the back (watch for restlessness) a beginning storyteller is likely to be nervous and speak too rapidly, and since much happens in the opening sentences of a folk tale the listeners need time to assimilate it. She feels that the beginner need not be much concerned with techniques and should not strive for dramatic effects. These things will come in time, and one will learn when to vary the pitch of his voice and the pace of the story, and when and how long pauses should be to be effective. (Two ways of learning these things are by observing other storytellers and by listening to recordings of other storytellers--and oneself.) The quality Ross believes to be the most important, and other librarians concur, is sincerity. And sincerity comes from finding the right story, from learning the story so well that it is part of the storyteller, and from a delight in the story by the storyteller.

Storytelling for the Very Young

A lot of librarians are now telling stories to children who are younger than those in traditional story hours. Sometimes these children are as young as eighteen months. Usually they are from two to three years old, and sometimes to three and one half. Storytelling for this age has special problems and demands special techniques. There are also rewards; when these children go into the regular story hours, they behave better than those who are starting new and you

may be starting today's increasingly sophisticated children
on the book and library habit.

The size of the group is important. Large numbers
of children are difficult to manage at this age, and several
librarians have suggested ten as the optimum number. That
means limiting the group in some way, possibly by registration. Limiting a group at a program in a public library is
sometimes difficult, and it is not exactly in accord with the
public library ideal. Nevertheless, if you are going to have
such a program, it is probably necessary. One can't always
be too rigid, though, and it might be better to accept one
or two extra if it seems as though there won't be a lot more.
Limiting a group also allows the librarian to give the children individual attention, an important item at this age.

The length of the program is also important, and it
is definitely shorter than the traditional storytime. There
is some difference of opinion here, although part of that
difference might be in the slightly different ages that librarians are dealing with, since six months can bring a big
change in very young children. A librarian who works with
children of from eighteen months to two and one half years
limits her program to fifteen minutes. Another who has
some children under two, but most between two and three,
runs anywhere from fifteen to thirty five minutes, depending
on the circumstances and on the children. Other librarians
vary: one said that twenty minutes was tops; another thinks
twenty to twenty five minutes would be the longest she would
run a program of this kind; and one who has children ranging
from two and one half to three and one half years manages
to keep them interested for a full half hour. Probably the
most important thing to remember is the word one librarian
said was the key to programming for this age group--"flexibility." Young children are, after all, individuals too, and
they don't always behave the way the books on child development say they will.

The space must be considered. It should be the same
space every time, so that the children will become familiar
with it and associate it with storytime. It should be a confined space, so they won't wander away. And distracting
objects should be removed. Don't have it in the stack area,
for example, or don't have any unnecessary furniture around,
or anything not connected with the program. The books that
are being used for the program--those that have been and are
going to be read--should be kept behind the storyteller and
out of reach.

Then there are the parents, who necessarily come with
young children. There is some difference of opinion about
where they are to stay. Most librarians like them right
with the children, holding the children on their laps or sitting
next to them. Some of these librarians think it's just too
much trouble to separate them, and that it is not the librarian's job to do the admittedly more difficult task of shep-
herding a group of very young children. A number of librarians also say there are positive aspects to having the
parents there. This group says the parents can help the
children learn to focus on the storyteller, and that they can
be role models by participating in the program. Others
have mentioned the pleasures derived by parent and child
from sharing an experience. Parents also learn stories,
songs and games they can repeat at home with the children.

Some librarians, however, do separate the children
and parents. One of these feels that although the parents'
presence is often comforting, it is also often distracting.
Ideally, she says, the parents should be moved a little way
off--visible to the children, but quiet. A librarian who works
with children eighteen months old says it is impossible to
separate them. But the librarian who separates them does take
in children who are under two. Maybe it all depends on the li-
briarian, the children, and what you are trying to accomplish.
It might be interesting to try it both ways.

It is useful, at the first session or prior to it, to
have a discussion with the parents. Regularity of attendance
should be stressed, says one librarian. They can be told
about the format of the program, what is expected of them,
and what your goals are. They can be shown the materials
to be used, and taken on a tour of the children's room--or
possibly the rest of the library, which they might not have
used before. Older siblings are sometimes a problem, and
an article in School Library Journal suggests some solutions. [10]
The parents can be urged to arrange for sitters. Other
staff members could watch them, possibly using pages for
this purpose. The Friends of the Library, or a similar group
can provide a volunteer. The parents can be told that the
older children can't come, which would limit attendance.
If there is a group of older children, and another storyteller
is available, perhaps they could have their own program at
the same time. It wouldn't have to be a story, of course.
Showing a film, for example, might better fit in with the
library's resources.

Make an effort to learn each child's name, and greet
each child by name. Name tags for both parents and children are useful. As for the format, the word "flexibility"
was used here too. The traditional storytime approach,
with the librarian standing in front of the group is not the
norm, according to one librarian, who said, "They are a
very mobile group and you must move with them." She sits
on the floor, kneels, or does whatever seems appropriate;
this is the librarian who separates parents and children.
Another librarian used the word "active" when describing
storytelling for this group.

The use of a puppet was mentioned by several librarians. The puppet can introduce the story, and can even
turn the pages. Children who are shy will sometimes talk
to the puppet before they will talk to the librarian. One
librarian said, "Children will be glad to introduce themselves
to the puppet (and you learn their names at the same time).
They will also listen quietly to the stories so that the puppet
can hear."[11] She also says that the children will learn that
when the puppet goes on the storyteller's hand, the story is
about to begin.

The program itself should be varied: stories are
interspersed with songs, games, finger plays and nursery
rhymes. One librarian even mentioned using films. Usually
they are animated—no doubt in both senses of the word.
They must be extremely simple, and last no more than five
or six minutes. This same librarian plays the guitar for
the children, because she says they like live music best.
Games with body action are good, anything that involves
stamping the feet or clapping hands, for instance. Sometimes
circle games are played. One librarian mentions improvis-
ing "simple physical activities suggested by the ... story...."
She says that these improvisations are better than more
difficult games and finger plays " ... because they extend
the fun of the story ... require imitation rather than verbal
instruction," and because two-year-old children " ... seldom
have the manual dexterity necessary for finger games of any
complexity."[12] Finger plays are commonly used with two-
year-olds, though. It was suggested that repeating them
would be helpful. That would give the child a chance to
master them and to be a success. "Eensy Weensy Spider,"
"Two Little Eyes," "Grandma's Glasses," "Two Little Apples," and "Here's the Bunny" were mentioned as the most
popular, although there are a lot of other possibilities.

The stories that are used are very short and simple, and have large, bright pictures, often of things the children will recognize--animals, numbers, common objects. Children will often say, "I have that" or something similar. A number of lists of stories for this age have been compiled, two of them in the fine School Library Journal articles cited above. Stories that have been mentioned by other librarians include Whistle for Willie and The Snowy Day by Ezra Jack Keats, Whose Mouse Are You? by Robert Kraus, Good Night Owl by Pat Hutchins, Freight Train by Donald Crews, Charles Shaw's It Looked Like Spilt Milk and Elephant Buttons by Noriko Ueno.

Some kind of visual focus is important and that's probably why a live musician is better than a recording and why a film would work. The children are, after all, probably used to television. Flannelboard presentations and filmstrips have also been used. All this variation of the program, and the use of short, lively elements is because of the short attention spans these children have, and because of the need for frequent physical activity. It was also suggested as important that the elements in a program (story, song, story, game, etc.) be given in the same order each time.

But, we've delayed long enough, It's storytime! One librarian sets up a semi-circle of tiny chairs with dolls in them. She says it gives the children the idea. She and the children sit on a rug in front of the chairs. "I've found it successful to present a participation type book first, to capture their interest and have them feel part of the group," we were told by one librarian we consulted. One doesn't read the story so much as present it, she says. Sometimes the children will tell you about the teddy bears they have. You can listen, discuss them, and then try to bring them back to the book. If the story isn't working, this librarian says she just cuts to the end, and "steps up the action" with a song or finger play.

A good way to finish the program, it was suggested, was to hand out one of the books to each child, and let them look at it alone. The librarian then circulates among them. She and the child pick out some pictures to look at and talk about, and the child learns to turn pages and how to hold the book. The parent would help in this activity.

There is one final note: it is better to over-plan the program, and then be flexible about what you do. That principle could apply to almost any kind of program.

Storytelling with Props

     A lone performer on a stage--without scenery, props, or costume--can present us with great theatre. That performer must be very good, however, and accessories do usually enhance the performance. Sometimes, of course, gimmicks detract from a performance, but a costume, an object, or a piece of furniture often is useful.

     Coni Dyckman of the Hendrick Hudson Free Library in Montrose, New York, likes props when she tells a story. She says they lend "visual excitement" to the story and give it an "added dimension." She does point out that you will still have to know the story well. The props are not crutches. Beyond that, props--far from interfering--will enhance the story. They will also, in Ms. Dyckman's words, " ... help make the transition from television, a recognized albeit troublesome fact of life to the storyteller."

     Ms. Dyckman uses a "story box" from which she takes the objects one at a time. As she takes them out, she talks about them, and she builds interest by letting the children handle them. Some of these props she finds at school fairs, some she makes, and some are made by friends. A number of them are found objects. She uses clothes pins, work gloves, egg cartons, and the cotton from medicine bottles. She is constantly seeking new ideas and reads all the crafts books she can get.

     One of the story boxes is in the shape of a pelican. For The Five Chinese Brothers, Ms. Dyckman will draw out five finger puppets. For Gertrude the Goose Who Forgot by Joanna Galdone, she has a duck which she dresses--as she tells the story--with a hat, shoes, socks, a shawl and a purse. And for Katy No Pocket by Emmy Paybe she uses a plywood kangaroo with an apron. When it comes to Lengthy by Syd Hoff and Crictor by Tomi Ungerer she uses stuffed animals which she has to carry in florist's boxes because of their size. Work gloves, egg cartons, clothes pins and a blackboard are the Handful of Suprises she uses for that book by Anne Heathers and Frances Esteban. Tico and the Golden Wings is a papier-mâché bird with detachable golden wings. The book is by Leo Lionni. Her "Snopp"--from The Snopp on the Sidewalk and Other Poems by Jack Prelutsky--is imagination run riot; she created it herself.

     In an extension of storytelling, Ms. Dyckman makes

headpieces of lions, cats, roosters and other animals. The children then act out the story, and a program develops naturally.

Another use of props in storytelling has been developed by Ms. Dyckman. She introduces the children to various cultures by telling them stories from that culture, along with showing them actual artifacts. For stories from Africa she uses Moroccan, Nigerian and Kenyan dolls, a Benin puppet, appliqué from Dahomey, a mask, a weaving tool and various carved pieces. Such stories as Why Mosquitoes Buzz in People's Ears by Verna Aardema, "Talk" from Cow Tail Switch and Other West African Stories by Harold Courlander and "Test of Friendship" from The Dancing Palm and Other Nigerian Folktales by Barbara Walker are used.

For stories from the Far East she uses items like Japanese and Korean dolls, fans, kites, chopsticks, an origami crane, masks, ceramic bells, an abacus, a screen, a newspaper and a map. And she tells Sadako and the 1,000 Paper Cranes by Eleanor Coerr, "Terrible Black Snake" from Sea of Gold and Other Tales from Japan by Yoshiko Uchida, and "Urashima Taro" from Fairy Tales, Old and New by May Hill Arbuthnot. Ms. Dyckman has developed similar programs for South America and the United States.

At some libraries, the storyteller dresses in a costume, and these can be very simple affairs. For a Halloween story hour, a librarian in The New York Public Library made a witch's costume. She borrowed a long, black dress from a colleague, made a hat from poster board (the brim was stapled to the crown) and bought (for thirty-nine cents) a Halloween makeup kit which included black wax to blacken her teeth. In Paducah, Kentucky, they use costumes for storytelling on a regular basis. A wardrobe has been built up and each piece or costume can be used many times. There they have dressed as everything from clowns to visitors from outer space.

Various media have been used in connection with storytelling. An overhead projector can be used to create an environment that is compatible with the story being read. The author of a Library Journal article suggests using a green transparency as a setting for A Tree Is Nice by Janice Udry. It will she says, "Flood the children in an environment of green."[13] A blue transparency with a sound effect recording of rain will do nicely for And It Rained by Ellen

Raskin. And for The Great Blueness by Arnold Lobel she
used a water-filled ash tray; each time the wizard changed
the color of the world, she added a different food coloring.

Another storyteller made imaginative use of a record-
ing; she read to the children the sections of the Laura Ingalls
Wilder books that deal with wolves, and then she played
Language and Music of the Wolves (Columbia C-30769).
Anyone who has heard this haunting record can appreciate
the dimension it added to the stories.

And if you do all these things with props, you too,
like Crictor, will be "Loved and respected by the entire
village" and you may "live a long and happy life."

Puppet Shows

One of the most popular kinds of programs for children is the puppet show. Sometimes it is a show presented
to the children by librarians or others, and sometimes the
children make the puppets, scenery and stage, and present
the show themselves. Either way, puppet shows are usually
howling successes. Some librarians have successfully made
puppet theatres and puppets themselves, and have put on
very professional performances. One children's librarian
has made two puppet theatres. One of them folds into a
compact box and can be made from materials costing (in
1973) about $25. The other does not fold and cost $10.
Plans for making the theatres were found in The Puppet
Theatre Handbook by Marjorie Batchelder (New York: Harper, 1947). Instructions for making puppets can be found in
a number of books, listed in the Bibliography at the back
of this book.

Puppet workshops might not produce productions as
finished as those put on by adults, but they are undoubtedly
more engrossing and of more value for the children. A
typical puppet workshop is described in the following excerpt
from an annual report.

A three-week puppet workshop drew 142 children
and many spectators. Session I was devoted to
demonstrating a variety of easy puppets; papier-
mâché, sock, finger puppets, stick, paper bag,
and paper plate puppets. Children were encouraged
to create their own characters using paper bags,

plates and socks. We provided basic materials, while the children provided material for special effects, i. e. sequins, special bits of ribbon or buttons, fur etc. Children tried making favorite fairy tale and TV characters. I suggested a variety of characters from books that might make for good puppet plays later on.

Session II was a group effort, resulting in a stick puppet presentation of Lionni's Swimmy. I began by explaining the technique of stick puppets. I read the story aloud to the group and invited children to choose the character from the book they would like to make. The choice of a neutral story (sans prince, or 'sissy stuff') made it easy to involve boys as well as girls in the production. There is nothing sissy about a six-foot electric eel, or an enormous tuna with tin foil teeth.

Younger children helped to decorate 'the sea,' a yard long roll of tissue paper which, with a collage of yarn, paper, and magic marker sea creatures, was used in the auditorium to hide from view our young puppeteers when on the stage. Children were given about forty minutes to construct their puppets, then all the characters were taken downstairs to our auditorium for a dress rehearsal. The sea was attached to the auditorium wall, a volunteer 'bubble blower' was recruited from the audience for atmosphere, and with me reading the book out loud, the puppets told the story on stage for parents and assembled friends. Two days later a second performance was scheduled. We asked for children to volunteer in assisting to manipulate the puppets. They seemed particularly elated to oblige. All together 25 children manipulated puppets on stage, quite a feat on our small stage.

Session III emphasized relating puppet characters to stories for plays with puppets. I demonstrated simple finger puppets and showed how cardboard boxes in varying sizes could be decorated for puppet stages; Shoe boxes made good finger puppet stages; cardboard boxes were used for hand puppets, the boxes varying in size from table top variety to a huge refrigerator packing crate. Working in groups, children chose a story to dramatize, worked on stages, and dialogue, and prepared for a formal puppet show. Finger puppet plays were

given of: Whistle for Willie, The Three Bears,
nursery rhymes, and an original fantasy called:
The Indian Family. Using an exhibit case as a
stage, hand puppet performances included: Cinderella, Red Riding Hood, and an original story, The
Cat Lover. A repeat performance was scheduled
for two days later, this time using our auditorium
and our full sized puppet stage. Audience and
performers were enthusiastic, and several asked
if the workshop could be repeated in the Fall."14

Dramatic Programs

From Finland (the Youth Theatre of the Tampere
Public Library) to Seattle (Let's Pretend with Fours and
Fives) libraries have long had active dramatic programs for
children and young adults. Boston, with creative drama
classes, Providence, with improvisational theatre, New York
City and Philadelphia, mentioned later in this section, and
various libraries in Westchester County, N. Y. , are committed to some form of drama in the library. Sometimes
outside theatre groups of adults bring programs to the library. Sometimes librarians themselves form groups of
children to perform. There are classes and workshops.
There are structured plays. And there is improvisational
drama. But, whatever forms they take, librarians in all
these places agree that dramatic programs are valuable and
that they serve a variety of functions.

The Free Library of Philadelphia has a long history
of working with children and drama. They have conducted,
for a number of years, classes for children in creative
drama and workshops for adults who teach those classes.
With funds from the library, a foundation, and the Library
Services and Construction Act, such classes expanded from
a modest beginning of three in 1961 to 36 classes in 1968.
The purpose and justification for this program are well presented in the program's brochure:

Creative Dramatics offers participants the immediate experience of 'doing drama. ' Unhampered
by scripts and memorized lines, children explore
the essentials of drama--action, plot, character,
dialogue--and use these as the building blocks
for their creating. The value to the individual
child evolves from his extemporaneous doing of

drama rather than from any attempt to prepare
a polished production for audience enjoyment.

... the purpose of the Creative Dramatics project
is to develop in youngsters an awareness of themselves as individuals and of the world around
them through experience in improvised drama.
Its intent is to foster an appreciation of literature
and interest in books while encouraging creativity,
improving the self-image of the child, and helping
him relate to others.... The Free Library Program generates in the child a curiosity and desire
to explore the world of literature through the art
of drama. Literary appreciation grows as children 'try on' characters from familiar as well as
unfamiliar tales and respond to poetry with its
range of expression and mood. Art, music, history, science, current events--any of the Library
resources--can provide a starting point for dramatization. 15

A librarian in New York City who was conducting a
drama workshop expressed some similar ideas. She said,
in conversation, that these workshops helped the child to
use his imagination, to gain confidence, and to get into the
story. She also said that they helped the child's reading
and awakened him to other areas of reading, especially plays.
She also stressed the lack of solemnity in her workshops.
She, above all, wanted the children to take pleasure in what
they were doing. She had had the experience of reading
funny stories to children who weren't sure they were allowed
to laugh, and of seeing children, in and out of school, whose
whole lives were structured and formal. "Children," she
said, "should be able to laugh."

The flyer for this workshop says, "These workshops
are designed to help your child improve his listening skills,
utilize his imagination, and improve his skill at self-expres-
sion. Week to week, we move from familiar concrete situations and characters (family members, dinner time, farm
animals) to more abstract, less familiar concepts (imaginary
animals, inanimate objects, sounds)."

This particular workshop was created for children
from five to seven years old. The librarian would usually
read the story and the children would be asked to act along
as the story was being read (they would all roar like lions

or swim like fish); or she would read the story first, and
then they would act different parts. At the conclusion of
the workshop there would be a recital which might take
various forms, depending on how the workshop developed.

TUESDAY, JULY 10, 10:30-11:30 a. m.

Mexicali soup--Hitte
When mother goes to make her famous Mexicali
soup, everyone in the family has a suggestion about
what to leave OUT. Join the family ... be mother,
father.

Terrible roar--Pinkwater
A little lion discovers he has a terrible roar. Every
time he opens his mouth a terrible roar comes out,
and every time he roars, SOMETHING VANISHES....
Be a lion, an elephant, a mountain, a star....

TUESDAY, JULY 17, 10:30-11:30 a. m.

The turnip--Donamaska
Grandpa planted one little seed. He never expected
such an enormous turnip. It got so large he had to
call the whole family and the farm animals to help
pull it up. Be grandpa, boy, dog, gaggle of geese,
a turnip.

I wish that I had duck feet--Geisel
Just suppose you suddenly grew duck feet, an elephant's trunk, a deer's antlers....

TUESDAY, JULY 24, 10:30-11:30 a. m.

Where the wild things are--Sendak
When Max was bad he got sent to his room, but instead he went to where the wild things are.... Make
a mask and be a wild thing too....

TUESDAY, JULY 30, 10:30-11:30 a. m.

Magic Michael--Slobodkin
Michael was always being something or other. Can
you be a stork, a light bulb, a book?

TUESDAY, AUGUST 7, 10:30-11:30 a. m.

What kind of sounds can you make?

> Mr. Brown can moo! Can you?--Geisel
>> Can you be a hippo chewing gum? A goldfish kiss?
>> A bass drum? A fife?

TUESDAY, AUGUST 14, 10:30-11:30 a.m.

> The buried moon--Jacobs
>> Once in the long ago, when the world was filled with
>> bogs and such, the moon came down from the sky
>> and was trapped in the swamp by the ghouls and
>> mooly things. Be a mooly creature....

TUESDAY, AUGUST 21, 10:30-11:30 a.m.

> Conclusion and recital.

At the same time, this librarian conducted a workshop for children age nine and older. This group started
with skits taken from books in the library. They then went
on to plays of one or two pages which they used as starting
points for improvisation. Still later they did dramatizations
from things like Alice in Wonderland and Stone Soup.

This librarian has done dramatics in two libraries in
widely different communities, and she has seen dramatic
differences in the children of the two areas. In the community with a preponderance of children from low-income
families, there were many poor readers and the children
had difficulty learning their lines; however, they were much
less inhibited and got into their parts much more than the
children from the more affluent families. The more affluent,
however, read very well and learned their lines more easily.
She concluded that the children from the higher income
families led much more structured lives, and needed an unstructured workshop.

In an article in Top of the News, Irene Cullinane and
Theresa Brettschneider list the activities for a ten-session
program in creative dramatics that was given at Poughkeep-
sie, New York.[16] This program was for children up to 13.

Sessions 1 and 2. RECREATING FAMILIAR PHYSICAL
> ACTIVITIES (throwing a ball, jumping rope, running in
> the wind) to activate the imagination, develop the powers
> of concentration, and to relax the body by encouraging a
> natural response. Charade games (guess what I'm doing?)
> are popular and effective.

Session 3. EXERCISES INVOLVING PHYSICAL SENSES (eating sour pickles, listening to the grating sound of fingernails on a blackboard).

Session 4. RANDOM WALK. Group walks in a circle and reacts to words called at random by a leader (sticky, afraid, ocean).

Session 5. ADDING EMOTIONAL REACTION TO AN AC-TIVITY (looking at a report card, an automobile accident, a banana split).

Session 6. CHANGE-OF-MOOD PANTOMIME. In small groups of two or three, children act scenes with a definite transition of mood (walking proudly in new clothes and being caught in the rain, being afraid of approaching footsteps on a dark night only to discover it is a favorite uncle).
   From this point on children are encouraged to think as someone other than themselves. They are eager to do this from the beginning but they need the discipline and stimulation of formal exercises in sensory perception and emotional responses.

Sessions 7 and 8. CHARACTER IMPERSONATIONS. Each child is handed a card (king, clown, detective) and walks as that character. Action cards (crossing a brook, riding a bicycle) are then distributed and each child amplifies the given character.

Sessions 9 and 10. FORMING SKITS. Small groups are given character and action cards and told to make up a story using all of the cards. Speech is a natural addition at this point. Each skit is presented to the group for approval and analysis. Some skits are expanded to include more characters and repeated with other members of the group.

   Cullinane and Brettschneider say, "the group is now ready for full-scale dramatization of their own plays or familiar folk stories such as Stone Soup, Three Billy Goats Gruff, Rumpelstiltskin." These techniques can be adapted for all upper elementary age levels. For those younger children who are not ready for interpretive dramatics, they suggest the imitation of animals, imitating characters in a story, simple games, pantomimes, finger plays and other such activities.

In another kind of program, students of a graduate
course in children's literature presented dramatized versions
of fairy tales and picture books. Their purpose was to
"entertain the children and to encourage them to listen, and
to read on their own."[17] One of the plays was a version of
The Giving Tree by Silverstein, complete with a seven-foot
cardboard tree that had real branches and a smiling human
face. The audience had to be restricted to ages seven to
eleven, because of the overwhelming response to similar
programs--an indication of the popularity of this kind of
program. The children's librarian believed that these programs "served a special role in linking the community, the
library and the children." This was partly so because the
performers were parents of the area, teachers in the local
schools and volunteer workers in neighborhood service groups;
thus they were linked to community, library and children in
several ways.

Librarians have gathered children together to put on
traditional, structured plays. One librarian has been over
(almost) whelmed with the response to her idea. She wanted
to form a theatre goup for children in the fourth through
the eighth grades. One hundred and fifty children responded
to her initial request. She selected the plays to be presented and, with the help of volunteer directors, held audi-
tions, selected the cast, rehearsed the actors, prepared the
publicity and presented the plays. Up to fifty or sixty children were auditioned for each play. Those that were not
given speaking parts were asked to work on other important
aspects of play production, such as publicity, props, costumes, stage crew, and ushering. No money was spent on
costumes or props, both for the sake of the children and because the library (so, what else is new?) had no money.

One extra benefit to the staff was that the children
became very excited about the plays; they made suggestions
about what plays should be produced and they continually
asked when the next production would be. It is times like
these that make programming seem very worthwhile. If
the response of children who wanted to be in the play was
greatly enthusiastic, the response from those who wanted to
attend was David Merrick's dream. One hundred tickets
were prepared for the first performance of Sleeping Beauty,
and they disappeared on the first day. At a second per
formance, after all the seats were filled, one hundred additional children wanted standing room. Performances were
later given at other libraries and, in additional spin-off, a
neighborhood group was formed to give backyard plays.

A children's librarian at the Caldwell (Idaho) Public Library presents what she calls "Instant Drama" once a month. She has formed a "Junior Library Club" of children from six to fourteen and there are about 90 members. When a play is to be given about 20 members are called in for tryouts for the important roles. This is about a week before the play, and she and the members who are present decide who will get the parts. If there is time, at that meeting, they run through the play once. Those with the parts take a copy of the script home for study. They are required to know when to speak and when to enter and leave, but word-for-word memorization is not necessary; they are told to ad lib, if they forget. A one-hour practice session is held on the day of the performance.

The children's librarian dramatizes fairy tales and other children's books. The script is kept simple, and sometimes merely the outline of the story is used, with the actors using their own words as they go along. The Three Bears, Three Billy Goats Gruff and Little Red Riding Hood were found to be fairly easy to produce in this way. With less familiar stories, she has found that there are often one or two natural actors who can carry the story and make it a success, regardless of the others.

Costumes are a mere suggestion, and scenery is kept to a minimum. Paper masks, a gold crown made of Christmas wrapping paper, a crepe paper cape and other easily made objects are used. A narrator is often found useful to fill in gaps in the story. Since there is neither stage nor curtains, the entire room is used as a theatre, with the audience in the middle. That is, different acts can be presented in different parts of the room, according to the dictates of the play. Such a system is good when there is action--the children running from one part of the room to another.

Chamber Theatre

A different kind of drama program is "chamber theater." It is described in another article in Top of the News[18] (a gold mine of information on dramatic programs). The advantages of chamber theatre are that it is easily produced, you can be flexible, and it costs very little in terms of both money and staff time. It is described as "an oral interpretation by two or more voices of a story or poem. It is not an adaptation of any sort, but rather a word-for-word presentation with all the 'he said's and 'she answered's left in."[19]   The material, the author suggests, should be carefully selected to suit the age group and it should have a lot of dialogue.   Thurber's "The Unicorn in the Garden" and "The Secret Life of Walter Mitty" are suggested as sure-fire stories.   She says that if you have enough talented readers, you can choose works that are basically narrative and that don't have much dialogue.   Henry James's "Beast in the Jungle" and chapters from Ray Bradbury's Dandelion Wine are possibilities.   They should be carefully divided to take advantage of the variations in prose and the talents of the readers.   For poetry, she suggests as examples, Eliot's "The Hollow Men," Frost's "The Death of the Hired Man," and Benét's "John Brown's Body."

The properties, sets, and costumes are kept very simple.   One device she considers effective is to have all the readers dress alike.   Certainly libraries will want to make adaptations depending on their circumstances and other work they are presenting.   This seems like an important program for libraries because of its effectiveness and simplicity.   It will certainly be important for the performers, for many reasons--not the least of which is that it will make them pay close attention to the words on the page, a consummation of the reading act "devoutly to be wished."

For those who want help with dramatic programs, the Children's Theatre Conference is available.   This organization, with headquarters in Washington, D.C., was formed in 1944 to "promote work in children's theatre and creative drama; to raise standards of productions and of informal dramatic work with children and to encourage excellence in training for workers in the field."[20]   It is divided into 15 geographical regions that sponsor local workshops, festivals and other projects.   Children's Services Division of the American Library Association has set up a committee to work with them. CTC can hold workshops for librarians to teach them the techniques of creative drama.   They can also provide an annotated bibliography of books on creative drama and children's theatre, and will suggest children's plays.   If they are already producing plays in the community, you can invite them to perform in the library.

Children's Discussion Groups

These programs, like adult discussion groups, take

several forms, and are perhaps even more varied than adult groups. In one case, three books by one author were discussed (one book in each session) and for the fourth session the children met and talked with the author. The program was entitled "Read and Meet." The children who attended were from grades four to six and refreshments were served. This program was given by the Manhasset (N.Y.) Public Library. They also had a one session discussion group at which the author was present. At another library, there was a parent and child one session book discussion group.

Three- and four-session groups seem to be common. In Manhasset, New York, they discussed Operation Peeg by Jonathon Gathorne-Hardy, Lizard Music by Daniel Pinkwater and Tuck Everlasting by Natalie Babbitt. The books were selected because they were outside the experience of the children, and because they were entertaining. When this librarian started discussion groups, she decided to give a book talk and let the children select, from the talk, the books to be discussed. It didn't work. The children couldn't agree on any book and she decided she would have to make the selections herself. Ten to twelve children attended this one--a good number for a discussion group.

Sometimes longer discussion groups are successful. At a branch library on Staten Island, New York, there was a six-session group that worked very well. Twenty-three children attended the first session, but the attendance dropped to ten for the others. This is a common experience in adult groups too and is to be expected. The program was advertised as being for grades three through eight, but the children who stayed were in the middle, ranging in age from 10 to 12. Name tags were used and proved to be helpful. Some experimentation on the time between sessions showed every other week to be better than every week. Discussions lasted about one hour, which seems a good length. The children were told to try two chapters of a book and stop if they didn't like it. Suggestions like that make the program seem less like school, as do the attitudes of the leaders during the discussion. It should not seem like a test or like a chore. One thing that should be stressed--as it should in all discussion groups--is that participants should read the book before the session. They should also be asked to come to every session, to achieve continuity.

At this group, there were two leaders (some successful groups have one leader) and one of the leaders gave a

brief introduction to discussion groups. He talked about
different kinds of conflicts in books and he discussed symbolism.

The first book discussed was Paul Zindel's The Pigman. They talked about the characters and the relationships
among them. Interestingly enough, the children saw the relationships differently than the leaders did. They also liked
the second book, Roll of Thunder Hear My Cry by Mildred
D. Taylor, but none of them finished the third book, Child
of the Owl by Laurence Yep. Most liked Summer of My
German Soldier by Bette Green, but some said there wasn't
enough action. The other books were Julie of the Wolves
by Jean Craighead George and Jonathan Livingston Seagull
by Richard Bach.

Two four-session groups were held concurrently at
the New Hyde Park (N. Y.) Public Library. One was for
children 9 to 11 and the other for ages 12 to 14. The younger
group discussed Hugh Lofting's The Story of Doctor Dolittle,
O. Henry's Gift of the Magi, Charlotte Dixon's Ali Baba and
the 40 Thieves, and Dickens's A Christmas Carol. Ten
children attended the sessions of this group and the discussions lasted 45 minutes to an hour. The racism in Hugh
Lofting's book was discussed and the attitudes of people then
and now were contrasted. Only five children attended the
sessions of the older group. That's enough for a discussion,
of course, but a slightly larger group is somewhat easier.
These children discussed "Harrison Bergeron" by Kurt Vonnegut, Ray Bradbury's "The Veldt," Louis B. Saloman's
"Univac to Univac," and again Dickens's A Christmas Carol
since it was Christmas time.

At Oceanside, New York, they have several years of
"very successful" book discussion groups for fifth and sixth
graders, with 19 or 20 children attending regularly. Their
sessions also last about an hour, and they have ranged from
three to five sessions. A single leader has been found to
be satisfactory. They have tried--as have the others--to
disassociate the program from a school atmosphere. The
children sit in a circle with their shoes off, and are given
candy or cookies. They are encouraged to express themselves freely, without criticism or a thought of being graded.
In past years, they have gone the traditional route of having
the group as a series of more or less related discussions.
For the most recent discussions, they have run them as independent programs--advertising each separately. They have

liked this format better, although it was more work, and
they have not found that it destroyed continuity. A core of
the same children continued to appear, just as they had in
previous years.

Fantasy is the most popular type of book in Oceanside. Among the books discussed were A Wrinkle in Time
by Madeleine L'Engle, Dinky Hocker Shoots Smack by M. E.
Kerr, Edith Maxwell's Just Dial a Number, Mrs. Frisby and
the Rats of Nimh by Robert C. O'Brien, and Tuck Everlasting by Natalie Babbitt.

At the public library in Port Washington, New York,
they had another variation. There was a "Twelve O'clock
Club" with the children bringing lunches. It was held on
five successive Wednesdays, and 15 to 20 children, aged ten
to twelve attended. (That seems to be the best age group.)
At each session there was a guest speaker, talking about a
genre or a specific book. Then the children discussed.

Arts and Crafts

Some imaginative programs for children have been
developed in this area by some unbound children's librarians.
These activities can easily be related to books (both imaginative and informative) and other materials. And there are
many art forms, art materials and formats around which
programs can be built.

One children's librarian planned a "Summer Arts
Festival." It was entitled "Pictures with Imagination."
Children were invited to "explore a variety of materials,
textures, and ideas as they make a different picture each
week." It was a series of six programs, for children five
years and older. The first session was a chalk-in, and it
was loosely based on The Tale of Peter Rabbit. The children were asked to draw a chalk picture of Mr. McGregor's
garden, or to make up a garden of their own. If the sun
was shining they were to draw outside on paper or on sidewalks. Rain would send them inside to draw in the library
to music. It did rain, but it was a very festive festival.
The brightly lit children's room with children all over it
drawing on large pieces of paper with colored chalk and
music in the background was a happy place to be.

For the second session, drawings and paper cut-outs

were used; children were asked to make pictures of their favorite fruits. Suggested were an apple tree with cut-outs of red apples, pumpkins and scarecrow, or berry patch and cut-out birds. Felt was used for the third program. They were asked to make felt cut-outs of characters from their favorite story or fairy tale, and to use them in making a story picture. A nature collage was the next art form used. Children brought in dried grass, leaves, feathers, twigs, hemlock cones and small stones and combined them with drawings that made pictures to express their feelings about nature.

The next picture was determined by a treasure hunt. Children were given instructions for the hunt; they hunted for objects, inside and outside the library, that had been hidden by the staff; then they made pictures using the objects they had found, so that no one knew in advance what kinds of pictures would develop.

An illustrator of children's books attended the last session. She talked, informally, about her work and about drawing, about how a drawing is made, and she answered questions from the children. Her books were exhibited during the program. The theme of the session was the sea. Children brought in shells, starfish, sand and pebbles; from these they made drawings and collages about the sea.

Materials for these program were supplied by the library at the cost of a few dollars. The attractive flyers used for publicity included very simple line drawings of flowers, birds, shells, etc. which were done by a staff member; they also featured quotations, appropriate to each session and adding much to the charm, from The Tale of Peter Rabbit, The House at Pooh Corner, Wind in the Willows and others. Most of the musical selections that were played during the indoor parts of the program were those that were familiar to the children, so that they would feel at home. The children's librarian did say, however, that she was experimenting to find out what kinds of music would best enhance the program for the children. In any case, the use of books, art work, and music in great variety, the visit of the illustrator as a culmination of the festival, and the interaction among children, librarians and materials provided an enriching experience for all concerned.

At another "Summer Arts Festival" the librarian described her goals in this way. "We wanted," she said, "an informal, relaxed atmosphere; activities that would lend themselves to broad themes and simple materials; an emphasis on the individual response. We also wanted books, the feeling of books, to be a real part of every program. Even if they might not be at the center of the activity they should at least be around--in exhibits relating to the week's activity, or on hand for the child needing help with ideas or in shaping the details of an idea." She went on to say that the word festival was the key to the tone and spirit of these programs: "we wanted most of all that everyone have a good time, that some good spirit be around, that everything that was to happen should spring from that."

The response to this festival was great. Children were waiting outside the library in the early morning before the first program. There were so many that they forced the library to open an hour ahead of schedule. Throughout the summer this response continued; they filled the children's room bringing to it "life and enthusiasm." Many arts were encompassed in this festival. The children drew murals, made nature collages, and made things from clay. There was a three-week creative writing session; during this activity, they sewed simple books, wrote stories and poems, and decorated them with pictures done in watercolors and pastels. There were also two storytelling festivals, American and European, featuring stories, folk songs and poetry.

Children came in bathing suits, on their way to a local swimming pool. Friends came in groups, brothers and sisters came together, and some children came alone. Some children had traveled widely. Others had never been as far as the local beach. But, during the summer, these children from a variety of backgrounds, shared their work, their experiences and their ideas. For various parts of this festival the following books and music were used:

American Folklore Festival

Macmillan, Cyrus. "Glooskap's Country" and "The Indian Cinderella," Glooskap's Country and Other Indian Tales, Oxford, 1956.
McCormick, Dell J. "Paul Bunyan and the Giant Mosquito Bees," Tall Timber Tales, Caxton, 1939.
Songs--group sing: "Clementine," "I've Been Working on the Railroad," "She'll Be Coming 'Round the Mountain," and "Swing Low, Sweet Chariot."
Recording--"Pete Seeger Sings America's Favorite Ballads."

Making a Book and Original Writing

(These books were used to show examples of children's
writing, poets writing for children, imaginative kinds
of books, unusual shapes of books, etc.)

Lewis, Richard, comp. Miracles, Simon & Schuster,
1966; and Journeys, Simon & Schuster, 1969.
Behn, Harry. The Golden Hive, Harcourt, 1966.
Mizimura, Kazue. I See the Wind, Crowell, 1966.
Hoffman, Felix. A Boy Went Out to Gather Pears,
Harcourt, 1966.
Sendak, Maurice. Chicken Soup with Rice, Harper,
1962.
Morrison, Lillian. Sprints and Distances, Crowell,
1965.
Larrick, Nancy, ed. On City Streets, Evans, 1968.

European Folklore Festival--The British Isles

Alger, Leclaire. "The Lass Who Went Out at the Cry
of Dawn" Thistle and Thyme, Holt, 1962.
Jacobs, Joseph. "The Rose-Tree," English Folk and
Fairy Tales, Putnam, n. d.; and "The King o' the
Cats," More English Folk and Fairy Tales, Putnam,
n. d.
Folksongs with guitar: "Fox Went Out on a Chilly
Night," "Cockles and Mussels," "Frog Went A-
Courtin'," "Down in the Valley."

Make Your Favorite Character in Clay

Some that were chosen were: the turtle in Voyages of
Doctor Dolittle, the rabbit in Rabbit Hill, the bear from
Helpful Mr. Bear, and Gollum from The Hobbit.

Still another "Summer Arts Festival" was centered
around a theme--"Celebrate the Earth." The series began
with a session on the creation myths. The following programs corresponded to the Biblical sequence of the creation
of the world. The second program, "Sun-Light-Awakening:
Moon-Stars-Darkness," tried to relate the growth and sleep
processes of nature. The titles of the other programs were
"The Ocean," "The Green Earth," "Creatures of the Earth,"
and "People." Simple techniques and materials were used:
colored paper, chalk, oil pastels, clay, collage, leaf-prints,
scratch-drawings.

At the beginning of each session in this series, the children's librarian met with the children to talk about the morning's theme. There were books on exhibit, and there were objects from nature for children to see and feel. "Foreign language poetry and picture books were especially helpful in conveying a deep feeling for the earth." The simple objects--leaves, shells, seeds--created a sense of wonder. They were passed around; the children held them, examined them, felt them. Many of the children had never before seen, or looked closely at a milkweed. Its beauty surprised them. Sometimes the children spoke of their own experiences; they told about making a garden, taking care of a pet, or vacationing at the beach. After they exchanged ideas, the children spent the rest of the time putting their images on paper.

For the "Celebrate the Earth" festival, the following books were used:

Creation Myths

Belting, Natalia M. The Sun Is a Golden Earring, Holt, 1962.
Leach, Maria. "Why the Birds Are Different Colors," How the People Sang the Mountains Up, Viking, 1967; and "Raven Finds a Clam," The Beginning; Creation Myths Around the World, Funk, 1956.
World Council of Christian Education and Sunday School Association. In the Beginning; Paintings of the Creation by Boys and Girls Around the World, Nelson, 1965.

Sun-Light-Awakening; Moon-Stars-Darkness

Selsam, Millicent. Play with Seeds, Morrow, 1957.
Webber, Irma E. Travelers All, Addison-Wesley, n. d.
Darby, Gene. What Is a Season?, Benefic Press, 1960.
Hugelshofer, Alice. Kuckuck, Kuckuck, Rufts aus dem Wald; and Wollt ihr Wissen, Wie der Bauer
Oberlander, Gerhard. Das Marchen von den drei Apfelbaumen

The Ocean

Lionni, Leo. Swimmy, Pantheon, 1963.
Lionni, Leo. Fish Is Fish, Pantheon, 1970.
McCloskey, Robert. Time of Wonder, Viking, 1957.

Huntington, Harriet E. Let's Go to the Seashore, Doubleday, 1941.

Engel, Leonard. The Sea, Time-Life, 1967.

Meyer, Jerome S. Picture Book of the Sea, Lothrop, 1956.

Abbott, Robert T. Sea Shells of the World, Golden Press, 1962.

Bevans, Michael H. Book of Sea Shells. Doubleday, 1961.

The Green Earth

Andersen, Hans Christian. The Fir Tree, Harper, 1970.

Topelius, Zakarias. "The Birch and the Star," Canute Whistlewinks, Longmans, 1927.

Carlson, Bernice. Make It and Use It, Abingdon, 1958 (used for tracing method).

Creatures of the Earth

White, E. B. Charlotte's Web, Harper, 1952.

The Golden Goose Book, Warne, n. d.

Flack, Marjorie. The Story About Ping, Viking, 1933.

Grzimek, Bernhard. Rhinos Belong to Everybody, Hill & Wang, 1965.

Schulthess, Emil. Africa, Simon & Schuster, 1969.

Periodicals: National Wildlife, Ranger Rick, Natural History

People

Lewis, Richard, comp. Miracles; Poems by Children of the English-Speaking World, Simon & Schuster, 1966.

Another similar series of programs was based on stories from around the world in honor of International Book Year. The first session was a Winnie-the-Pooh Birthday Party. The children made birthday books, ate cakes and drank punch, and blew soap bubbles. (There was only one disappointed child who kept looking for Winnie.) The series ended with a Topsy-Turvy Nonsense Party. This series, in addition to the older children, was opened to pre-school children. The mothers assisted the staff in helping and encouraging the children. In one case, an infant slept in a portable crib in the midst of all the activity.

A number of children's librarians have conducted workshops in which the children made their own books, writing, illustrating and binding them. A librarian, who obviously feels the importance of atmosphere in these programs, has described, the scene in this way:

> Tuesday mornings, a little before 10:30, the children arrive to work on making their own books. It is good to go down into Stapleton's cool basement meeting room, a pleasant place graced by cut-out paper designs made by artist Paul A. Lobel for a Paperteer workshop program earlier this year. Near the round tables where the children work are a few pictures done in bright, clear colors, of animals, of a knightly figure, and of children's book illustrator Elsa Beskow's unspoiled countryside, somehow adding their special presence, as does the bouquet of garden flowers brought each week by two young sisters who come to the arts program. Soon each child finds the material he needs (earlier he has chosen to work with watercolors, pastels, oil pastels, or a magic marker pen set), and after a look at the previous weeks' work in his folder, is ready to carry his book a step further. Some titles of the tales that are unfolding are: 'The Magic Dodo Bird,' 'The Flying Dragon,' 'The King, The Princess, and the Little Boy,' 'Wildlife,' 'Bambi and the Bear,' 'The Mouse, the Owl, and the THING.'

Each child's book is quite different from the others, for it is his own. With each session everyone including the children's librarian seems to be discovering that it is a happy thing to work this way, imposed ideas giving way to attempts to give thoughtful help, as needed. It is good, too, to hear one child telling another, "Don't forget, keep your colors clean and clear."

The Free Library of Philadelphia obtained a grant to conduct an unusual arts program. At bookmobile stops, they gave sidewalk demonstrations of printmaking, and invited the children to participate. They also gave an eight-week instructional course in printmaking at six branches. [21]

The Dallas (Texas) Historical Society has conducted workshops for children that seem natural to that part of the country but that would certainly be appropriate anywhere else. One of these was a "Pioneer Crafts Workshop" in which children aged ten to thirteen made soap, candles, quilts, and learned something about spinning and weaving and the pioneers' techniques for food preservation.

Workshops for making Halloween costumes, making toys from other countries, learning about stamp collecting, learning backgammon and learning Spanish have been conducted by libraries around the country. The public library in Springfield, Massachusetts has even given piano lessons.

Notes toward a simple arts and crafts program*

The following materials are listed according to how necessary they are, and how easy they are to obtain. The first list, marked "Essential," consists of materials which are necessary for the beginning of even the most basic arts and crafts program, according to our experience. The second list, entitled "Useful," consists of materials which have been helpful in crafts programs, but not necessary, and which may be expensive to obtain. The third list, marked "Save," contains materials which are useful to crafts programs, and which are often found in homes and children's rooms.

Essential	Useful	Save
crayons	crepe paper	newspapers
construction paper	felt	magazines
white paper	foil	used desk blotters
small pencils	waxed paper	material scraps
magic markers	pins	whole nut shells
scissors (small, blunt)	needles	wrapping paper
paste	ink pads	ribbons
white and black thread	spools	paper towel and toilet paper rolls
string	macaroni	cartons
yarn	oaktag	medicine bottles

*Reprinted, slightly altered, by permission of The New York Public Library.

tempera paint	paper bags
brushes (small, medium)	paper cups
dish pan	brown paper
paper towels	plastic tablecloth
stapler	modelling clay

Children's Science Programs

Children of various ages can be interested in science programs. One science museum takes a variety of programs--at different levels--to libraries. For children from kindergarten through the third grade, they have an "animal adaptation" program in which they talk about habitat, coloring, shape and senses. The children can see and touch rabbits, iguanas, boa constrictors and bull frogs, to name a few. They also have a botany program for the same group. Roots, leaves, seeds and spores are shown and talked about.

Botany for grades four to six focuses on parts of plants, habitat and reproduction. For these ages, there are also vertebrate and invertebrate programs. "Insects, worms, clams and snails" are among the animals without backbones that are shown. The five classes of vertebrates are described, including such aspects as skin covering and reproduction.

"Chemo-demo" as the name implies is a chemistry program. It is for all ages. It is very dramatic, and is good for large audiences, with lots of smoke, sparks and colors. Electric circuits--with batteries, wires and bulbs--and a program demonstrating the working of simple machines are some of the other subjects covered.

At the Manhasset (N. Y.) Public Library they have had a program in which the children (ages 10 to 12) learned computer games. Because of the nature of the program, it had to be limited to 12 children. A college instructor did the teaching. A portable terminal was hooked up to one of the library's telephone lines, but although the whole program lasted more than an hour, it was only on-line for about ten minutes altogether. One interesting feature noted by the librarian was that the children who attended were not library-users.

Children's Film Program

Many of the principles that govern showing for adults and teenagers also apply to film showing for children; the same care must be taken to see that the equipment is in order and that backup equipment is available; the films should be previewed, and they benefit from being introduced; and attention should be paid when selecting films to the intended audience, and to the order in which they are shown. Some of these principles are, of course, applied differently to film programs for children, and there are some factors that are applicable only to children.

Children are usually divided into several age categories: pre-school (up to five years), ages six and seven, and age eight to about twelve. Many children's librarians, however, point out that there are not sharp delineations, and that the child's experience with films and his level of sophistication also influence the choice of films. Furthermore, age, intelligence and experience are likely to vary widely within any audience. Ultimately, experience is the best guide and even then the results are not predictable. One children's librarian believes that "all you can do is aim for a good film program" and the experience of the Children's Film Theater was that they "couldn't always predict what kids will like."[22] Other librarians have found children attending, and enjoying, film programs planned for teenagers and for adults. "One clear thing about planning a film program," said a children's librarian, "is that it is a creative process." Another said, "What you put together will depend on your own taste and your instincts which will grow surer as you gain in experience."

When one is dealing with young children, there are several things to watch out for. Safety is an important factor. Children are likely to want to explore the screen and the projector and to knock them over if one is not careful. Or they might grab the film or pull on a cord, etc., etc., etc. They may also need to use lavatories and get drinks of water. For these reasons an extra staff member to watch the children is essential. Sometimes young children are afraid of a dark room so it is wise to have them enter when the lights are on, and become familiar with the surroundings. Chairs are sometimes a problem in programs; one must have enough, they must be set up and taken down. But with children, particularly young children, it might be better to let them sit on the floor; they like to do

it and it creates an informal, cozy feeling. When seating
children, it is best to seat those that are there on time at
the front; that way latecomers can be seated without disturbing the others.

Unlike programs for adults, talking at children's film
showings is not looked on with disfavor. One children's
librarian even says that "Talking is an integral part of the
child's enjoyment of the film. It is a sharing and learning
process."23 And the Children's Film Theater has a similar
experience. 24 They found that some problems in the films--
"scary parts, plot resolutions, questions of reality"--were
resolved by the children's talking among themselves. They
also found that too much or too loud talking was resolved by
the children, and that they didn't need to interfere. ("The
kids are also very adept at quieting their vociferous peers.")
Another children's librarian points out that the film program
may be the child's first social activity. She says, "They
may spend considerable time looking around at the other
children instead of at the screen. They may even walk
around and visit between films." A child, of course, shouldn't
be allowed to disrupt the program, and sometimes the librarian must step in. One commonly used technique is to
let the troublemakers help you. They can be used to turn
lights on and off, for example, or to hand out materials.

When The New York Public Library trains its children's
librarians, it offers the following guidelines for evaluating
films:

The film must show respect for the child's intelligence.
It should not be coy, patronizing or have forced
humor.
It should have originality and beauty, both in language
and visually.
The subjects and style should appeal to children.
It should avoid stereotypes.
Although some educational films are used, the didactic
is generally avoided.

Within those guidelines there are many possibilities.
One can build a program around a theme or subject. For
example, there are some fine films that are appropriate to
seasons such as winter or spring or to holidays such as
Halloween or Christmas. If animals were to be the subject,
one could have programs about pets or about wild animals.
Places or peoples--Africa, American Indians, Eskimos--

might be the subjects, or one might choose to feature individuals, such as Harriet Tubman or Frederick Douglass.
Or films could be shown about a variety of other subjects
such as circuses, cities, trains, comedy, myths and legends.

If a theme or subject doesn't seem appropriate because of differences in age and experience or because you
can't get the films you want, have a variety program. One
can not only vary the subjects, but also the style, technique
and mood of the films. Balance such qualities as realism
and imagination, and comedy and drama, or have animated
and live-action films, or films with and without narration.

The order in which films are shown is important.
A short, lively film could open the program and be followed
by a longer, more serious or slow-moving film. Or a scary
film might be followed by a funny one. Some librarians like
to end with a relaxing film, to prepare the children for the
close of the program. In any case, think about the relationships among the films and change the pace and mood.

It is important to introduce the films. For one thing,
an introduction gives the children time to settle down. One
can also explain parts of the film that might be puzzling,
suggest things they might watch for, and introduce to the
children some books that are related to the films. Thalia
Mannon-Tissot of the Brooklyn (N.Y.) Public Library described an incident that showed the importance of an introduction. 25 She showed a sing-along film, Frog Went A-
Courtin' (Weston Woods), to two groups of children on the
same afternoon. For the first showing, she suggested that
the children might like to sing along. Few did. At the
second showing, the children were "specifically told that the
fun of the film was their singing along and the results made
the library resound." One can also use such things as
poetry, finger plays, a puppet, a short story or music to
set the mood for the films. Such things are useful between
films too, especially if there is any trouble with the projector or other equipment. The children could sing a song
or merely listen to a recording.

Programs can be scheduled in a number of different
ways. Showings can be designed for special occasions such
as Book Week, Black History Week, National Library Week,
Christmas or Halloween. There could be seasonal showings
such as a spring or fall series or there could be series related to a day and time such as Saturday morning or Sunday

afternoon. Vacation series such as summer films or Christmas or Easter vacation showings are often used. Some libraries have monthly, biweekly or weekly showings during
a school year or they have shorter series such as six-week
or four-week series.

The length of a film showing for children must be
carefully considered. For pre-school children, librarians
have suggested 20 to 30 minutes, and 30 to 40 minutes.
Doubtless this would vary with the experience of the children.
One librarian suggests a "lights on" break every 20 minutes.
Another librarian conducting a pre-school series starts with
showings of 25 to 30 minutes and increases the length to
about 45 minutes as the series progresses. She also increases the length of the films (to no more than 15 to 18
minutes), and uses more abstract films. But short films
are the general rule with this age and there are many good
films of six, seven, eight and ten minutes. Other estimates
of program lengths are: for six- and seven-year olds, 30
to 40 minutes; for age eight and up, 30 to 60 minutes; and
a program for all ages, 30 to 40 minutes. Sometimes--
and the possibilities will have to be determined by previewing
--a film can be cut short if it seems too long and/or the
children are bored or restless.

Since children in groups usually present more problems than adults in groups, the size of the audience is a
factor. From 20 to 40 children seems to be an ideal size.
Films have been shown to children in groups up to 70 and
even 100, but one must be especially sure the program runs
smoothly, and that everybody can see and is comfortable.

There are subjects, kinds and styles of films that
appeal to children. They like animated films, films about
animals and about other children, fairy tales, films with
puppets and comedy with slapstick. They like straightforward
stories with realism more than abstraction, but sometimes
they will respond to some element in the film. (Dance
Squared, in which geometric shapes divide and gyrate to the
rhythm of a square dance, is such a film and children respond to its rhythm.)

For pre-school children, one librarian suggests using
one or two story films (based on picture books they know or
can borrow from the library), and possibly a short abstract
film showing colors changing to music, or a documentary on
zoo animals. Story films can either be the iconographic

films, of the kind produced by Weston Woods, or the animated type. Bright colors are important and are to be preferred to black and white unless the film is exceptional. (An exception, it has been pointed out, are the Lotte Reiniger silhouette fairy tale films.)

For school-age children, one might show a feature-length film one time and two or three shorter films the next. Programs might consist of films showing a variety of subjects and techniques or they might be built around a subject or be all of one type.

In addition to merely showing the films, one can do a number of other things that will enhance the value of the showing. Children are likely to be interested in how things work; younger children can be allowed to watch the projectionist thread the film, and older children might be taught how to do it. Thalia Mannon-Tissot has described the ways in which she encouraged children to learn about the techniques of filmmaking.[26] Between films she would ask the children questions about the theme of the film, what scenes accomplished the theme, what role the music or background noises played, and what parts they liked and why. Sometimes they ran parts of the film without the sound, or the sound without the picture, to help the children see the functions of each. At other times, they used stories that appeared in both books and films (Whistle for Willie, Five Chinese Brothers) and compared the two media. When a Marcel Marceau film was shown, the children mimed various actions between films. Sometimes stories were used to provide background.

Those engaged in the Children's Film Theater have used stories in several ways.[27] They had "great success" with reading the stories on which the films were based. They also had success in getting the children to spontaneously make their own sound tracks: a film would be shown without sound while a tape recorder was left running; the children unknowingly provided a sound track and the film was then rerun with that recording.

An interesting variation that was enjoyed by the children was to run a film, without sound, backward. Films with a lot of live action and no narration (Jet Car, Young Directors' Center) worked best. But be forewarned! Running a film backward can ruin it, and your budget may not allow that.

Painting, drawing and various kinds of artwork can be related to films, and are stimulated by films. The Children's Film Theater had the children make transparencies for the overhead projector; they showed Glittering Song,* an animated film using a collage of broken glass, and afterward the children made their own collages of colored pieces of plastic/acetate gels which they projected. They also wrote their names on the collages with grease pencils and enjoyed seeing them projected. Having children mark blank film á la Norman McLaren is an activity that has been described by several librarians and others. Magic markers, felt-tip pens, crayons and even pins have been used. A recording can be used for the sound track, and the children have then made their own movie.

Multimedia Programs

As with adult and young adult programs, there are many opportunities to produce multimedia programs, or variety programs that are festival in nature. One can celebrate holidays, special events, special subjects and themes. The Houston Public Library celebrated National Children's Book Week with a variety of programs. [28] A new central library was being built and like all such construction it was surrounded by a wooden fence. Children were invited to a paint-in, during which they painted their favorite storybook characters, cartoon characters and graffiti on the fence. A hundred children, 3 to 13, participated and the event was covered by three television stations. For the adults there was a Meet-the-Author reception, with about twenty authors and illustrators of children's books, and luncheon program during which the book editor of a local newspaper discussed new directions in writing for children.

In Portland, Oregon, they held a folklore festival for National Children's Book Week. There were programs in the central library and in the city's 18 branches. Children's librarians told folk tales before each program. There were two puppet shows dramatizing a Slavic folk tale. There were African, Norwegian, Irish, Balkan, Mexican, Maori and Scottish dances. There were Swiss songs and yodeling, Chinese music and a bagpiper. And there was an origami

---

*This film is now distributed by Ceskoslovensky Filmexport: Vaclazske Nam, 28; 111 45 Prague, Czechoslovakia

demonstration and displays of German toys, Russian games and Indian artifacts. There were also talks about the customs of various countries.[29]

The Greenwich (Conn.) Public Library held a multimedia festival with the ambitious title, "All the Arts for Kids." Certainly many arts were included and the title was nearly realized. The whole library was utilized for the purpose. Throughout the library there were art slides flashing and there were banners made by Greenwich school children. Events were held in several parts of the library. One program, an electronic concert by local high school students, was a multimedia event in itself; the musicians were accompanied by films, slides and dancers. Other events during the four week festival were a showing of the Beatles' film Yellow Submarine; a marionette production of Gilbert and Sullivan's Pirates of Penzance; a lecture on "Golden Days of Greek Gods"; a demonstration of various art techniques; and a sculptor who demonstrated the two-hour inflating technique for a piece of vinyl sculpture. The opening event, entitled "See, Touch, Discover and Create," allowed children to touch and play with various pieces of sculpture and other works of art, after which they were invited to create their own art objects from business and industry discards.[30]

In the public library of Westport, Conn., a series of summer programs concentrated on Africa. There was storytelling for all ages, featuring folk stories, animal stories, fairy tales and stories of children in contemporary Africa. A film series, also for all ages, covered similar ground. There were also reading clubs for grades one and two, and for grades three and up.

The Bloomfield (N.J.) Public Library created its own holiday, "Children's Day," and held a party to celebrate it. The party was held on the Town Green, opposite the library, and included a folk singer, free soda (the children brought picnic lunches) and a "Things Not to Do" contest.

A Scandinavian holiday program was presented by a library on Staten Island. It was a morning program for ages six and up, and it was held during the Christmas vacation. Two films were shown: Ashlad and His Good Helpers (Modern Learning Aids) and The Seventh Master of the House (Modern Learning Aids), Scandinavian folk tales were told, Scandinavian food was served, and there was a drawing session for the children.

One children's librarian took advantage of a current interest to have a multimedia program. She read to the children the sections of the Laura Ingalls Wilder books that deal with wolves <u>Little House on the Prairie</u> was then being shown on television), and then she played the recording, "Language and Music of the Wolves" (Columbia C-30769).

There need be no special occasion for multimedia programs; they can be built around themes, subjects or moods. There are hundreds of possible subjects, and materials for children abound in all media. Often a story will be available in a book, film, filmstrip and recording. The point to remember is that material should be selected to supplement and enhance the other material and not used simply because it is there. One librarian has said, "Adding imagination to the use of an audiovisual item may add more than another switch or plug. You don't need to be plugged in to tell a story which will make a film more meaningful." One must also keep in mind that every additional mechanical device multiplies the complications. It is best to start modestly with two or three items until one is at home with the workings of all the equipment, with the transitions from one medium to another and the other problems of running a complicated program, and until one sees the ways that one medium works on another. It is better to have a limited well-run, well-integrated program than a grand failure.

The New York Public Library's Office for Children's Services suggests to its children's librarians that they keep notes on any ideas for the juxtaposition of materials that occur to them when they are reading, viewing or listening to books, films or recordings. They further suggest using things that feel right. Putting together a multimedia program is, after all, largely subjective and experimental and one doesn't know in advance what items will work together for a particular audience. (And what will work with some members of an audience won't work with others.)

In its training sessions for children's librarians, The New York Public Library offers the following programming suggestions:

Sample Program Themes and Materials for
Multi-Media Programs

(Symbols indicate forms in which material is available:
B Book; F Film; FS Filmstrip; R Recording)

NAMES
Caterpillar and the Wild Animals (Perennial) F
Farjeon. "The Flower Without a Name," from
The Little Bookroom. Walck. B
Flora. Leopold the See-Through Crumbpicker.
Harcourt Brace. B F
Grimm. "Rumplestiltskin." B R
Mosel. Tikki Tikki Tembo. Holt, Rinehart &
Winston. B F FS R

ART
colors
Lionni. Little Blue and Little Yellow. Astor
Honor. B F
O'Neill. Hailstones and Halibut Bones. Doubleday.
B F

drawings come to life
Crayon (Paramount) F
Emberley. Ed Emberley's Drawing Book of Animals.
Little Brown. B
Hearn. "The Boy Who Drew Cats," from Japanese
Fairy Tales. Liveright. B
Lathrop. Dog in the Tapestry Garden. Macmillan.
B
Leisk. Harold and the Purple Crayon. Harper.
B F FS R
Leisk. A Picture for Harold's Room. Harper. B F
Zemach. Awake and Dreaming. Farrar Straus. B

A HUNTING WE SHALL GO
Milne. "In Which Pooh and Piglet Go Hunting and
Nearly Catch a Woozle," from Winnie-The-Pooh.
Dutton. B
Moonbird (Radim) F

VALENTINE'S DAY
Belpré. Perez and Martina. Warne. B R
Cooney. Cock Robin. Scribner. B
Fillmore. "Forest Bride," from Shepherd's Nosegay.
Harcourt. B

Langstaff. Frog Went A-Courtin'. Harcourt. B R
Various romantic folk songs available in our record
collections: "Fiddle Dee Dee," "Riddle Song" (I Gave
My Love a Cherry), "New River Train" (Honey, You
Can't Love One)

CHICKENS

Boiled Egg (CRM/McGraw-Hill) F
The Chicken (CRM/McGraw-Hill) F B
Sandburg. "Shush, Shush, the Big Banty Hen," from
Rootabaga Stories. Harcourt. B

KITES

Kite Story (Churchill) F
Yolen. The Seventh Mandarin. Seabury. B

BLACK MUSIC IN AMERICA

Film: excerpt from Black Music in America from
Then till Now (Learning Corporation)
Filmstrip: Black Folk Music in America (SVE)
Recordings:
Theme from Shaft, Hayes (Enterprise 5002)
Zungo! Olatunji Afro Percussion (Columbia CS
8434)
Fisk Jubilee Singers (Scholastic 2372) and selections
by the Jackson Five, Aretha Franklin, James Brown
Books:
Hughes, Famous Negro Music Makers, Dodd, 1955
Hughes, First Book of Jazz, Watts, 1955
Locke, The Negro and His Music, Kennikat Press,
1968
Moore, Somebody's Angel Child: Bessie Smith,
Crowell, 1969
Southern, The Music of Black Americans, Norton
1971

MAGIC PROGRAM: TRANSFORMATIONS

Theme Music: Magical Mystery Tour, Beatles
(Capitol SMAL-2835)
Film: People Soup (Learning Corporation)
Storytelling: "Don't Blame Me" from Don't Blame
Me by Richard Hughes, Harper, 1940
Performance of Magic Tricks
Related books:
Leeming, Fun with Magic, Lippincott, 1943
Rawson, The Golden Book of Magic, Golden Press,
1964

Severn, <u>Magic Shows You Can Give</u>, McKay, 1965
Wyer and Ames, <u>Magic Secrets</u>, Harper, 1967

Other Sample Programs

Friendship program for picture book age:

Recording: "My Little Rooster," from <u>American Folk
Songs for Children</u> (Atlantic 1350)
Filmstrip: <u>Corduroy</u>
Film: <u>Queer Birds</u>
Introduction of related picture books

Whale program for story hour age:

Poem from <u>Beyond the High Hills</u> by Guy Mary-
Rousselière
Recording: <u>Songs of the Humpbacked Whale</u> (Capitol
ST 626)
Storytelling: "Living in W'ales," from <u>The Spider's
Palace</u> by Richard Hughes
Recording: "The Whale" from <u>Burl Ives Sings the
Little White Duck</u> (Columbia HL 9507)

"Shape-changing" program for story hour age:

Storytelling: "Telephone Travel" from <u>The Spider's
Palace</u> by Richard Hughes
Film: <u>The Windy Day</u>
Poem: "The Twins" by Henry Sambrooke Leigh in
<u>Poems for Pleasure</u> edited by Herman Ward

Finally, a committee of the New York Library Association suggests the following multimedia programs for two
age groups:[31]

SAMPLE MULTIMEDIA PROGRAM FOR PRIMARY CHILDREN (35-40 minutes)

THEME: A LAUGH-ALONG

Introduction: Tell a joke
Picture book: Mosel--<u>The Funny Little Woman</u>
Break: Riddles from Cerf--<u>Book of Animal Riddles</u>
Picture book: Calhoun--<u>Old Man Whickutt's Donkey</u>

Poems: Choose several from Prelutsky--The Snopp on
   on the Sidewalk; Lear--Complete Nonsense Book
Song with flannel board: "I Know an Old Lady Who
   Swallowed a Fly"
Film: The Foolish Frog (Weston Woods)

SAMPLE MULTIMEDIA PROGRAM FOR OLDER CHILDREN (ages 9-12)

THEME: SCARY STUFF

Story Collections:
   Ainsworth- The Phantom Cyclist
   Fenner--Ghosts, Ghosts, Ghosts
   Hoke--Monsters, Monsters, Monsters
   Leach--Thing at the Foot of the Bed
   Mendoza--Gwot! Horribly Funny Hairticklers
   Nic Leodhas--Gaelic Ghosts
   Sechrist--Heigh-Ho for Halloween
   Spicer--Thirteen Ghosts
Poetry:
   Brewton--Shrieks at Midnight
   Prelutsky--Nightmares; Poems to Trouble Your Sleep
Records:
   Disney--Chilling, Thrilling Sounds of the Haunted House
      (Disneyland DQ-1257)
   Price--A Coven of Witches' Tales (Caedmon TC 1338)
   Price--A Graveyard of Ghost Tales (Caedmon TC 1429)
Films:
   Ghosts and Ghoulies
   Monsters: Mysteries or Myths? (Films, Inc.)
   Winter of the Witch (Learning Corporation of America)

NOTES

1. Vanko, Lillian. "A Metropolitan Library Reaches
   Out," Illinois Libraries, Sept. 1971, pp. 462-6.
2. A footsie "consists of a hoop to which a length of cord,
   weighted at the end is attached. The hoop in placed
   around one ankle and the idea is to swing the weight
   around with one foot while jumping over the revolving
   cord with the other foot!" For further information
   on the footsie contest and other programs see:
   Quimby, Harriet, "Brooklyn Grooves," Top of the
   News, April 1970, pp. 283-9.

3. New York Public Library. Circulation Department Memo. No. 21, pt. II, p. 20.
4. Greene, Ellin. "The Preschool Story Hour Today," Top of the News, Nov. 1974, p. 83.
5. Ross, Eulalie Steinmetz. The Lost-Half Hour; A Collection of Stories, New York: Harcourt, Brace & World, 1963; pp. 183-4.
6. Ross, p. 186.
7. Ross, p. 188.
8. Greene, p. 83.
9. Ross, p. 189.
10. Kewish, Nancy. "South Euclid's Pilot Project for Two-Year-Olds and Parents," in School Library Journal, March 1979, p. 97.
11. Markowsky, Juliet Kellogg. "Story Time for Toddlers," in School Library Journal, May 1977, p. 30.
12. Markowsky, p. 31.
13. Stroner, Sandra. "Media Programming for Children," Library Journal, Nov. 15, 1971, p. 3812.
14. Goldfarb, Elizabeth. Children's Room Summer Report. Great Kills Branch, New York Public Library; pp. 2-3 (unpublished).
15. Fertik, Marian I. "A Crescendo: Creative Dramatics in Philadelphia," Wilson Library Bulletin, Oct. 1968, pp. 160-4.
16. Cullinane, Irene and Theresa Brettschneider. "Creative Dramatics in the Public Library," Top of the News, Nov. 1969, pp. 57-61.
17. Goldfarb, Elizabeth. Children's Room 1971 Summer Report. New York Public Library, West New Brighton Branch; p. 3 (unpublished).
18. McChesney, Kathryn. "Chamber Theatre; An Exciting New Tool to Stimulate Young Readers," Top of the News, April 1970, pp. 292-3.
19. McChesney, p. 292.
20. Elgood, Ann. "The Children's Theatre Conference," Top of the News, Nov. 1970, p. 66.
21. "Roundup of Art Action in Libraryland," Wilson Library Bulletin, April 1971, p. 758.
22. Rice, Susan, comp. and ed. Films Kids Like. Chicago: American Library Association, 1973, p. 15.
23. Mannon-Tissot, Thalia. "Innovation Through Trial and Error." Film Library Quarterly, Fall 1969, p. 14.
24. Rice, p. 18.
25. Mannon-Tissot, p. 14.
26. Ibid.
27. Ibid.

28. Library Journal, Feb. 15, 1974, p. 519.
29. Ibid.
30. Library Journal. Jan. 15, 1974, p. 168.
31. Films for Children; A Selected List. Prepared by New
    York Library Association, Children's and Young Adults
    Services Section, 4th edition, November 1977, p. 22.

7 ★ PROGRAMS FOR SPECIAL NEEDS

SENIOR CITIZENS

As the authors age, their interest in the aged also
increases. And if one is to judge from the news around
the country, everyone else's interest in the aged is increasing too. Senior centers are active, nursing homes are
thriving, and organizations of the elderly are into all kinds
of activities. Libraries are part of this trend, delivering
books to the homebound, sending them through the mail,
and giving programs for senior citizens, both in and outside
the library.

What we, as a country, are discovering is that the
elderly are not all grandfathers and grandmothers rocking on
the front porch, or vegetating in old age homes, waiting for
death. They are as varied as it is possible to be--as anyone who opens his eyes can see. There are, nevertheless,
characteristics common to most older people: eyesight and
hearing do fail, climbing steps becomes harder, and reactions may be slower. We all know the little old lady who
is sharp as a tack, of course, but even Henry Aaron and
George Blanda had to give up professional sports.

As for kinds of programs, there is no reason to
think there is any limit. Libraries have discussion groups,
poetry workshops, film programs, plays and many other
kinds of programs both for the elderly only, and for audiences
that include the elderly. And, as with the kind of program,
there is no limit to the content either. The authors remember one elderly couple who attended every program the library produced, and were seen elsewhere in the city going
to other activities.

People of a similar age are likely to have some
things in common, of course, if only because they remember

the same things. One must remember, though, that even
those we term elderly can be thirty years apart in age.
One thing those of a certain age are likely to have in common is music, because they will remember many of the
same songs. The Grand Prairie (Texas) Memorial Library
has put this interest to good use. They have found "sing-
a-longs" to be very popular, particularly in the nursing
homes--with songs ranging from "Alice Blue Gown" to "Pis-
tol Packin' Mama." To enhance this program the library
has compiled 30 copies of a large print song book, which
is distributed before each program. They have also made
transparencies of the songs so that they can be greatly enlarged on a screen by using an overhead projector. The
staff has also developed a bingo-like game that they call
"Singo." It has proved so popular that they get requests
from other groups for its use. In this game, a bit of the
song is played and participants must guess the title. A
small prize is given each winner.

There are also a number of concerns the elderly
have in common. One of these is the fear of being a victim of a crime and quite a few libraries have presented
programs dealing with this problem. One branch of The
New York Public Library held a three-session program for
those who wanted to avoid being mugged, defrauded or bur-
glarized. They learned what they could do in their homes
and on the street, what the police would do for them, and
what social service agencies would do if they became crime
victims. Programs dealing with other problems of particular
concern to the elderly include avoiding accidents, defensive
driving, nutrition, and income tax assistance. All these
and more have been given by the Grand Prairie library,
which is obviously very active in behalf of its senior citizens.

Grand Prairie also had great success with a twice-
a-week exercise program, something we clearly need as we
age. Another library, in a similar program, presented
"Tai Chi for Senior Citizens." Tai Chi is an ancient Chinese
health exercise that involves slow movements. It can strengthen
muscles, improve breathing and posture, and reduce stress.
Furthermore, it need only take 15 minutes a day. All in
all, it sounds ideal for those of us who are getting older.
Anyone not getting older will need something more strenuous.

In a somewhat related program, a branch of The New
York Public Library conducted a course entitled "Intimacy

and Aging; sexuality in the later years." This program involved information and informal discussions on health, and on physical changes that take place as one ages. There were nine sessions of an hour and half each.

According to a report of the Grand Prairie library, genealogy is now the third largest hobby in the country, and any librarian working with the public can believe it. Acting on that trend--always a good programming bet--they co-sponsored a genealogy workshop. Related to this program was a local history project. Citizens were asked to bring in old photographs, which were copied and added to the collection. Then an "Identification Party" was held. The older citizens of the community were asked to come and identify the pictures. It was a drop-in affair but most of the guests stayed all afternoon. The library gained much valuable information, and pictures continued to come in some time after the party. The program obviously caught the imagination of the community and the older people enjoyed "being needed by the library." This last comment suggests a programming principle: in a report from Grand Prairie, the point is made that the most successful programs for the elderly were those in which the audience took an active part.

In Oyster Bay, New York, the public library has also had a local history program involving senior citizens. They have centered their program around Theodore Roosevelt, the town's most famous citizen. Books about him were discussed, a videotape of old newsreel footage was shown, articles from contemporary local newspapers were read, and the elderly were asked to share their memories of Roosevelt and of the town. The proceedings were videotaped.

On Staten Island, New York, the local museum conducted a program adaptable to libraries. It was called the "Black Man on Staten Island" project. Elderly black people were asked to talk about the past, and a slide-tape program was created. In New York's Harlem, a library conducted an "Ethnic Heritage Studies" course for senior citizens. The culture and development of Jewish, Italian, Black, Hispanic and Chinese groups were studied. The cultural characteristics of the country of origin were traced, and the ways they were changed in this country were described, including the impact they have had on our culture. The elderly were again asked to share their knowledge.

Older people are often concerned about the direction that the country is taking. Senior citizens interested in changes from the past to the present--and the future--took a course in one library entitled, "America, Where Are You Going?" Trends in crime and punishment, education, race relations, religion and politics were discussed.

The arts are of interest to all, but the elderly often have more time for them, and many libraries have taken advantage of that. One small group of librarians, and some others, formed an acting company (they had had experience) and they gave one-act plays for the elderly. One library had a play-reading course, covering plays from ancient to modern. The group read and discussed the plays, including such subjects as the development of the theatre, "what is acting," different types of theatre, and recent changes. A course in art appreciation, and a course in music appreciation have also been library offerings for the retired set.

As was suggested above, programs in which there is audience participation are apt to be the best, and everybody can take part in the arts. Painting, drawing and sculpture have all been the subjects of library programs for the elderly. Writing workshops, both in prose and in poetry, have been quite successful.

A successful poetry workshop for teenagers was broadened, in an experiment, to include the elderly. The response was "overwhelming." The group ranged in age from thirteen to people in their eighties. There had been doubts and anxieties from both groups, but they disappeared on closer acquaintance. The participants found that the enthusiasm of the young and the experience of the elderly were mutually beneficial, and some interesting poems resulted. Some of the older people had not had any formal education and they could neither read nor write. The leader overcame that handicap by using a tape recorder and by writing out their work for them. And they learned to express themselves in what the leader/poet described as "a unique and artistic manner." This unusual program was best summed up by one woman in these words: "My God, I just can't believe this is possible and me eighty-eight and a part of it." When the poems that were produced in the workshop were put together in a magazine, the name that was chosen was (significantly) Possibilities.

Meanwhile, in Grand Prairie, Texas, the library held

a combined art show and tea, exhibiting paintings by those
over 55. Twenty-four artists exhibited forty paintings to a
large number of people. Programs like these benefit all:
they benefit the elderly who can participate and be recognized;
they benefit the public; and perhaps as much as anyone they
benefit the library staff who can feel much satisfaction at
doing something worthwhile.

A branch of the Brooklyn (N.Y.) Public Library put
together an unusual series for the elderly which was centered on the arts. It consisted of four sessions. The first
was a slide talk about the collections of the Brooklyn Museum.
For the second session, the group took a bus trip to the
Museum and were given a guided tour of a specific collection.
The third session presented a film about Georgia O'Keeffe.
Finally, there was a workshop in which the participants were
invited to experiment with a variety of media. Another
series--on a differend kind of art--combined films about
gardening and a trip to the Brooklyn Botanic Garden.

Film programs are enjoyed by people of all ages.
The authors have presented films--Charlie Chaplin, for
example--that were attended by audiences ranging from the
very young to the very old. Nevertheless, there are considerations when showing films for the elderly, for as some
of us are learning, the stairs are getting steeper. So,
avoid having a lot of stairs that the elderly will have to
climb. Open the doors to the screening room early enough
to give people who move slowly--those with walkers, for
example--a chance to get a seat. Have a staff member on
hand to help with the seating. He should also have a flash-
light--a good idea for any film program. The exits should
be well lit, and there should be restrooms and outside seating areas near the screening room. Some of the audience
will be hard of hearing and that makes sound levels a problem.
Adjust the sound as well as you can to satisfy everybody,
something you may not be able to do. No program for the
elderly should run too long without a break, probably after
about forty-five minutes.

As far as the content of these programs is concerned,
older people are just people who happened to have lived
longer. They have all the variety of tastes and interests
that any group of people has. According to one film librarian, there is an assumption among those who plan programs
for the elderly that they will want silent comedies or bland
travelogues. Plan as you would for any film program, and

if you have a chance, ask the audience what it wants. You
may be surprised.

Videotape has been used in an interesting way in
another program that was planned to involve senior citizens
and teenagers. Members of each group were gathered together for a discussion of whatever topic seemed of interest.
The main subject turned out to be dating problems--today
and in the past. The discussion was videotaped. Then the
tape was played back, and the participants continued the discussion in light of what they had just seen and heard. The
video camera thus became, in a sense, a participant in the
discussion by jogging memories and stimulating further discussion. The two groups started by thinking they would
have little in common, and they ended with an increased
understanding and the realization that they had had many of
the same problems. This program was held at the Port
Washington (N. Y.) Public Library, long a library leader in
the use of videotape.

When a program for the elderly is being planned (and
we are talking about the mobile elderly and those not confined to institutions) there are some points to consider.
Studies have shown that most old people do not travel more
than five blocks from home in the normal course of things.
Since many don't drive, and public transportation is often
inadequate, this is probably so. It is also a generalization
with numerous exceptions, like all generalizations. Nevertheless, it is something to think about. Programs will often
have to be taken to the audience. A related discovery that
has been made in studies of the elderly shows that many do
not use senior centers. Therefore, if a program is being
taken on the road, one would have to consider (in addition
to the senior centers) going to churches, synagogues, clubs,
and other places that attract the elderly. Sometimes parks
are such places, and--just as there are park programs for
children--so there could be for people at the other end of
the life span.

The time of day is important, with the mid-morning
to mid-afternoon range being the best. Again there are
exceptions. Winter is often the best time of year for library programs, but if a lot of snow can be expected or the
sidewalks are likely to be icy, the elderly might not venture
out. Paying attention to local weather patterns will help in
planning.

There are various ways to choose, plan and publicize programs. An advisory group of the elderly has been described elsewhere in this book, or one can merely talk to people and ask them what they would like and how they would like it. The Brooklyn (N. Y.) Public Library has found a way to choose, plan and publicize programs for the elderly that is unusual, and what's more it works. They have been given a grant to hire advisers. These people are over 55 themselves (which has the added benefit of giving them work) and they live in the neighborhood of the branch to which they are assigned. They usually speak the language of the main ethnic group in that neighborhood. They are given an intensive, five-week training course, and they work under the supervision of the branch librarian. Then they do everything connected with programming; they find films, speakers and performers; they organize the event, plan the publicity, and reach the potential audience. One of their charges is to reach those who would not normally use the library. In this they have been successful, and their programs for the elderly attract a wide range of people.

A number of qualities are considered in choosing these "Senior Assistants." Among these are physical health, sensitivity, flexibility, and enthusiasm for the project. The training covers a wide range of subjects. They are taught to run projectors and how to run a good film program. They are given discussion group leadership training. Training is given in book talks, and other programming ideas are discussed. The "Myths and Realities of Aging" are discussed and they talk about the purposes of the program. Any such special staff members must be given a good grounding in the rules and the services of the library. Anything else will result in misinformation, bad service and bad public relations.

When it comes to publicity, the Senior Assistants themselves believe word-of-mouth to be the best method. It is important in any kind of programming. Unfortunately, people who don't use the library, or are not acquainted with those who do, won't get the message. In fact, all forms of publicity must be utilized, unless you have such a large potential audience that the space will be overwhelmed.

Programming for any special group such as the elderly usually has extra satisfactions, because they are so appreciative. Some old people may complain a lot as will some younger people. Take it good-naturedly and shrug it

off while being sure the complaints are not valid; that's part
of the job.   Sometimes the elderly will want to talk a lot.
Sometimes the talk seems more important to them than the
service being rendered.   But a librarian's job is a bit like
a bartender's: listening is part of the job too.

THE HANDICAPPED (GENERAL)

In the next three sections we deal with programs for
three kinds of handicapped persons: the deaf, the mentally
retarded, the emotionally disturbed and neurologically impaired.   In one case (the deaf) we have included some programs for those who live and work with them.   But there
are other handicaps.   Unfortunately, space and time have
their limits, and we have not covered them.   Certainly libraries may want to consider programs for the blind, those
who lack some limbs, those with cerebral palsy, and so
forth.   Programs for those who live and work with handicapped persons, as well as programs for the general public
about handicaps, would be most useful.   Such programs
could deal with the nature and problems of the handicaps,
jobs, rights, resources and facilities for handicapped persons.   Because of their disabilities, handicapped persons
often do not have access to the recreational events enjoyed
by the rest of the community, and libraries can often provide
the necessary techniques and facilities for that kind of program, as no other institution can.   At the same time, because the handicapped are out of the main stream of life,
very often, libraries will have to do a great deal of work
to reach them.

Many libraries will be located in communities where
only small numbers of persons with a particular handicap
live, and they may not be able to produce programs for so
small a number.   A branch library on Staten Island, New
York solved this problem by producing a series of programs
dealing with a variety of handicaps, and we offer it as an
example.   The series was called "Living with Handicaps"
and it was designed for "parents, teachers, siblings, handicapped individuals and people who are just concerned."   There
were six sessions, a week apart, of approximately two hours
each.   Films, speakers and discussion were the vehicles.
A sign translator for the deaf was present.   The building is
accessible to wheelchairs and the library announced itself
ready to provide any special accommodations needed.   The
program follows:

I. Subject: Introduction
    Film: "Who Are the DeBolts?" (This Emmy Award
    winning film tells the story of a California family
    that adopts a variety of orphans, some with multiple
    handicaps.)
    Discussion: Led by a children's librarian

II. Subject: Who Are the Disabled?
    Film: "He's Not the Walking Kind" (Brian Wilson is
    a spastic, confined to a wheelchair. Shows how
    family, friends, and his own perseverance help him
    develop.)
    Film: "Language of the Deaf" (Life on the campus of
    Gallaudet College, the college for the deaf. Provides
    insights into their lives.)
    Discussion: Led by the Borough Director of United
    Cerebral Palsy

III. Subject: What is the Impact of Mainstreaming?
    Film: "Moira: a vision of blindness" (A blind teenager
    is shown in school, at home, writing poetry, etc.)
    Film: "I'll Find a Way" (A young girl with spina
    bifida is shown in school, with her family, etc. She
    discusses her feelings about mainstreaming.)
    Discussion: Led by a clinical psychologist

IV. Subject: How do/should we react to disabilities?
    Film: "Marsha" (The life of a retarded teenager.
    Shows the limits on her, and the mixed feelings of
    her family.)
    Film: "Blind Sunday" (A young man is attracted to a
    pretty girl, and then finds out she is blind. He
    tries to understand what it is like to be blind, as
    the relationship develops.)
    Discussion: Led by a clinical psychologist

V. Subject: What rights do/should the disabled have?
    Film: "Exit" (Young woman in a wheelchair attempts
    to make a pay-phone call. Film shows the obstacles.)
    Film: "To Live On" (Handicapped persons discuss their
    work as watch repairers.)
    Filmstrip: "Disabled: No Longer Handicapped?"
    (Discusses the movement for equality for handicapped
    people. Shows political action, as well as the
    problems of everyday life.)
    Discussion: Led by an employee of H. E. W.

VI.   Subject: Is Equality Possible for the Disabled?
      Film: "Like Other People" (A man and woman, both
        spastics living in an English residential care unit,
        wish to marry. They struggle for freedom and
        privacy.)
      Film: "Day in the Life of Bonnie Consolo" (Follows
        the daily life of a young housewife, who was born without
        arms. Show how she has compensated by learning to use
        her feet.)
      Discussion: Led by the Director of Public Education
        for the Borough Developmental Services Office.

                       THE DEAF

        With 15,000,000 deaf persons in the country, it be-
hooves librarians to provide them with services. A number
of libraries now do so, but many more could, and should.
Given the financial condition of many libraries, one might
think an extra service is impossible, but "it ain't necessarily
so." Although some libraries have been given grants for
such services, at least one library, in Indiana, has produced
many programs and provided other services for the deaf,
without any extra funding and without having anyone on the
staff who knew sign language. Money always helps, of
course, and it is possible to raise it from foundations, businesses and other organizations. Service clubs such as
Lions, Kiwanis, Pioneers and others have money for such
purposes.

        It might be useful to think about why special library
services to the deaf are necessary. Clearly, they are shut
out of many experiences. Radio, most television programs,
and most movies are not useful to them. Neither are tele-
phones, unless a special device is attached. Their reading
levels--and educational levels--are often low because of the
difficulty of learning, and because they start way behind
other children. There are also the deaf with double handicaps: the elderly, various minorities, and those who are
foreign born.

        There is a wide range of hearing impairment, and
there is a wide range of abilities, intelligence and education
among the hearing impaired. And just like everybody else,
they have a lot of different interests. Therefore, they must
be seen as individuals, not just in terms of their deafness.

(This principle applies to all groups, as we must keep re-
minding ourselves.)

Before one gives programs for the deaf, one must
find them. The chances are that not many use the library,
and since deafness can't be seen, they are invisible. So
they must often be sought after. There are organizations
for the deaf in most places and there are private and governmental organizations working for them. There are also
publications for the deaf that may help. Schools and rehabilitation centers are obvious places to look, and so are stores
selling hearing aids. Some churches provide signed services.
Centers for the aged, and any social service agency may
have leads. As with any special group, building a mailing
list is a useful device.

Having found the potential audience, the next step
is to decide on the program. The best way always seems
to be to ask the target audience themselves. They may
not, however, know what they want, simply because they
won't know what you can offer. Provide them with a list
of choices. You might also establish an advisory board of
the deaf and of those who work with the deaf.

As we have indicated, a great variety of programs
are possible, because--like the rest of the population--the
deaf have a wide range of interests. It's just that their
limitations must be considered. Some silent films, especially
those of the comedians such as Charlie Chaplin and Buster
Keaton, are popular with everybody of all ages, and they
should provide a good source for this group. A number of
nature films have little or no narration. White Throat (Dan
Gibson Productions) comes to mind. Some contemporary
films that are thought-provoking and good discussion material
are not narrated. Two of these (and there are others) are
The Hand and Two Men and a Wardrobe (CRM/McGraw-Hill).
Many foreigns films, with sub-titles, would be useful. And
there are other films for people of all ages that are signed
or captioned. There are several sources for these films.
The U.S. Department of Health, Education and Welfare oper-
ates Captioned Films for the Deaf Distribution Center. One
must get an account number to borrow the films. (Write
to Captioned Films for the Deaf Distribution Center, 5034
Wisconsin Avenue, N.W., Washington, D.C. 20016. There
are children's films in depository libraries and one can get
a catalog from Special Office for Materials Distribution,
Indiana University (Audio Visual Center, Bloomington, Indiana

47401). The Edward Miner Gallaudet Memorial Library is
another source, Gallaudet College, 7th and Florida, N.E.,
Washington, D.C. 20002. When one is borrowing or renting
films from a distance so that they must be mailed, it is a
good idea (as in any film program) to have a backup film
available--possibly something like a silent classic that can
be borrowed locally. The hearing librarian may find it
difficult to judge the effect of a film on a deaf person if it
has some narration or it has sound effects. If there is a
question, watch the film without the sound the first time you
see it.

Video is a related medium that is also useful for
programs with the deaf. Captioned and signed software is
available from many sources, including Alexander Graham
Bell Association for the Deaf, Public Television Library,
and a number of film distributors.

Theatrical productions provide opportunities, especially
mime--an art that can be equally enjoyed by hearing and
non-hearing people alike. Then there are theatrical companies such as the National Theatre of the Deaf and the
Gallaudet Theatre Touring Company. Perhaps local schools
for the deaf will have performers.

Storytelling is, or can be, a theatrical performance,
and it is used successfully with the deaf. The Metropolitan
Cooperative Library System of Pasadena, California has compiled some information on working with the deaf and they
give some tips for storytelling. The most important point
to remember, they say, is that the visual should be emphasized, and the use of visual aids, such as flannel boards,
is suggested. In this connection, it is recommended that a
short section of the story be told, with the interpreter signing as you speak, and that the appropriate pictures be then
shown to the entire group. Otherwise, many children will
lose the signs (or the pictures). Unlike your usual expecta-
tions for a story hour, this one will probably be noisy.
"Since deaf children cannot hear themselves, their exuberance
is vocal and uncontained, even after months of library visits."
Books with a straightforward narrative are suggested as
being easier for deaf children to follow. Stories dealing
with sounds, such as Why Mosquitoes Buzz in People's Ears
by Verna Aardema, are obviously to be avoided.

Two follow-up techniques are recommended. After
the story is finished, ask the children some questions about

it. "You may find it necessary to tell the story a second time." And if you have been working with the same group, you may want to have a child act out a part of the story after you have told it. Such a technique is particularly good with action stories such as When the Drum Sang by Ann Rockwell. This device would help the understanding, and more importantly involve the children with the group.

There are a number of possible programs to draw deaf persons into the library. The Philadelphia Free Library held a wine and cheese reception to honor several outstanding deaf individuals. A number of libraries have given tours of the library, with instructions on its use, for deaf persons. Similar to this program, or perhaps combined with it, is an open house. This is particularly useful if the library has materials, services, or equipment of special interest to the deaf. If, for instance, the library acquires a TTY (telephone-teletypewriter), which a number of libraries have done, an open house might be held to demonstrate its use. At the same time, that's a good way to publicize a new service.

The deaf have some special needs and libraries have held programs serving those needs. The District of Columbia Public Library gave a workshop entitled "Deaf Consumer Rights and Protection." In Philadelphia they had a program on law and the deaf. Programs on employment opportunities, and workshops for improving skills, are other possibilities. A library in Indiana even taught dog obedience training using signs. Those who live with deaf people, work with them, or just associate with them can benefit from a number of programs. The Free Library of Philadelphia held a "Family Night" workshop for deaf parents and their children, in order to encourage better communications within the family. The program started with refreshments, always a good ice-breaker. Then, after an introduction, there was a film (Deaf and Bright), there were "Family Life Skits," discussion groups, and a wrap-up session. The same library, logically, held a workshop for the parents of deaf children. At that program, the parent of a deaf child spoke on, "Due Process and the Handicapped Child's Right to Quality Education." Then a panel of deaf adults talked about their educational experiences, and a teacher of hearing handicapped persons answered questions.

Many hearing persons would benefit from learning sign language, and some deaf persons don't know it. Libraries have had everything from "mini-sign language lessons" (Philadelphia again) to a full-fledged course. Hearing children would undoubtedly find such a program enjoyable, hearing library staff members would find it useful, and anybody living or working with the deaf would find it essential. One would need to find out which form of sign language was used in the area. SEE and AMESLAN are two different methods used.

Most of us would benefit from gaining a better understanding of deafness and the deaf and there have been library programs designed to do that. For any library serving the deaf, sensitivity training for the staff should be the first program. Some libraries have had week-long programs to promote understanding, to bring the deaf into the library, and to bring the deaf and the hearing together. The City of Brotherly Love, living up to its name, must again be cited. They had a "Deaf Awareness Week," with programs all over the city. Publicity included news articles, radio and television, and a mayoral proclamation. There were ten exhibits including a collection of equipment used by the deaf (a portable TTY, a TV-phone, a baby crier, a door bell flasher, a fire alarm system for the deaf, and the world's first radio for the deaf). There was also a collection of antique hearing aids. Among the programs were signed story hours, workshops, seminars and sign language lessons. Hearing tests were conducted at several branch libraries, and they were a big attraction.

The District of Columbia Public Library also conducted a week-long series of programs which they called "Deaf Pride, Deaf Culture, Deaf Heritage." There were films, speakers, workshops, and a play. Such large scale programs are a lot of work, but they can generate a great deal more publicity than a group of individual programs would. A lot more help will then be freely available from outside sources.

Other program possibilities include book talks and other kinds of talks, discussion groups, and all kinds of crafts programs. There should be interpreters, of course, for most if not all programs for the deaf, but if the library is producing such programs it is likely that an interpreter can be found. If someone is giving a talk in sign language, then another interpreter is needed to translate it back into sound. If the program involves a darkened room--for a slide show or movie without captions--there must be a light on the interpreter so that he can be seen.

MENTALLY RETARDED

"Exhausting but satisfying," is the way one librarian who has worked with retarded adults put it. Another librarian who has worked with retarded children said, "Working with the retarded ... does a world of good in ways that you can't possibly measure." Most people who work with any special group that has some kind of handicap find such work thoroughly satisfying. Although your main aim is to help the group in question, the knowledge that you are doing something worthwhile is very good too.

As with most groups that are lumped together because of some handicap or disability (the deaf, the elderly, the foreign born) the mentally retarded vary widely in age and intelligence, not to mention interests. Therefore, librarians who have worked with the retarded suggest getting to know the group first. One librarian has said that being "open and loving" is very important, and another suggests patience, love, and an open and flexible attitude. She has also said one shouldn't look for quick results, or, in some cases, any results at all. Otherwise, one is bound to be discouraged. Touching and talking in an affectionate way have also been suggested (with children) as well as giving frequent praise-- praise for the ordinary things such as waiting in line, sitting quietly, and so forth. Even rewarding them for good behavior by giving them something to take home has been recommended.

It is a good idea to talk to the group's teacher, or other adults who know the participants, ahead of time. One can find out about interests, what to expect, behavior problems, possibly disturbing materials, and other things that will make for a better, more easily handled, program.

Be prepared for unusual behavior. A librarian who works with children says they will talk louder than normal. They may interrupt more, and you may want to let them. On the other hand, they should learn the rules of behavior, such as not disrupting the library and respecting the rights of others. A librarian who works with retarded teenagers has found that they will interrupt, sit on your lap, hug you, stroke your hair. She recommends not pushing them away, but saying something nice about them, and gently suggesting that they go back and sit down with the others. A librarian who has worked with retarded adults has found very good

behavior among them--with the exception of one temper tan-
trum--and she also reports that the retarded have much
appreciated library visits and obtaining library cards.

A children's librarian has suggested that routine and
consistent discipline are important. She starts each program
with the same format, for example. Each child is provided
with a mat or chair, so that his or her space is defined.
The retarded have short attention spans, so that brief programs, or short segments of programs are called for. They
may have other handicaps such as poor sight or lack of
coordination, which add to the difficulties of handling materials or equipment. Clearly, a lot of patience is needed.
Repetition is something that is stressed by everybody who
works with the retarded. So are programs in which the
audience can participate. Everything sould be bright, clear
and simple. At the same time, one should create a sensory-
rich environment that appeals to all the senses; use music
and props with storytelling, for example. Tie-ins with
school projects are good, as learning is reinforced. The
teacher can be asked what they are studying, and the program built around the subject. Finally, the retarded can
be included in many regular programs. Both the retarded
person and the normal audience may benefit.

There are a number of programs that are possible
with the mentally retarded, and, as with most other groups,
films are one of the most popular kinds. One librarian has
not found films to be as useful with the retarded as storytelling. Others--while they tentatively agree with this assess-
ment--have said the retarded enjoy films a lot. Much, of
course, depends on the amount of retardation, and on what
one hopes to achieve. In Berkeley Heights, New Jersey,
where the library has done much with the retarded, a librarian has said, "While it is doubtful that the severely
retarded get much out of the films, hospital supervisors
feel that the greatest value of the library visits lies in getting
the participants out into a social situation and in familiariz-
ing them with normal community activities in an atmosphere
where they attract no special attention."[1] Moreover, the
librarians have said that to their surprise the retarded who
now most frequent the library are the very retarded. Since
this group doesn't read, the films seem to have been useful. A New York City librarian who works with teenagers
has also found films to be useful with the very retarded.
Short, simple, rhythmic films, with no dialogue, work well,
she says.

Librarians in Berkeley Heights have also used videotapes frequently. Library-produced videotapes included
special performances, role playing, job interviews, sports
and other subjects. The retarded had to be taught the basics
of television-watching and how to gain information from it.
These people had never understood these concepts before,
but with training, most of them learned to recognize themselves and others in the group on television.

In any case, many retarded people can enjoy films,
and in Berkeley Heights they have found that films emphasiz-
ing music, color, and action are the most popular. Comedy,
animal stories, travel and sports were some of the subjects
mentioned. At the Half Hollow Hills (N. Y.) Public Library,
where they also have regular visits from groups of retarded
persons, comedy films with Laurel and Hardy, Abbott and
Costello, Harold Lloyd, and W. C. Fields were found to be
popular with mentally retarded adults. They also liked Black
Music in America and were able to compare it to Roots
which was then being shown on television.

A report from the Altoona (Pa.) Area Library[2]
suggests the following guidelines for using films with the
mentally retarded:

1. Preschool Programs: Films with loose story-lines
   and few if any words. Familiar sounds, music,
   bright colors. Five to ten minutes.
2. Primary grades: Lively animation is best. Elementary vocabulary. Sound film strips not generally
   successful. Ten to fifteen minutes.
3. Intermediate grades: Most films can be used at
   this level, as well as lively sound film strips.
   Fifteen to thirty minutes.
4. Young adult/adult: Films with mature themes, but
   simplified plots and vocabulary. Twenty to forty
   minutes.

Another standard library program that is used with
retarded children is storytelling. Repetition is one of the
keys here. One librarian has told us of reading a story as
many as fifteen times to a group. She was rewarded for
that act of "heroism," when one of the children jumped up
and told the story, even imitating her manner. It follows
that stories that contain repetition within them are good ones
to use. Rhythm, simple story lines, and large pictures
without too much detail have also been mentioned as being

important attributes. Pictures should also relate closely to the story. The relative brevity of the story has been mentioned by many librarians. A fine article on the subject[3] suggests that, although that is one feature of stories used with this group, one objective is to increase attention spans; therefore, the length of the stories should be gradually increased. This same article (which is packed with information) makes a number of other suggestions for those choosing stories to use with the young mentally retarded. Since retarded children are literal-minded, abstractions are likely to confuse them. Obsolete or obscure words, and foreign words and phrases should be avoided. Sometimes an unusual work is necessary to the story, and then it would need some explanation. The setting of the story should be familiar. The humor should be obvious. And the story should be about something specific, not one that merely creates a mood.

When it comes to presenting the story, the storyteller should anticipate any problems that group might have with the story. Therefore, a brief introduction is desirable. The previously cited report from Altoona gives a number of other helpful tips for storytellers:

1. Preschool: Use visual aids. Puppets, flannel board figures and drawings are useful. Concrete objects the children can touch are the best.
2. Primary: Involvement is greater on the part of the children. Have them take part as much as possible by acting out parts of the story, answering questions, or finding things in pictures. Large storybooks can be used, but techniques such as tell and draw should be used in combination with them.
3. Intermediate: They can follow storybook presentations, mature themes, and enjoy plays, particularly if they are given a role. They may have some problem speaking the parts, so they should be allowed to act out the story while it is being narrated.

Storytelling is also useful with mentally retarded teenagers, and there are a number of points to remember with this group. A librarian who has told stories to these teenagers has advised against using anything that might be sexually stimulating, because they have the feelings and don't know how to cope with them. A similar experience

was described by a librarian who had mentally retarded
adults visiting. One of the women saw a picture of a nude
male and became very upset. It took a good deal of time
to calm her down. With mentally retarded teenagers--even
those that are very retarded--one shouldn't use books that
are about children. They will be sensitive to the fact that
children's books are being used with them. Some children's
books can be used, however. With the very retarded, such
books as Leo Lionni's Little Blue and Little Yellow have
been suggested. They like silly humor, on the level of a
three- or four-year-old child. Books with photographs of
animals have also been suggested. In any case, the story
should be short and simple, using simple words in the
telling.

With the slightly retarded teenager, complete, simple
stories should also be used. Again children's books can be
used, if they are not about children. Harry the Dirty Dog
by Gene Zion and George and Martha by James Marshall
are examples. Folk tales about adults can be used. The
Grimms' The Fisherman and His Wife is a good one, but it
needs to be shortened because of limited attention spans.
Books about animals are good with this group too. Many
of the Time-Life publications, for instance, are useful to
show to them because of the photography. Finally, for any
mentally handicapped person, scary books are not recommended.

Musical programs and crafts programs can be successful with the retarded person, and once again we can turn to
the fine report from Altoona, Pennsylvania for suggestions
by grade level. For musical programs the following recommendations are made:

1. Preschool: Finger plays set to music, action songs
2. Primary: Simple songs with repeating verses
3. Intermediate: Rounds and songs involving several
   actions
4. Young adult/Adult: Folk songs with guitar accompani-
   ment or records. Rock music is often liked.

For crafts programs try these ideas:

1. Preschool: Simple activities involving one or two
   skills, such as coloring pre-cut feathers and gluing
   them on the body of a turkey. Avoid cutting activities unless you have a one-to-one situation.

2. Primary: Cutting, coloring, pasting and folding.
   Paper bag puppets is an example of a good activity
   at this level.
3. Intermediate: Use unusual objects for appeal such
   as pine cones, styrofoam, sponges.
4. Young adult/Adult: Should center around a particular
   craft with a mature finished product that does not
   look childish.

EMOTIONALLY DISTURBED AND
NEUROLOGICALLY IMPAIRED

When giving programs for these groups, there are
points of similarity with other groups, such as the mentally
retarded, but there are differences. These children obey
their impulses: they may go to sleep, fight, do or say
obscene things, and generally go where their impulses lead
them. Presumably, they would be brought to the library by
a teacher, or other adult who was working with them. That
person should be asked some questions. You may not be
able to seat two children close together, for example, because they will fight. Ask if any of the children are medi-
cated. If they are, you may not get any response, setting
up anxiety in you and the children. Avoid flashing lights,
or other rhythmic things (a metronome, or even a fan) or
ask the teacher if they would present problems. Flashing
lights can set off an epileptic seizure, for example.

It is important to be firm at first, perhaps firmer
than normal, then one can ease off later. Don't do anything that might be interpreted as hostile or aggressive,
however, and don't tell stories that have these traits. One
librarian said she found they could handle films portraying
that kind of behavior better than they could stories. It
seems likely that the impact of a film is less than a live
performer, or that it seems less directed at the audience.
Using sarcasm or teasing are out. Be firm, but gentle
was the way one teacher put it.

The children should be confined in an area, either
through the use of strict ground rules, or by physical barriers. Otherwise, they may wander off in the middle of
your carefully prepared story. Repetition is important here.
As one teacher said, "You can't say it too often." And you
should speak slowly. These children have short attention

spans, so a change of pace, or a change of medium is important. They also have trouble being passive listeners. So, if you are telling a story, use one they can act out or respond to, such as Caps for Sale or It Looked Like Spilt Milk. They may not understand the nuances of language (puns, metaphors, etc.) so these things, if they are used, should probably be explained. Humor is good, but it obviously can't be too subtle. Also, it shouldn't be too broad, or it may stir them up too much and you won't be able to regain their attention. One teacher says that if they are stimulated (such as at a playground session) they don't come back down the way ordinary children do. For that reason, you may want to schedule them in the morning.

The question of using props, or several mediums, seems ambiguous. The children are easily distracted and it may be best to focus attention on a person or thing, such as the storyteller. But a teacher we talked to tries to give them multi-sensory experiences, because life is full of that kind of experience and they need to adjust to life as it is. Perhaps it would be best to start simply and expand the program as you gain experience and confidence. Again, the teacher would doubtless be the best guide.

All of this seems difficult and clearly a lot of patience is required, but having a success with a group like this is rewarding and worth the effort.

PROGRAMS FOR PRISONERS

All kinds of library programs are now being presented in prisons, jails and detention centers. Some of these are being done by librarians in the library of the institution and others by visiting librarians at institutions where there is no library. Library service often appears to function at the discretion of the prison administrator, and programs at such institutions can clearly present problems. There are several reasons for these problems: institutions are often short of staff; they lack trained library personnel; and the attitudes of some administrators are negative. Librarians are not strangers to any of these conditions, however, and are doing fine work.

The attitude of the administration of the institution is undoubtedly the most important factor. Some officials

Programs for Special Needs / 189

have requested library service, and others have come to
learn its value.   But some administrators don't seem to
want programs, possibly because they perceive programs as
making more work for them, or making their work more
difficult.   Prior approval for each program must often be
obtained.   The visiting librarian will probably have to be
screened before starting his service and establishing service
can be a long process.   In the words of one librarian, who
spends his full time visiting correctional facilities, "It takes
patience and determination."

    Censorship is another problem, and there are two
kinds.   First, there is the official variety.   Materials about
the use of guns, the techniques of karate, the art of lock-
smithing are not allowed.   Unofficial censorship presents a
greater problem.   One librarian has said, "In one institution,
while discussing inmate requests with an administrator, we
were surprised to hear him tell us not to bring 'any political
garbage' into the institution."   Material about Cuba, China,
the Puerto Rican independence movement, Black American
politics, modern Africa and "any Commie stuff" were not
welcome.   It was strongly suggested that, even if such material was brought to the prison, it wouldn't reach the prisoners.   Material on these subjects was purchased, and--as
it happened--that administrator was transferred.   This librarian tells us that most censorship is of the unofficial
variety, and that it is not an uncommon problem.

    There are some things to remember when dealing
with prisoners.   (One would do well to remember them
when dealing with other segments of the population too.)
It is important to establish a feeling of trust.   If there are
groups who speak languages other than English, materials
in those languages will be necessary.   Following through on
requests is important; if they perceive that you don't keep
faith with them, they will be--in the words of Gwendolyn
Brooks--"long gone from the store."

    Film programs can be popular in prisons, as they
can be everywhere.   Administrators, also, often welcome
them, because large groups of inmates can be kept occupied
--with little trouble--at no cost to the administration.   The
New York Public Library's prison visitor has most success
with films at a center for teenagers, all males, who have
enjoyed sports and action films, and films featuring fighting
and violence.   A film about a roller derby was a big hit,
for example.   Films about social problems have not gone

well. That shouldn't surprise anybody. They often don't
go well with the public at large, either.

Roots has been far and away the most popular film
program given by this librarian, although there was some
violence between racial groups after the showing. Discussions of this, and other films, has proved difficult. Careful planning and "good priming" are important if a discussion is planned. He goes on to say, "The audience may be
too large, too hungry, or simply too restless to be good
participants." There have been good discussions, however,
and among the films that stimulated them were The Time
Machine, The Third Man, and King Kong. Of the films that
did not provoke discussion, Green for Danger, The Man Who
Knew Too Much, and Foreign Correspondent were cited.
Probably nothing in their experiences made them connect
with the people in the latter films.

Prisoners have a lot of time to think. Not surprisingly,
there have always been prisoners who wanted to write those
thoughts down. Doubtless, Cervantes gathered material in
jail, if he didn't actually write there. In recent years,
writing workshops have been held in prisons across the
country, and quite a lot of prison writing is being published.
To give one example, a "Creative Writers Club" grew out
of activity at the library of the Fox Lake (Wisconsin) Correctional Institution, and the librarian became the advisor.
She brought writers into the club's meetings in the institution,
and she took the men out to writers' conferences in the
area. The inmates (as a group) became members of the
Wisconsin Regional Writers Club, and they entered contests
sponsored by that organization--producing statewide winners
in six different years.

This imaginative librarian has conducted a number of
other kinds of library programs. Among these have been
a variety of contests, some of which have had the useful
purpose of building library skills. Prizes were often given
to the winners, as inducements to enter. For one contest,
fifty pictures of "20th-century notables" were attached to a
bulletin board, and each picture was numbered. Entry blanks
were numbered one to fifty, and the inmates consulted library books to identify the pictures. Dictionaries, which
she says are always at a premium, were given as prizes to
those identifying the most pictures.

For a "General Knowledge Quiz Program," the men

were divided into teams of three. Questions were divided
into categories such as spelling, history, literature, and
trivia. A team was asked a question and given thirty seconds
to answer. If they could not answer, each succeeding team
was given a chance. An answered question gave the team
one point, and the team with the most points at the end of
the hour was the winner. Cigarettes, she says, are "money"
in an institution, and the winning team got two packs per
man. Interest built up from week to week, and those who
came to watch, at first, later entered the contest. And
that should be remembered by all programmers.

Another program that built interest as it went along
was a spelling bee. Eighteen men entered the first one,
for which the prizes were five dollars and a book. When
it was over, others asked when there would be another one.
As the librarian said, "It always takes a little getting the
feet wet before interest is stirred up."

A contest was the culmination of another program.
This was a four-week library skills course called "Seek and
Find." The course met an hour a day, and it stressed
such basic tools as the card catalog, the Dewey Decimal
System, and various reference books. Audiovisual materials
on library skills supplemented the talks. To hold interest,
each inmate (they were adult males) decided upon a subject
on which he would like to do research. He then looked up
his subject in each tool, and reported some fact he had
learned from every source.

A trivia quiz was given for the final examination.
Each man was given a different question. When he found
the answer, he showed it to the librarian and earned a point.
The man with the most points at the end of the hour was
given a blank book--to encourage him to write his own.
The men were reportedly sorry when the course ended.

Book talks are popular at the Adobe Mountain School,
an institution for teenagers in Arizona. These are informal
programs. The librarian reads from a variety of books
and talks about them with the inmates.

At the Fairfield School for Boys, in Lancaster, Ohio,
the librarian has taught storytelling to the inmates. They,
then tell stories for outside groups.

The Free Public Library of Woodbridge (N. J.) has

come up with a different kind of program. This one is not for the direct benefit of the prisoners (although they benefit indirectly) but for the prisoners' children. The Rahway State Prison, near Woodbridge, has long visiting hours (11 a.m. to 4 p.m.) on Saturdays and Sundays, and the children are not permitted to bring in any books, games or toys. Disciplinary problems arose, as a result of this situation, and the prison asked the library to provide some programs for the children. A group of volunteers were assembled, and they, along with some librarians and library clerks, visited the prison each weekend. Many different programs were held each day. Craft programs, such as working with clay and finger painting, were conducted. Films were shown regularly. Librarians read to the children. And games were played. Fifty to one hundred children (ages three and up) participated each time.

In addition to the volunteers and the library staff, some of the inmates assisted at the programs. The main problem was in attracting, and keeping, volunteers. Although there were special circumstances connected with this program, that is always a problem with volunteers, and should not be surprising. The program eventually was run by two part-time employees, with the assistance of inmates, and it lasted for the three-year term of their grant without difficulty. Funds were provided by the state agencies running institutions and schools, and by the New Jersey State Library.

Libraries are now conducting various kinds of programs that will prepare prisoners for their release. One such program, entitled "Guides for Living," is conducted at the Kettle Moraine Correctional Institution in Plymouth, Wisconsin. It is a 24-session course and its objectives (according to the librarian who teaches it) are the "Development of positive thinking, planning for goal setting, and growth in self understanding and understanding of others." Books, films and cassettes are used in an attempt to help the prisoners learn to solve their problems without reliance on drugs or alcohol, to help them get rid of unwanted negative emotions, and to help them develop a positive attitude. Group discussion is the method used to help them achieve these goals.

NOTES

1. Montgomery, Helen. "Special Report: Outreach to the

Retarded," in <u>Wilson Library Bulletin</u>, May 1976, p. 688.

2. Forer, Anne-Marie, and Mary Zajac, in cooperation with the Altoona Area Public Library. <u>Library Services to the Retarded.</u>

3. Baskin, Barbara H., and Karen H. Harris, eds. "Storytelling for the Young Mentally Retarded Child," in <u>The Special Child in the Library.</u> Chicago: American Library Assoc., 1976, pp. 114-117.

Radio and television provide two ways of reaching out to many different kinds of people, in many different places, without ever going to those places. Indeed, if the library owns a station--as some libraries do--one need not even leave the library. Furthermore, by owning a station, the library is free to broadcast any program they want to, at any time they want to. Most such libraries, in fact, find the main problem to be filling up the available time. Owning a station presents other problems as well. As one librarian put it, it "takes a lot of time and a lot of money ... and we never felt we had much of an audience." We agree, in part. It does take time and money, and when you are talking into a microphone or facing a television camera, you do feel that nobody is out there. There are more listeners or viewers than you imagine, however. And you have to keep at it. Build up an audience, just as you would with any other kind of programming. The size of the audience can be estimated, too, so it won't all be guess-work. Ask for responses or suggestions, for example. The number listening will be many times the number who respond. The experience of the Danbury (Conn.) Public Library is instructive. They have their own television station, and a survey showed them to have an audience of better than 5,400. Even if only a few hundred watched any one program, not many libraries can boast that kind of attendance.

Although both staff time and costs are often in short supply at libraries, do they not seem desirable expenditures if the potential audience is so great? Again the experience in Danbury is interesting. The library produces six to eight hours of original programming a week, with a lot of programs coming from other organizations. But the station is on the air 24 hours a day, seven days a week. They do this with the use of a message wheel that revolves in front of the camera and gives municipal and community information. For

libraries, such a device has infinite possibilities. Many
people in the community have also been trained to use the
video equipment and to produce programs, thus providing
more potential programs and reducing the burden on the library staff. All this is estimated to cost $25,000 to $30,000
a year, even with growth. That is not a large sum for the
possibilities inherent in the situation. There are a lot of
ways to cut costs. The Half Hollow Hills (N.Y.) Public Library happened to have a trustee who built them a radio
station. Probably not many libraries will be so lucky, but
if you really wanted a station, it might be quite possible to
find a person, or persons, to build one, and to find businesses or others to donate pieces of equipment.

People are always volunteering to work in libraries
these days, and volunteers in a radio station can help cut
costs. They are usually willing, if not eager, to broadcast,
and they can be trained. Many people will also be willing
to appear as guests on radio and television programs without
a fee. Finding volunteers to do the necessary clerical work
around a station may be more difficult.

All kinds of programs can be borrowed. A lot of
places, including libraries, are making videotapes. Canned
radio programs are available from a number of organizations.
Radio Canada, The United Nations, the American Chemical
Society, the National Institute of Mental Health and the National Retired Teachers Association are some places that
supply free programs. Some legislatures and some individual
legislators and other officials will do the same.

In short, the costs need not be overwhelming, and it
may well be worth a library's time and money to own a
station. Indeed, it seems to be a logical place to have one,
given the large amount of material available to a library and
the large numbers of people a library would like to reach.
Furthermore, even if there are local stations, they may not
be readily accessible to a lot of groups or for many kinds
of information. Libraries can provide that access.

For most libraries though, using somebody else's
station will be the easiest and cheapest method, and local
stations will usually provide a time slot--and be glad to do
so. The public library in Ocean County, New Jersey, for
example, has produced many television programs without
owning any equipment and without employing a technician.
Most of the programs have been taped in the television

studio by company personnel and on company equipment. If
the library does have its own videotaping equipment, its use
will be another programming source, of course.

If the station isn't owned by the library though, one
can't dictate the time a program will be on. As we all
know, prime time is the name of the game. Two a. m.
on a Monday just won't make it. But if you have a good
program and you build a reputation, the audience will be there
at any reasonable time. Programs should be on at a regular
time, probably once a week, although that shouldn't preclude
specials. Having to do a regular program can seem burden-
some, but it's the way to build an audience.

Another way to build an audience is to aim your
content--and your publicity--at a particular group. The
elderly, the homebound, the rural, parents with young children, are all groups for which library radio and television
programs would be helpful. Any sizable number of foreign-
born people in the community would be a good group to aim
at. They might be drawn into the library, and they could,
at least, be helped to cope with their new country. The
public library in Framingham, Massachusetts has presented
a bilingual program of survival information, as well as programs of news and cultural events which were aimed at the
Puerto Rican community. Many of the groups just mentioned
will scan newspaper and radio television listings regularly.
Your program(s) should be there.

Programs can be taped, or they can be live. Many
people are terrified of appearing on radio and television--
especially of doing a live show! Remember what F. D. R.
said in another context and have no fear. There will be
experienced people at the station who will, figuratively at
least, take you by the hand. A good television floor manager
can lead a novice through a book talk so he will feel like
an old pro. Taping does have obvious advantages. You will
undoubtedly be less nervous, and you can go over and over
a script until it is smooth and free from warts. Live programs seem fresher, however, and sometimes a little bit of
nervousness is a good thing, giving it a slight necessary
tension and avoiding dullness.

Timing is the essential element. With a couple of
practice runs you can fit a script into the allotted time, and
you will soon get to know just how long a script should be.
On a 15-minute radio book talk, for example, we found a

six-and-a-quarter page, double-spaced typescript fit the
allotted time almost exactly. About two minutes were left
over for opening and closing announcements. As with any program, the completeness of the script is a matter of choice.
Since you are not seen on radio, you can read it, if you can
do so without seeming to. Novices will probably feel more
comfortable doing that. After some experience, an outline
will be all that is necessary. A complete script can be
prepared for television too, and if you practice a few times
you can consult it without actually reading it. It will also
be useful if the station's program director has a copy of the
script.

Even if the program is done live, though, you will
probably want to tape it. Tapes are useful for re-runs, and
re-runs are not all bad, even if the big commercial stations
use them ad nauseam. For one thing, you can catch different audiences at different times of the day or week, or
just catch those who missed the program the first time.
Danbury, as do some other libraries, makes the tapes available to anybody at any time they want to go to the library
and watch them.

As with library programs generally, the kinds of
radio and television programs you can dream up are almost
endless. Attention must, of course, be paid to the medium
being used. Television requires a lot of visuals, to avoid
the talking heads problem. Performers, people making
things, animals, still pictures and other variations may be
used to enliven television programs. For both media, a
mixture of general and special interest programs, of those
that are light and serious, will be best. It's always useful
to relate library materials to the program. And library
services and other events can be announced.

Interviews are one of the most obvious kinds of programs for both radio and television. Poets, novelists, dramatists, authors of non-fiction, musicians and lexicographers
are a few kinds of people who might be worth interviewing,
especially local representatives of those genres. For a
television program, an editor or a book designer might talk
about the physical book, and show examples.

The New York Public Library has had a successful
expanded interview-type program going on now for over
twenty years, a half-hour show called "Teen Age Book Talk."
It is taped on Friday afternoons after school at the city's

municipal radio station and broadcast the following Sunday
morning.   The program consists of a group of six to ten
teenagers and a librarian/moderator who discuss a book
(usually a recently published title) with the author.   A monthly
listing of the books to be discussed are mailed to interested
teenagers who then select the program each would like to
be on and arrange to pick up a copy of the book two to three
weeks before the program.   It is completely unrehearsed
and therefore spontaneous.   The only requirement is that
the teenagers read the book before the program.   The librar-
ian/moderator does prepare a script ahead of time with an
introduction to the author and questions addressed to the
author and the panelists, but the latter are both encouraged
to ask their own questions of each other and make observations and comments.   The moderator's job is mainly to keep
the program moving and progressing in some kind of order
so that the radio audience will be able to follow the discussion, and also to bring the show to a smooth close.   Over
the years the guest authors have included Eleanor Roosevelt,
John F. Kennedy, Kurt Vonnegut, and writers of teenage
books such as Robert Cormier, Walter Dean Myers, Francine Pascal, Rosa Guy and Jay Bennett.   Everyone involved
in these programs benefits from them.   The authors enjoy
meeting their teenage readers and getting feedback from
them, and the teenage panelists enjoy meeting the authors
and, in addition, develop critical acumen, become more
articulate, and gain greater self-confidence as a result of
the experience.   For the library it means good publicity as
well as pride in having helped young people in their personal
development.   For the listening audience it means an entertaining and informative program.   Most libraries would not
have the large resource of authors that New York City has.
However, this type of program has been done successfully
in some libraries without the authors, and this has proven
true with "Teen Age Book Talk" also when the authors occasionally have had to cancel due to illness or other reasons.

     Variations on this theme might include, along with
the interview, a scene from a play (previously videotaped),
the reading of some poems, the performance of music, and
the display and use of objects related to the book or subject.
During one library television program, involving an interview
with a naturalist, the television camera was put to excellent
use when an item was displayed that was connected to the
naturalist's book.   He had brought a toad with him and he
placed it on the table in front of him; as the camera zoomed
in for a close-up, the toad snapped up flies with its long

tongue, making for effective theatre and making the toad a
star performer. One might mention, at this point, that all
performers are not stars--some of them are duds. It therefore behooves the librarian to try and find out first if his
projected guest is likely to be a good interviewee. (This
is a principle that applies to any library program, as we
have said more than once.)

There are many more people to be interviewed. The
Half Hollow Hills (N.Y.) Public Library conducts a radio
interview program they call "Women on the Move." They
mainly interview women with unusual occupations. Among
others, they have talked with a minister, an assemblywoman,
a garbage commissioner, and a woman who heads her own
public relations firm. This is a series that could certainly
be of interest to many people, and could be useful to them
as well. Questions were asked about how they got started,
problems on the job, and any problems their jobs might
have created with their families.

At the Natrona County (Wyo.) Public Library they
interview political candidates at election time for their (the
library's) television station. Such interviews need not be
confined to election time, of course, nor need they be confined to elected officials. Any official might be interviewed
if there is some issue demanding public information, or
simply to explain what they do. One library has interviewed
a member of a town council, a state legislator, a school
superintendent, a human rights commissioner and somebody
in charge of a public assistance program. Many possibilities
in this and other areas will come to mind. At the public
library in Stamford, Connecticut, for instance, they find
their interviewees right in the library--discussing the library's services with staff, trustees, and users of the library.

Instead of an interview, you can simply have a talk,
which is easier, and may be better in some cases, especially
if you don't have a skillful interviewer or your guest is more
at home with a straight talk. Book reviews or book talks
are the first things that will occur to you. Again, the
possibilities are endless. In Stamford, Connecticut they
have had reviews of books about antiques, parenting, pre-
Columbian art, planning your own wedding, and women writing about women, among others. Book reviews need not be
long. The Dallas (Texas) Public Library airs two-minute
book reviews on the radio four times each Monday.

For talks on subjects, you will have to depend on whom you can get, but since many people seem to love being on radio or television you are not likely to run out of sources. The Ocean County (N. J.) Library has had talks on television about haunted houses, palmistry, decoupage, embroidery, divorce, child abuse, drug and alcohol abuse, local vegetation, canning, and preventive dentistry--that's variety! But it's not all. They ran a program called "Signs of the Zodiac," and if anyone doubts the potential popularity of library radio and television programs, it ran overtime in response to great viewer interest. To satisfy the demand, they produced two other programs on the subject.

Radio has long been used for reading to listeners. One can read novels, short stories, plays, speeches, essays, letters, poems, biographies, books of travel and that's enough to keep you busy for 99 years--or even for the rest of your career. The Half Hollow Hills (N. Y.) Public Library staff read, on their radio station, the first chapters of novels to entice listeners to come in and borrow the book. If an entire novel is going to be read, an episodic novel such as Pickwick Papers might be chosen. Then if a chapter is missed by a listener it really doesn't matter much. Short stories are obviously well-suited to this medium, and plays used to be a radio staple. For this activity (reading) you may need permission, and permissions are sometimes hard to get. There are, of course, many books in the public domain, so there will be no lack of material.

Some libraries answer reference questions on the air. The Ferguson Library in Stamford, Connecticut, for example, answers questions from both the children's and adults' reference departments. Questions would probably be best mailed or called in beforehand, but you might try having them called in during the program, answering them later in the program or on the next one. One idea might be to describe how you went about the search. Of course, you would be leaving yourself open to possible criticism from your colleagues ("Why did he look there?") but try to overlook such petty comments. In any case, a program of this kind would help to show the kind of work we do (something that is badly needed) and any reasonably-sized library gets enough unusual questions to make an interesting, sometimes humorous, and worthwhile show.

The air waves are filled with music and the library's

air waves may as well be too, because there is room for a
lot more, and a lot more different kinds than are played on
commercial radio. If the library has a record collection,
as most libraries now do, that will be a good source. Such
a program can publicize that part of the library's collection.
If the library owns a radio station, it may be able to get
free records from various record companies. There will
be no need to run out of ideas for musical programs on the
radio. The selection on most commercial stations is limited.
Listen to what they offer, then play something else. The
library will be doing the community a useful service. No
doubt popular music really is the most popular, but there
are audiences for all the other kinds too. So do try Gregor-
ian chants, Chinese folk songs, Ukrainian Liturgical Music,
La Clemenza di Tito, Prokofiev, and Bessie Smith, in addition to the more popular material. Maybe you will build
an audience.

There are numerous other possibilities for programs.
Quiz programs have long been popular on both radio and
television, and in North Carolina they created a library
version called "Book Bowl." The schools select three students in each grade that they consider the best readers, and
schools challenge each other. The program, usually half an
hour, is heard throughout the schools on the intercommunica-
tion system. Librarians prepare short questions with definite answers. They try to pick questions that will stimulate
reading, and that will be fun. They pick books they would
expect most children of a particular age to have read.

The Tucson (Arizona) Public Library created an original television program. They made a film, "The Information
Place," instead of a written annual report. Then they broadcast it on a local television station. The film included part
of a story hour, and staff members reporting on various
services--reference, technical, programs, and the bookmobile.

If the library has its own station, all kinds of programs dealing with local subjects can be broadcast. The
very active television station of the Danbury (Conn.) Public
Library does a number of them. "Sports Break," for example, is a fifteen-minute, weekly program about local
sports. On every other Friday, they do a weekend magazine
that covers local events, local arts and other features. Then
there is a program in which current, local issues are examined and they do a local news program, some of it with
in-depth coverage.

The most novel and certainly the most exciting idea
for a television program is taking place in Columbus, Ohio.
Warner Communications is (in late 1979) experimenting with
a system called Qube, in Columbus. The system allows
viewers to talk back to their television sets, through a special
device and by telephone. The public library is taking advantage of that fact, and is conducting "Home Book Club," a
monthly discussion program. A panel discusses the book in
the studio, and the viewers respond. The viewing audience
even votes--via the television set--on which book to discuss.
Viewers can have the book mailed to them in advance, again
by ordering through the television set. As many as 200
copies of one book were mailed out, indicating the popularity
of the program. The possibilities of this device boggle the
mind, and since Warner is planning expansion (at this writing)
to Houston, Cincinnati and Pittsburgh, the prospects are
promising. Libraries should get in on the ground floor.

Children are a large potential audience for radio and
television--which all good commercial stations know. But
some libraries have also realized this, and they have been
broadcasting to children for years. Such programs have
often been aired early on Saturday and Sunday mornings, no
doubt on the theory that young children need to be entertained
while their parents sleep, and quite likely because no one
else wants to produce programs at those times. Actually,
they are both fairly good reasons to have at least some
programs.

Storytelling is particularly suitable for radio, and the
Dayton and Montgomery County (Ohio) Public Library[1] has
had a very successful program of this kind, as have a number
of other libraries. This fifteen-minute program is aired on
Sunday mornings at 7:45, and is designed as a breakfast-
time program for the whole family. The program is taped
during the week, and the theme song, "Frère Jacques," and
the standard opening and closing announcements are added
at the program. Stories are chosen for broad appeal, literary quality, fast action and a minimum of detail. Folk tales
often fit these criteria. Stories about Paul Bunyan and
Pecos Bill, for example, are fast-moving and have humor,
and they have been found to be good choices. Animals stories
and stories about everyday life have also been successful.
If the permission of the publisher of the story is necessary,
it is usually granted. But if there is a fee, the story is
not used. Sometimes the length must be cut, and details
and some passages can be left out. If the story is too short,

they might play more of the theme song, read a poem appropriate to the story, or make more announcements about the library.

The librarian from Dayton has given some helpful hints about storytelling on the air. Enunciation should be clear, and the story must not be read too fast. One should learn the value of dramatic pauses, but if the pause is too long, radio listeners may think you have finished and turn the dial. Also, the stories should be read in a natural, conversational manner. Since the microphone is a delicate instrument, it will pick up all noises made in its presence. Be careful, therefore, not to make any extraneous noises, such as rustling papers or moving chairs. Some noises, though, such as a cough, or a laugh, might add to the naturalness of the program. Even if you cut some things out of the tape, you might consider leaving them in.

Many other kinds of programs for children are possible both on radio and on television. The Paducah (Ky.) Public Library does so many unusual television programs for children that they are worth citing at length. These programs are produced at a local television station which gives the air time free, as a public service. Their program is called the "Uncle Briggs Show" and it is on for a half hour a week. Holidays are naturals for program ideas, and in Paducah they celebrated the 4th of July by having a staff member dress as Uncle Sam, and having others wear red, white and blue hats. They sang songs from the Yankee Doodle Song Book. Another staff member--dressed as the Statue of Liberty--showed some books about American History. For another dress-up program, a staff member put on a King Arthur outfit, and led a "round table" discussion. Books about King Arthur and knighthood were introduced.

Singing is clearly a good idea on both radio and television. At another program in which singing was the central part, the programmers led 45 "Head Start" children (the studio audience) in "The Zoo Song," "The Elephant Song," and "The Boa Constrictor." The children and teachers were then interviewed about library services. Live animals were some of the performers at a program on pet care, which featured four kittens, two children, and some books about cats.

Craft demonstrations can make for good television,

and some librarians from Paducah--using The Rainy Day Book by Alvin Schwartz--constructed a paper bag puppet and a spool doll. Many crafts programs will come to mind. Using a country or an area is always a good way to focus a program, so at another program, books about France, famous French people and French cooking were discussed. Then they gave a reading (in French and English) of "La Petite Famille." Some other television programs from Paducah have included a discussion of the Newbery and Caldecott awards, a puppet show of "Jack and the Beanstalk," and an open house on the bookmobile.

NOTE

1. Mathy, Margaret. "Folklore and Flapjacks," Top of the News, April 1970, pp. 199-201.

There are some activities that just don't seem to fit in anywhere, although they are undeniably programs. Contests are included in this category. At the Prince George's County (Md.) Memorial Library they have had a photography contest for teenagers, although such a contest could be held for children or adults. The judges came from newspapers, photography studios, camera stores, high schools, and colleges. Prizes were donated by stores, civic associations, and fraternal organizations. The winning entries were criticized for all who attended, and there was private criticism of the others for those who wished it. The photographs were then used as exhibits.

For a cooking contest at the same library, the judges and prizes came from restaurants, 4-H clubs, Campfire Girls and the Boy and Girl Scouts. The winning entries in this contest probably didn't last long enough to be exhibited.

A really different contest was held in Boise, Idaho. There they made a bookworm of nine hula hoops, purple and yellow material for the body, and shocking pink for the face. The worm also has a red nose and wears blue glasses. All in all, he must be striking. It takes nine children to walk this sixteen-foot creature when he goes to parades and such. At any rate, having made a bookworm they had to name him, so they held a contest. Children under twelve could enter. A prize of a book (what else?) was awarded to the winner, and other participants were given certificates. The winning name was Longfellow, and the prize was awarded at a party --at which Longfellow was, of course, present.

A children's Art Festival was held at a Staten Island, New York library, and a contest was again the main feature. Children three to thirteen years of age submitted original works of art, mounted for display. These works were exhibited at the library for six weeks, and were judged by a committee of artists, community leaders, and various people who worked with children. There were prizes of money, and the winners were purchased by the library for its permanent circulating collection of original art works. Local artists helped with mounting and display, and individuals and community groups gave the prizes. Prizes were awarded at the usual reception.

Art has been the focus of assorted other programs. In one case, the artists--whose works were on exhibit-- attended a reception, and talked with those present about their philosophies of art and about the techniques they used. In another instance, an interior mural had been painted in the library by an artist and some of the local youths. Again a reception was held when it was finished.

Tournaments are also a part of this miscellany. We are not talking about jousting knights but about such things as chess and backgammon tournaments. One library decided to have a chess tournament following a successful lecture/demonstration on chess, since the interest appeared to be there. Registration was necessary, since the number of players had to be limited. A simple registration form was adapted from a form in use by a local chess club. Players were asked to bring chessmen and boards, a notation pad, and--if they had one--a tournament clock. The tournament was open to all, except that the players were required to know chess notation. The tournament was run according to the rules of the United States Chess Federation. It was divided into two parts, one for members of the Federation, and one for non-members.

It was held on three consecutive evenings, with each participant playing two games per evening. Fifty players registered and the ages ranged from eight to about sixty; many of the players were teenagers. It is believed that many more would have registered with more widespread publicity. Because of space limitations, however, publicity was held down. The event itself generated much additional publicity; the local newspaper printed several news stories, mentioned it in their weekly chess column, and printed a photograph of the players in action--if action is the word to describe chess players. No fee was required, and no prizes were given.

Quite a lot of space was needed for this tournament,

although it might have been held in a smaller space if the
right kind of furniture had been available. Round library
tables had to be used in some cases. It was held in a
large children's room, which opened off the adult department,
and which was little used during the evening hours. Library
patrons could thus wander through and watch the play. It
was, needless to say, a fairly quiet kind of program, and
thus ideally suited for a public service area--although occasionally "the hum from either army stilly sounded."

A collector's fair was an unusual library event held
in Salt Lake City, Utah. This four-hour program was spread
out from the sub-basement to the third floor, and featured
twenty-two collections. People were invited to browse and
to quiz the collectors. Collectibles included comic books,
stamps, movie photos, sheet music, mice, toys, thimbles,
buttons, bottle openers, hats, and railroad memorabilia. A
directory was printed. The budget was $200 for the fair
and the public response was overwhelming. If such a program
is successful, the public relations value is great. This
program was a great success and they are repeating it.
It is being expanded to two days, and a number of auxiliary
programs are being added. These new programs will include instruction in the restoration of old furniture, old
books and old cars, and a program on how to conduct an
auction. There will also be 42 collectors this time. One
should always learn from inevitable mistakes. The fair
organizers learned to have more directional signs, and to
have the exhibits ready as soon as the library doors opened.

To celebrate anniversaries, or other events, or for
no reason at all, libraries sometimes have a kind of carnival, that is, a number of activities going on at the same
time, usually throughout the library. The Port Washington
(N.Y.) Public Library, for example, has a yearly "Happening." The idea is to have a "summer party," with a "very
festive atmosphere," so that everybody can just have a good
time. For the first three years, events for all ages were
held at the same time, so that it could be a kind of family
affair. In the fourth year, they decided to divide it into
two parts, since the children tended to get restless. Now
the "Happening" for adults and teenagers is on Friday evening, and that for children on Saturday morning.

The adults and teenagers were greeted by a communal
weaving session in the foyer. At the same time, bluegrass
music, juggling and mime were being performed in the

reading room, and in the children's room a Spanish guitar
was being played and caricatures were being drawn. Holograms were also displayed in the audiovisual department.
That part of the evening lasted an hour. Next, the group
assembled in the meeting room to see a juggler and scenes
from a play, and to listen to a harmonica, a guitar and more
bluegrass. The evening wound up with disco dancing.

The children's "Happening" had a similar format.
Games, fortune telling, accordion playing, caricature drawing, a "Penny Count Drawing," and a "happening" tunnel
occupied the first part. In the meeting room there were
mime and movement performances. In past years, there
have been sea chanties, Chilean singing, tap dancing, Chinese dancing, short films, star gazing, weight lifting, belly
dancing and a graffiti wall.

A branch of the Milwaukee (Wisc.) Public Library
celebrated its 25th anniversary by looking back to the 1950's
when the branch opened. Those attending were asked to
dress in fifties costumes, with appropriate hair styles, and
to bring harmonicas, kazoos and hula hoops among other
things. At the library they could listen to the music of the
fifties, ride unicycles or pogo sticks, and participate in
numerous other events reminiscent of that decade.

Open houses are similar events that are frequently
given by libraries. They are particularly useful if they can
attract groups that are not accustomed to using the library.
Port Washington had an open house for foreign-born residents
and their children. Refreshments are appealing at this kind
of activity and library resources and services can be displayed to good effect. A short film can be shown, a story
told, a historic newspaper displayed, new readers registered,
and so forth. One difficulty is to attract the group at which
you are aiming. Publicity should include the language(s)
of the group(s) you want to come, and events should obviously
be designed to appeal to their needs and interests. Parents
can frequently be persuaded to come by their children, and
the children are likely to be the most reachable.

Bus trips are sponsored by a number of libraries.
Some are day trips, or parts of days, and some are for
overnight. Usually the participants pay the fare, but the
library makes all the arrangements. Some go to operas,
plays, historic houses and other interesting places. These
trips are favorite activities for the elderly who can't, or

don't want to, drive. But they might be useful for any group. Sometimes a trip is the culmination of a library program. In Spring Valley, New York a bus trip to the Pompeii exhibit at the American Museum of Natural History followed a slide lecture on the art and artifacts of Pompeii. And from the Rosenberg Library in Galveston, Texas a group flew to Guatemala and Yucatan, following a year-long series of programs about Guatemala and Mayan culture.

NOTE

1. Boise Public Library credits Spokane (Wash.) County Library for bookworm idea.

PART II: FINDING AND SELECTING PROGRAMS

10 ★ PROGRAM SOURCES
(Where you can find them and how you can get them)

Some libraries provide money to pay speakers and performers who appear at library programs, but many do not. One must therefore be prepared to do some scrounging. There are quite a lot of sources of free programs, if one gives it some thought. The first thing to do is to look around you. You may even find the grail in your own castle. Inquire among your staff, or the families and friends of staff members. You never know where you will turn up an expert in some field of knowledge. These sources have provided discussion group leaders, poets, musicians, dancers, and people to give demonstrations and workshops in a variety of arts and crafts such as sewing, macramé, origami, and gardening. Sometimes one thing leads to another. One staff member knew a t'ai chi expert who knew some musicians and a lecturer on Chinese poetry. The library produced a program using all of these people; they, later, found other performers and a second program evolved from the first.

Local colleges are a rich field for exploration; among both faculty and students there may be actors, poets, musicians and experts in any number of subjects. Furthermore, they are often willing to perform for a local institution, such as the public library, without charge. You have nothing to lose by asking, and we have often been pleasantly surprised at the willingness of such talented individuals, and even their eagerness, to participate. College faculties on Staten Island have supplied, among others, a speaker on film history, a chamber music group and an actor to read a story by Charles Dickens. Students in a graduate course in children's literature presented some dramatized stories and gave some puppet shows. Other libraries have found student musicians and students in speech courses to give dramatic presentations.

212

Zoos and aquariums provide obvious possibilities; a herpetologist we know (who arrived with a boa constrictor that crawled around his neck as he talked, and a rattlesnake that didn't) put on one of the best shows we have ever seen in a library program--or anywhere else, for that matter. Zoos have veterinarians who could give talks on pet care and diseases. Aquariums could supply people to talk to amateur aquarists. Museums will have experts--or they will know people who are expert--in the arts, sciences and local history. They might provide entomologists, microscopists (an arachnologist would make a great program), anthropologists, archeologists, an expert on the local flora and fauna, or an expert in the detection of art forgeries. One museum known to the authors has an agrostologist and an expert on diatoms connected with it.

Don't overlook scientific and historical associations and societies. They frequently have members who have become expert in some field, and who are willing to share their knowledge. Such a program may also attract members to their organization. Many people, for example, are interested in local history, and in genealogy which often accompanies it. The Audubon Society or the Sierra Club may have local chapters, or there may be strictly local organizations for such subjects as archeology or geology. Poetry and literary societies are possibilities in those subject areas. Be sure they are not just mutual admiration societies, though.

City, state, federal and private organizations in the fields of law enforcement, health, consumer affairs, work with the aged, child care, mental health and business are usually willing to send speakers, and often films, to library programs. City and state police and the Federal Bureau of Investigation may be willing to supply speakers on a variety of subjects. One very popular library program, on protecting the home from burglars, was conducted by local police. In a series of programs for the elderly, a representative of the Better Business Bureau told some fascinating stories of frauds on householders; he also told his audience how to avoid being cheated.

In the same series, a nutritionist talked about food for the elderly and a speaker from the Social Security Administration talked about changes in his field. A psychologist from a mental health society conducted a lively series of discussions on child raising. Films were shown to spark the proceedings. The same mental health society was approached about a program on violence in our society. The program, it could have been a series, never happened, but the Society was interested and would have provided free speakers or discussion leaders.

Many organizations dealing with specific diseases or other aspects of health care are sources of programs. The American Cancer Society, the Epilepsy Foundation, Muscular Dystrophy Associations, heart associations, the Arthritis Foundation, county medical societies, city and county health departments and optometric societies will frequently provide both films and speakers. Drug abuse and drug rehabilitation centers will provide programs; they can send both the people who work with addicts and sometimes the ex-addicts themselves to talk about problems of addicts, methods of rehabilitation and to give information about drugs and their effects. Organizations that work with the physically and mentally handicapped can talk about the training, employment and care of their clients. Organizations that work with the blind can talk about the psychology of the blind, services for them, and their rehabilitation; libraries that serve the blind, for example, can give marvelous demonstrations of their services and of the materials they use.

There are city, county, and private agencies that serve the elderly. They can provide speakers on retirement, on activities for the elderly, and on their problems. Human rights commissions can discuss the employment of minorities. City and county planning commissions can discuss zoning, urban renewal, commercial development, public housing, and related topics. The League of Women Voters will supply speakers and discussion leaders on a variety of local, national and international topics that are of importance to the citizen.

Local drama groups sometimes attain considerable skill; often they include actors or a director with professional experience. These groups may be willing to perform plays, scenes, or give dramatic readings. There are probably struggling young poets in every community and they often write with power. Many libraries have provided showcases for them. They can be found through the English departments of high schools and colleges and often among your readers. There are music groups that are not affiliated with any institution, for example, rock groups, string quartets, pianists, singers and chamber orchestras. As with theatre groups, musical societies often include performers with professional experience and a lot of skill. Clubs and organi-

zations such as the American Association of University
Women or the Junior League may have a variety of performers among their members; one might find people with
expertise in many different crafts, or people who are, or
could be trained to be, storytellers, puppeteers and discussion leaders.

There are many clubs in most communities; they all
have programs with speakers, demonstrations, performances,
and films; often the speakers are drawn from among their
members and are experts in some phase of the club's special
interest. These clubs--which are often looking for meeting
space--can be encouraged to meet regularly in the library,
and to have meetings that are open to the public. Such an
arrangement benefits the club by stimulating interest in the
subject and providing them with publicity and it benefits the
library by providing ready-made programs. A geology club,
for example, had an interesting series of programs in a library; subjects included caves, fossils, and micromounts;
they were presented through the use of speakers, slides and
films.

Some businesses are glad to provide programs. They
can supply information about a subject without promoting
their own businesses; if it is known where they are from,
they will regard that as advertisement enough. Stockbrokers,
for example, can give information talks about investments
(which often are very popular programs) without drumming
up business for themselves. Karate schools have given
striking demonstrations to crowds of boys of all ages (including middle-age); they love the board-breaking parts.
Garden supply stores or plant nurseries can send speakers
to talk about gardening on any subject from azaleas to zin-
nias. People from pet stores might talk about the care,
training or diseases of pets. One library arranged for a
butcher to talk to housewives about cuts and grades of meat.
Businesses in the arts and crafts are a good source of
speakers and demonstrators.

Publishers are businessmen who have a stake in libraries. Their publicity departments may be able to get an
author who has a new book on their list to speak in a li-
brary--incidentally promoting his book. Publishers can also
tell you how to get in touch with an author, if you want to
contact one directly. If you can interest him, he may be
willing to come for little or nothing. Any local author is
certainly worth a try. You may not have the winner of a

Pulitzer Prize living in the neighborhood, as we did, but
local authors are usually of interest to the local population,
and they are usually willing to speak without a fee in their
community library.

Ethnic groups often form associations. If you want
to put on an ethnic program, and there is a local Italian
club or Sons of Norway, they may be able to supply performers or they will know of performers. Two very successful programs on Chinese culture were produced in this
way by one library. Often your readers, or other individuals in the community who are unaffiliated with any organization, will prove to be experts in something you can
use.

One of the authors worked in a library that was used
by a local fireman who had become an expert photographer;
he had learned this skill solely through the use of books in
the library. He talked to a group on the techniques of
photography, and at the same time served as a great advertisement for the library. There are many crafts that
lend themselves to this kind of possibility; macramé, needle-
craft, Christmas decorations and pottery are some library
programs that have developed from contacts with library
users. It is useful, in many ways, to know one's readers.

Local newspapers frequently print articles about
people in the community who have unusual hobbies or occupations or who have unusual backgrounds. Through newspaper articles, we have discovered two poets, a sculptor,
a man who made model ships for a living, a World War I
pilot, and an American Indian who have provided, or will
provide, library programs. The American Indian, for
example, gave a wonderful performance, talking, dancing
and singing before an enthusiastic audience. A great many
flyers and brochures come across every librarian's desk.
And, although we all regard this kind of mail with impatience,
it should be glanced at if you are looking for program
sources. One may as well utilize the groundwork that has
been laid by other libraries, museums, and other kinds of
organizations that do programming.

Having found all these people, one should record them.
A card file or looseleaf notebook is useful since one should
record their names, addresses, telephone numbers, speciali-
ties, the fee if any, where they have performed, and any
observations on the quality of their performance. Naturally,

such a file must be kept up to date. Somebody should be responsible for seeking out program' sources, and for maintaining a file; some library systems or regions do this centrally and notify their branches or member libraries of available programs.

When asking people to speak or perform on a library program, we have usually found that a telephone call, followed by a confirming letter, worked well. If there are any details or problems to be ironed out, you may want to meet with them, at THEIR CONVENIENCE, to do it. Theatre groups may want to measure the stage or confer on lighting, props and dressing rooms; speakers may want a lectern or not want a lectern; and anyone showing slides or films will need to discuss arrangements.

There are several things one must definitely do: speakers and performers should be invited well in advance of the program, sometimes months ahead; they must be notified in writing--a busy person can easily forget--and they should be given one or more reminders, tactfully and without bothering them too much. It must be clearly stated that you can't pay them a fee, if that is the case. The library's role in the program and the visitors' role must be clearly defined; some individuals, and groups, tend, consciously or unconsciously, to take over a program for their own purposes, if everything is not spelled out in advance. (They make too many demands or make of the program something you hadn't intended.) Speakers should be given a time limit, which can, of course, be flexible; some speakers will be too brief and most will go on too long. They should be told the purpose of the program and, if possible, indicate the kind and size of audience they might expect. Sometimes, in spite of all precautions, thing will get out of hand. Ways of handling such problems will be discussed later.

Now that all those speakers, actors, musicians and poets have been found, is it desirable to invite them sight unseen? If their reputations are big enough or good enough, one might. If possible, however, it is desirable to see a performance first. The contents of the program is important as well as the quality of the performance. One might rely on somebody else's opinion but one must be careful. As E. B. White said somewhere, "One man's Mede is another man's Persian." If no one can see a performance, reading the play or poems may suffice. The programmer will have

to judge his sources. These precautions are important for
several reasons. There may be something in the content of
the program that will make you decide not to use it. The
quality of the performance may not be up to your standards;
your standards may differ, however, depending on the objective of a particular program; if the program is designed
to present new, young poets, high quality and polish can't be
expected. Finally, even if you use the program, you will
want to be prepared to answer any objections that might
arise.

Eventually one runs out of free sources of programs.
Or one gets caught up in the excitement and stimulation that
programs can offer and wants to do things that cost money.
If you are in that predicament, you might consider applying
for a grant. At this writing, grant money, both from federal
and state governments and from private sources, is much
tighter than it was a few years ago. Nevertheless, money
is still available. One has only to look at the bulky volume
entitled The Foundation Directory, with its thousands of entries, to realize that this is so. Therefore, if you have a
good idea and present it in the right way, you have a chance
of getting money for your project. The authors have had
the very satisfying experience of obtaining such a grant;
the money restored a theatre in a branch library and brought
hundreds of programs to a neighborhood that had been cul-
turally barren. Now, when the footlights go on and the new,
red curtain goes up before an enthusiastic audience, we feel
that all the effort that went into library programming has
really been worthwhile.

Getting a grant, however, requires some thought and
some work. The first thing you need is a good idea that has
been thoroughly and clearly thought out. A successful grant-
getter and a reader of grants for a foundation have both told
us that there are two main reasons that grant applications
are not successful. One is that they are cloudy and unspe-
cific; that is, they probably have not been well thought-out.
The other is that they are overwritten and overlong. It has
been estimated that some foundations receive a thousand
proposals a year. Obviously the clear, concise proposal
will get more attention.

You have to subject your idea to some close scrutiny,
to decide if it is really valuable and is going to benefit
somebody, other than yourself. Other resources and sources
of funding must have been exhausted. You have to study the

budget very carefully and make sure it is realistic; don't assume you have to ask for more than you need.

The next step is to find out what foundations might consider your application. The amount of money they have to give and the purposes for which they give it are the key factors. There are several sources of information on foundations. The seventh edition of The Foundation Directory published by The Foundation Center lists 3,138 of the larger foundations. There are about 22,000 foundations in the United States, but the ones listed in this directory account for 85 percent of total foundation assets. In this directory you will find the names and addresses of foundations, their purposes and activities, financial data, lists of their officers and trustees, and application procedures. It is arranged by state so you will be able to identify the foundations in your area and it contains a subject index to foundation program areas. The Foundation Center has offices in Washington, D. C. , New York City, Cleveland and San Francisco. These maintain files of tax returns of foundations that show the grants they have made. The Center supplies materials to regional depository libraries in large cities in every state across the country, and there is no charge to the public for consulting these materials. Files of annual reports of foundations are also kept. To find out the depository library closest to you, you may write to The Foundation Center, 888 7th Avenue, New York, N. Y. 10106. They will also send on request, free of charge, a list of their other publications and pamphlets on proposal writing.

Another useful publication is Foundation News, a bimonthly periodical that keeps information on grants up-to-date. This is published by The Council on Foundations (1828 L Street NW, Washington, D. C. 20036) and includes in each issue a Grants Index of current grants put out by The Foundation Center. These are later compiled in an annual volume by the center. It is also possible to see the tax returns (IRS-990-PF and 990-AR) of foundations by visiting the office of the director of Internal Revenue for the district in which the foundation is located. Consult the Bibliography for further information on these publications.

After the project has been thought out, and likely foundations identified, it must be put in writing for submission to the foundation. As we said above, these applications should be clear and concise. In giving guidelines for the writing of applications, one foundation begins each of the

major points with the word brief. Another foundation speci-
fies a short letter. Proposals should be typed (double-
spaced) on white paper. The project should be described,
and the need for the project should be indicated; your own
observations and any documentation should be included. You
should also indicate the qualifications you have for carrying
out the project. The objectives should be spelled out and
the procedures you intend to use as well as the methods you
plan for evaluating the project described. A budget must be
carefully prepared and it should be compared to the written
proposal to make sure they go together and all points are
covered.

Fund-Raising Methods

If the library has some kind of support group among
the citizenry (such as Friends of the Library) there are a
number of ways that group can raise money for programs.
These activities are similar to programs themselves, and
--as with any program--the librarian must work with the
group on the details. Without careful planning, a potential
disaster is in the making--resulting in ill will all around.
Better not to have had the event in the first place. At any
rate, the date and time have to be selected. The method
of gathering the materials to be sold must be decided on and
transportation arranged. Supplies have to be provided, somebody has to clean up afterwards, and--above all--there must
be good publicity.

A book sale seems like an obvious event for a library
to engage in. Everything will have to be priced, and maybe
a local book dealer will do the job as a public service.
Prices can be reduced toward the end of the day, or books
can be sold by the pound or by the bagful. After it's over,
those items that are left should be stored for next time, or
they must be disposed of. A bake sale is another event
common to non-profit groups. Each item should be priced
beforehand and marked clearly. The cakes and cookies
should be delivered early. Portions should be evenly divided.
Unusual items may be raffled off, but perhaps there won't
be a problem in disposing of the remains at this event.

An art show is another fund-raising possibility. At
this one, local artists would donate work to be sold for the
benefit of the library, or the library would get part of the
money.

Volunteers

In the last few years, the subject of volunteers in libraries has been surfacing regularly. Everybody thinks it's easy to run a library, and since libraries are short of money.... Let's start off by saying volunteers cause problems. They can also provide a lot of help, particularly for programs. Just be careful! Volunteers may not show up when they're supposed to. They may call at the last minute and say they can't come. They may give misinformation to the public and so forth. Of course, sometimes the paid staff do these things too. Volunteers, then, should be carefully selected for your purposes and they should be well-trained. Sometimes there is a diffidence about supervising volunteers. That feeling has to be overcome. They should have time sheets and they should perform in the same way as the rest of the staff. They should not, of course, do the same jobs.

There are, however, quite a few duties connected with programs that they might do. Publicity is time-consuming. If you can find volunteers with some artistic skill or writing ability, so much the better. If not, there will probably be some who can do the job as well as the librarian, and as we have indicated in our chapter on publicity, it doesn't take a lot of skill; it's mostly a lot of work. So, they can do flyers, write press releases, distribute publicity, make telephone calls, and other things--all under your supervision, of course.

Volunteers can act as ushers and ticket takers. They can try to help maintain some kind of order when what seems like 4,000 children appear at a puppet show on a rainy afternoon. They can run projectors and other equipment and they may turn out to have a skill or some knowledge that will enable them to be the center of a program, such as lecturing, demonstrating gold panning techniques, or performing a soft-shoe routine.

Volunteers will probably be retired, be unemployed housewives, or be in school. The Port Washington (N.Y.) Public Library, for example, has a summer program for Junior Aides. These are students who have completed the 5th or 6th grade. They work three hours a week and they help with story hours, make posters, and help with equipment. Letters are sent to schools and school libraries outlining the program. They have time sheets and regular

222 / Library Programs

assignments. They report to a librarian when they arrive, and they wear a badge that says Junior Aids. The Caldwell (Idaho) Public Library has a Junior Library Club and members help with their puppet shows among other things. They also have a volunteer who is an experienced puppeteer. She is seventy years old. At a school for the deaf in Rochester, New York, the Salvation Army Senior Citizens have gone to the school to do craft work with the children, and the librarian has said, "It is rewarding to see the women come in, a little unsure of what this experience will bring; to see them leave, each telling about 'My kids.' "[1] Organizations like the American Association of University Women have done volunteer work in libraries, and teenagers have performed a variety of functions. So, programming help is out there, waiting to be found and organized.

NOTE

1. Sangster, Collette. "Library Service to the Deaf," in The Bookmark, New York State Library, Winter, 1979, p. 60.

11 ★ CHOOSING THE RIGHT PROGRAM

After you have found out what programs are available, you must decide which ones would be desirable and useful, and which will fit into your particular library. No matter how worthy a program may be, if it won't work in your library, you might better concentrate on something else. A program on welfare rights in a wealthy suburb or one on investments in an urban or rural slum just won't play. Don't be too quick to judge, however. There may be scattered people in your community who are interested in a particular subject, and sometimes audiences can be built up over a period of time.

When selecting a program, there are two main areas for consideration. The first is the subject matter: one must find out what subjects a group of people in the community is, or might be, interested in. The second area for consideration is the equally important, but more mundane, matter of physical accommodations--plus a few nagging little problems that are related.

One way to find out what people are interested in is to ask them. And one way to do that is to form a club or advisory board and let them help select--and possibly help plan--programs. This has been done with various age groups, as well as with groups including people of all ages. Because of their interests, energy and enthusiasm, teenagers can make a useful advisory board. It is important to remember a few things, however. Following through on their suggestions is essential. Naturally, a library can't do everything, and for one reason or another not all ideas will be workable. But it will be important to bring some recommendations to fruition. Nobody likes to see his or her work go to waste and teenagers can probably handle it less well than adults. It will be necessary to be sure the money, equipment, staff, and administration approval are there before programs are

planned. Some of the suggestions may startle you. The
library has never done anything like that, or done it in that
way. Be flexible! Maybe the library should. The library
administration must be convinced that something different
should be tried. If there are objections, perhaps you can
find a way to get the money, find the space, or otherwise
answer the objections.

An article in The Bookmark suggests a number of
points to consider when forming such a group. 1 They may
want to elect a president. In some libraries, a representative to the library board may be useful. A variety of teenage interests should be represented. If it's a large group,
the advisory board may want to divide into sub-committees
according to interest (film, music, literature). Frequent
reminders of meetings are necessary. Telephone members
close to the date. Give each member a specific job to do,
with a deadline, so that some of that enthusiasm is used.
Introduce the advisory board to the rest of staff, and convey their ideas to the staff too. They must not be made to
feel like interlopers.

At the other end of life, the Cleveland Public Library
organized the "Live Long and Like It Library Club" to do
programming specifically for the elderly. This group was
organized, not because all the programs were of interest
only to the elderly, but because that group seemed more at
ease with each other and more willing to attend programs.

Meanwhile, for those of us "Nel mezzo del cammin
di nostra vita" the Plainfield (N.J.) Public Library has organized a Mother's Club. This group, as do similar groups
in other libraries, meets while their pre-schoolers are having
a program in the children's room. The mothers decide, in
conjunction with the librarian, what programs they want.
They have had programs with titles like "Helping Young
Children Form Healthy Attitudes Toward Sex" and "Sex Education for Adults." But it's not all sex in Plainfield. They
have also wanted to find out what their schools were doing,
about the pros and cons of abortion, how to help their children with music, about television programming for children
and about gardening and various other arts and crafts. The
library has been able to provide programs on these subjects.

One advantage of such groups is that they also may
be the source of the contents of a program, as well as suggesting the subject. As with the more general friends of

WANTED!

Did you know the Finkelstein Library has a Young Adult Librarian and a Young Adult Book Collection? We plan to do more . . . have programs and special events . . . But we need your help and advice . . . .

Your name: Your age:
Your address and village:
Your phone number:
Your school:

1. Would you be willing to join the Young Adult Advisory Board to help plan Young Adult programs and activities at Finkelstein?

   Yes _____   No _____

2. What's the best day and time for meetings for you?

   _____

3. What types of programs would you like to see for Young Adults at Finkelstein? (Please circle).

   Science Fiction Films   Movies   Music
   Book Discussion Groups   Car Maintenance   Student Rights
   Self-defense Demonstrations Sex Education
   Crafts (which ones?) _____

   List any other ideas?

4. Do you have a special talent you could teach or share with others?

5. Would you be willing to read and review new Young Adult books?

   Yes _____   No _____

6. Please circle the kinds of books you like to read for pleasure.

   Romance   Teen novels   Poetry   Sports biographies
   History   Mystery   Adventure   Others?
   Biographies   Science Fiction Science

7. Is there anything else you'd like to suggest?

FINKELSTEIN MEMORIAL LIBRARY

the library groups, these clubs can supply or find speakers, performers, money or materials.

Another way of having a program advisory board is to form an ad hoc group for a particular purpose. This method is useful if you are planning a lot of programs on a particular subject, and it has been used with success in Port Washington, New York. In one case, they held a month-long "Celebration of Women." Fifty local women spent two months "meeting in small groups, exploring community resources, enlisting friends and neighbors in creating workshops and programs, assembling a diverse array of events." The result was a series of films, lectures, workshops and discussion groups on everything from birth control to business management, and including home repair, yoga, unusual occupations, resumé writing, Chinese cookery, and a variety of cultural programs. The women who did the planning were assembled from social, cultural and religious groups, as well as women who were active in various fields.

Another group at Port Washington is--at this writing --planning a series of programs under the heading of energy. This committee includes a high school teacher, a college president, a nuclear engineer, a member of the Audubon Society, a power company executive, a science writer, and a member of the League of Women Voters. They are recommending materials, suggesting speakers, and helping plan the formats of the programs. Before the first meeting, the group was given a form to fill out, which helped focus the discussions. It is shown below.

There is one general caveat for libraries assembling such groups: it must be made clear to them that the library is making the selection of the program and doing the planning and the group is a helping and advisory group. There are always dangers when programming with any outside organization or with individuals. Sometimes, if you're not careful, they'll eat you up. On the other hand, it will probably work fine.

```
NAME:
ADDRESS:
TELEPHONE--business:
            home:
```

1. What do you think are the most urgent issues regarding Nuclear Energy?

   A.

   B.

   C.

2. Are there particular areas in which you think the public is lacking in information or is misinformed?

3. What format for programs on energy (and specifically nuclear energy) do you think would be most interesting?

   Films   Debates
   Talks   Slide-talks
   Panel discussions   Videotaped interviews
   Public forum   with playbacks

   Other, please specify--

4. What about the timing of these programs ... Do you think, for instance, that we should try to schedule a program on nuclear energy right away because of recent public concern or do you think we should wait until the fall?

   Should we devote a block of time for concentrated programming in this area or should we spread it out and devote one program a month over a period of time?

5. Do you have any suggestions for resources for library programs or materials?

   Films or other media materials:

   Books:

   Exhibitions:

   People: (please identify their connection)

> Are there organizations in the vicinity which you think
> we should be aware of who might be interested or
> helpful?

Have Them Fill Out Forms

Another way of asking people what programs they
want is to devise a form that can be filled out and that can
be distributed to all kinds of people in all kinds of places.
This form can be given to library users; it can be distributed at meetings of clubs or other organizations at which one
is speaking, or merely attending; and when one has started
to have programs, it can be given to those attending. Libraries that do a lot of outreach work have even taken them
door-to-door along with other library publicity. Such a form
should be simple and easy to read and to fill out--otherwise
people won't bother. The following form is a sample of
what one library used. Depending on your library, you
may want to include other subjects, kinds of programs,
or categories of people. Remember, many people who
say they want a particular program won't show up when
you have one. Still, a form like this is useful, and it serves
several purposes.

1. Underline below the subjects which interest you.
Animal life	Dance	Photography	Travel
Art	Drama	Poetry	Other ____
Cooking	Music	Pollution	
Crafts	Occult	Sports	

2. What kind of performance would you like to see?
   Discussion   Film   Lecture   Workshop

3. Would you like to receive notices of programs?
   YES   NO

4. If yes, underline age levels which apply.
   Adult   13-17   under 13 years

5. What day of the week would you attend a program?
   Mon.   Tues.   Wed.   Thurs.   Fri.   Sat.

6. What time would you attend a program?
   Morning   Afternoon   Evening

PLEASE PLACE YOUR NAME, ADDRESS, AND ANY HOBBY
OR SKILL ON OTHER SIDE.

Another kind of survey, specifically designed for teen-agers, was tried. From part of a book stack, facing the front door of the library, some shelves were removed. A poster was put in that space. At the top of the poster were the words: TEENAGERS! WHAT TYPE OF PROGRAM WOULD YOU LIKE? Below were listed many subjects, with a row of boxes next to each subject for checking preferences. A wide range of subjects from candle-making to horseback riding and drag racing were included. A head and hands were drawn and cut out, and they were placed as if looking over the top of the stack at the poster; the teenagers especially liked this feature. Their response was excellent, and for some subjects very great.

JOHN DeGREGORY JR.

What Do They Read?

     But it is not necessary to form a club or take a survey before having programs. Every librarian knows what subjects interest his readers. If any sizable group is taking out books on a particular subject, that is also a good subject around which to build a program. This should be the easiest and most successful kind of program to have. Library patrons are the most used to going to a library, they are the easiest group to reach with publicity, and they usually have a variety of interests. If the readers take out a lot of books on antiques, they will be interested in a speaker who brings along a Queen Anne tea table or an 1884 Britannia chafing dish. Civil War buffs may be interested in seeing films like The True Story of the Civil War (CRM/McGraw-Hill) or Some of the Boys (Hank Newenhouse), which would supplement their reading. People who take out books on sewing, crocheting, and macrame will always be interested in demonstrations, and certainly anyone who reads poetry will want to hear it read.

Current Interests

     As everyone who selects books for a library knows, readers do not have only long-term interests; there is always some new subject that becomes popular for a time. These subjects may be essentially frivolous or they may be of tremendous importance. Responding to these current interests, not only in materials but in programs, is an important service. The American Indians, the occult, ecology, women's liberation, breadmaking, and acupuncture are just a few of the subjects that have become popular in the last few years.

     There are also needs, as opposed to mere interests, that surface from time to time. These needs have usually always been there, but interest in them grows from time to time, and as interest grows, more materials become available. These subjects should also make useful programs, and they will attract audiences when interest is high. Venereal disease, abortion, energy alternatives, job hunting, and inflation, are a few subjects of this kind. Programs that respond to current needs or interests may have the added benefit of attracting people who have not been library users. Perhaps a survey like the one on the following pages, used by The New York Public Library, would be helpful.

YOUNG ADULT INTERESTS SURVEY

Age _____ Sex _____ M _____ F _____
Which school do you go to? _____ Grade _____

What kinds of books do you like to read?

love stories _____   biographies _____
sports books _____   career books _____
mysteries _____   hobby books _____
books about women _____   poetry _____
science fiction _____   history _____

other: _____
_____
_____

Would you come to see a special program in the library
auditorium if it's about:

poetry _____   crafts _____
sports _____   sex education _____
drugs _____   women's issues _____
job information _____   Black history _____
cars _____   Puerto Rican history _____
dance _____   music _____
art _____   theater _____
film making _____   hobbies _____

Would you like to exhibit your art work in the library? _____

Would you like to perform in the library? _____

What kinds of writing workshops would you like to attend?

poetry _____
writing stories and/or articles _____
playwriting _____
journalism _____
other: _____
_____

What kinds of craft workshops would you like to attend?

jewelry-making _____

origami (paperfolding) _____
macrame _____
silkscreen _____
knitting, crocheting _____
model making _____
kite making _____
other: _____

_____

Would you like to participate in audio-visual workshops?
_____

film making techniques _____
video-tape _____
photography _____

Would you like to attend workshops in fashion, beauty, health and grooming?

skin care _____
make-up _____
how to dress _____
other: _____

_____

What kinds of table games would you like to play?

chess _____
checkers _____
backgammon _____
other: _____

_____

If you would like to be on our mailing list please fill in:

Name: _____
Address: _____ Apt. No. : _____
         _____ Zip: _____

Reaching the Unserved

That leads us to consider an important group, or groups--the people you are not serving. The community must be examined to see what groups are in it. Then one

must think about what those groups might want in the way
of programs. If there are large high schools or colleges
in the area, or the library is in a retirement community,
these things will influence your choice. The kind of high
school or college will also be a factor. If it is a vocational
school or a high school devoted to special subjects, that
will be important. If a large group of elderly people is
served, that will not only influence the subject matter, but
the time of day and the place in which the program is held.

If Blacks, American Indians, people of Italian or
Albanian descent, parents, housewives, or many Zoroas-
trians are served, those facts will help you decide on your
program. Within those groups there will also be differences;
there will be different levels of sophistication, language
problems, income, educational, and occupational differences.
Large numbers of people on welfare will be a consideration.
Do they live in private houses or apartments? Are the
apartments public housing? Are they rent-controlled? What
are the industries in the area and how do the people make
a living? What problems do these industries present? What
part of the country are you in? All these things should be
taken into consideration when planning programs.

They also have to be thought about; one can't make
superficial judgments. If your library mostly serves people
who live in apartments, you may not want to have a gardening
program (except for house plants), but you can not necessarily make that assumption. One of the authors worked in
a library that exclusively served people who lived in apartments; many of them, however, had summer homes and they
used gardening books extensively. Industries that pollute the
environment also support the population; programs about such
local problems need to present all the alternatives. If you
are serving black people, do they want to hear a black poet,
or do they want jobs, or do they want both? Knowing the
statistics is important, but one must also know things that
never appear in a census report.

What Is Being Done?

One must also look at what other programs are being
presented in the community. Museums, community centers,
colleges and all kinds of organizations are putting on programs. The question to be decided is whether to duplicate
what is already being done, or to do something different.

Your town may be garden clubbed to death, but have no
poetry readings. On the other hand, maybe they don't want
poetry readings. And you can't assume that because there
are already a lot of programs on a subject, more won't be
needed; the garden clubs may not be reaching everybody.
Indeed, we have found that the subjects most presented are
the programs best attended. It sometimes seems as though
everybody is interested in the same thing at the same time.

Recently, a program on Chinese culture (dance,
poetry, music) was to be presented at a branch library.
It was discovered that a local college was doing almost the
same thing on the evening before the library program. The
interest, at this date, in things Chinese caused large crowds
to turn out for both events. We have sometimes assumed
that certain films, or subjects, that had recently been shown
on television would have been seen by all who wanted to see
them. We have been proved wrong in those assumptions.
The television programs merely stimulated interest.

--And What Is Not?

It may be just as interesting, and more useful, to
explore those subjects about which nothing is being done. In
any community, there will be plenty of those. Libraries
can, as most other institutions cannot, provide programs for
small groups; those interested in spiders or--as Ezra Pound
said--the 23 persons interested in the Provençal poets. If
the readers of poetry are few and far between, they can
nevertheless be found and brought together to hear poetry
readings. It just takes some time and effort. One can't
expect instant success in such endeavors, but audiences can
be built up as the programs become known.

When deciding on what programs to have, there are
many mundane details to think about. How much staff do
you have and how many will you need for the program? Will
they object that all, or some, of the jobs connected with producing a program are not part of their work? (It has happened.) Will the staff have to work overtime? Might you
have problems with the custodial staff? Union contracts as
well as personalities have to be considered. You will have
to think about the need for ticket takers, ushers, the charging
out of books, and someone to introduce the program, among
other things.

Not having enough staff does not necessarily mean you can't have a program. Volunteers can be used for many purposes. They have been used as discussion leaders, story tellers, ushers and servers of refreshments. Libraries have frequently also trained these volunteers to tell stories or lead discussion groups. Friends of the library groups in libraries throughout the country serve refreshments and do other jobs connected with programs.

The Available Space

The amount of space available, and its location in the library, will help to determine the type of program; discussion groups don't need much space but a Chinese ribbon dance does. Don't necessarily give up if the space seems too small. One theatre group presented dramatic productions in an unbelievably small space; the director was imaginative and used the space in ways we hadn't thought of. Think about the different parts of the library and how they can be used. A library that had only a small story-hour room available for programs used it for discussion groups during the morning. Another library with no separate space ran film programs on mornings that the library was closed for borrowing. Children's rooms can often be used, when they are closed. A combination stack area and work room was used for evening discussion groups, in one case. Sometimes there are basement areas that can be transformed with some light and paint and by getting rid of accumulated junk.

Noise may be important during library hours; libraries don't want to chase out the readers they already have. This is another reason for having some kinds of programs when the library is closed. Otherwise, some experimentation may show you that you can even find space for a rock music concert. When thinking about the location--in the library-- of the program, one must think about security. Library materials, purses, and even persons may have to be guarded. The condition of the program space is important. In a karate program that we watched, participants were hampered by slippery floors. Dancers in bare feet may not want to pick up splinters. For all these things, the performers are, naturally, the best guide. They should be brought in to test the space, before the program is decided upon.

Furniture and Equipment

There are even more mundane matters to think about, when selecting a program. Are there enough tables, chairs, or other furniture? If not, can you get more? Can you transport them, or have them transported, if you can get them? We have been offered wonderful programs that needed a piano; however, transporting and tuning it turned out to be too expensive. What equipment do you have, or can get? You may be able to beg, or borrow (we don't recommend stealing unless you are eager to work in a prison library) movie projectors, slide projectors and other equipment. Performers may need, or want, lecterns, microphones, screens, blackboards or other items. Those needs have to be determined beforehand, and you have to decide if you can get what they want.

Complaints

When selecting a program to present, as when selecting library materials generally, one must be aware of the possibility of complaints. A program, unlike a book in the collection, sticks out like a sore thumb. And like a sore thumb, it is likely to get hit. It is produced on a stage and presented in front of (one hopes) a large crowd. It is also publicized throughout the community. These features bring the program to the attention of many people who would never think about the library, which is why you are having it in the first place.

When the Salt Lake City Public Library produced a series of programs in an effort to reach the Spanish-speaking community, word reached the local newspaper. They didn't like the whole idea; they said it was the work of "slick-talking racist agitators disguised as librarians and university professors" who were out to make "a pitch for armed revolution among loyal and patriotic Americans of Mexican descent. "[2]

Another library was visited one calm morning by a young man who said he represented the John Birch Society. He complained about their showings of films about David Harris, Malcolm X, W. E. D. DuBois and Angela Davis. He asked why they didn't show films about George Washington Carver and Booker T. Washington. The librarian told him that they had shown such films in the past, but now they were showing films about people of interest today. The young man replied that these people were communists, pimps and anti-Americans. He said the John Birch Society had films of positive, pro-American approach for rent. He also said he would attack the library's choice of films in the news-papers. There are some other points the librarian might have made. She could have said that the films in question were only four of forty-nine being shown. She could have pointed out that the program was really balanced: the film on Angela Davis was paired with The Weapons of Gordon Parks, a film with a decidedly different point of view.

The point is that one must be aware of the possibility of complaints, and be prepared to handle them. If the ma-terial has been carefully chosen, and one has sound reasons for having chosen it, self-defense is a lot easier. Librarians shouldn't self-censor their programs any more than they would the books on their shelves, but they have to be ready for attacks when they come.

Nothing further came of this complaint, which is what happens to nine-tenths of complaints, but if it had, the li-brarian could have taken some steps. If the incident seemed likely to grow, she could have contacted her state Intellectual Freedom Committee. Failing that she could have contacted the Office of Intellectual Freedom of the American Library Association. These groups can help librarians decide how to handle such situations.

One case of a program that did blow up is fully described in Film Library Quarterly. [3] It concerns a film program for teenagers in the Los Angeles Public Library that became a community-wide issue. Typical charges of Communism, corrupting youth, etc. were made, and the article describes all the action. It is a good example of the kinds of things that can happen and it tells how one library handled a difficult situation.

NOTES

1. Wilson, Evie. "The Young Adult Advisory Board," The Bookmark, New York State Library, Winter 1978, pp. 55-59.
2. Library Journal, July 1972, p. 2326.
3. Sigler, Ronald F. "A Study in Censorship: The Los An-geles 19," Film Library Quarterly, Spring 1971, pp. 35-46.

PART III: PRODUCING THE PROGRAM

When you have committed yourself to a program, or
to a series of programs, you may experience a slight sink-
ing sensation. Don't worry. You are normal. Nevertheless, careful planning is now necessary. (Publicity, an essential ingredient in that planning, will be treated separately
in another chapter.)

Where to Have the Program

The first thing to decide is where to have the program. In and around the library--depending on the nature
of the program--it might be held in a meeting room, the
children's room, the basement, the parking lot, the yard,
or the front steps. If the program is to be held away from
the library, you have a world to choose from. Libraries
are having programs wherever there are people. Stories
are told on beaches, in parks, and on the front steps of
apartment houses. Films have been shown in vacant lots,
at migrant workers' camps, in prisons, in nursing homes,
at drug rehabilitation centers, at shopping centers, and many
other places. There have even been programs, such as
walking tours, that have moved from place to place.

There are several good reasons for taking programs
out into the community. Members of minorities, people
who don't speak English well, people who are poor and who
lack an education often think libraries are not for them.
Libraries are often forbidding, official-looking buildings, with
(all too often) forbidding, official-looking people working in
them. Breaking down barriers is important, and when these
people are persuaded to go to a library they must be received with warmth and treated well. A brusque clerk or
a "too-busy" librarian can end their library visits. But the
library can be taken to them, and even if they never come

to the library building, they will be provided with the service. By working at it, however, they often can be persuaded to come.

On Staten Island a few years ago, a store front neighborhood center called the Martin Luther King, Jr. Heritage House was about to open. Many of the residents of that area were not library users. One of the authors met with the board of directors of that institution. After two very dry martinis, he committed the library to co-producing six programs in one week. They were to be held in the Center, during its first week of operation.

We obtained some posters with giant photographs of Martin Luther King, Malcolm X and others. We also borrowed an exhibit of pictures and other materials relating to black inventors, explorers, doctors and others who had made important contributions to civilization. With these items, and with books and recordings devoted to black history and culture, we set up a large display that was to run through the week. A large supply of special booklists devoted to those subjects was also on hand, to be given out to the audiences at the programs.

A program was planned for each weekday evening, and for Wednesday afternoon, it being Lincoln's birthday and a school holiday. Films were selected to appeal to a variety of ages and interests. Library staff members showed films of black history, and films about black political leaders, athletes, musicians and various professional men. There were poetry readings, book talks, dance and drama programs, and lectures given by both librarians and members of Heritage House. Several hundred people attended the week's activities, in spite of a heavy snow on the day before the opening that had almost halted transportation. Many booklists were distributed, library card applications were taken, and reservations for books were taken. Much information about the library was disseminated informally by staff members.

As a result of these programs, a black music discussion group was organized, and held in the library. We were invited back to Heritage House to give a series of story hours, some more poetry readings and more book talks. We also know that one direct result of this activity was that a number of persons began using the public library for the first time. And, not the least benefit was that several hundred persons enjoyed a variety of cultural and recreational activities that would otherwise have been unavailable.

The New York Public Library's South Bronx Project, which deals primarily with Spanish-speaking people, has conducted many programs outside the library in almost every conceivable place and frequently under very trying circumstances. Puppet shows have been given in parks, at a street festival, and on the sidewalk at a bookmobile stop. One of their most trying, and probably most rewarding, experiences was giving a puppet show in a vacant lot.

> One of the high points of the summer came in early July when Dr. Eismann, a psychologist at Lincoln Hospital, contacted us. He said that he had obtained permission from a Baptist Church in the Hunt's Point area to use their adjacent vacant lot as a gathering place for the young people in the area. He was looking for an evening outdoor program with some sort of stimulation for the children. We decided to do our puppet show as well as show the film "Puppets" which gives excellent ideas on making various types of puppets. The children on the block were expecting us as we drove up to the lot on Fox Street in Mr. Hampton's red VW bus. They were all, of course, more than willing to help us with the puppets. The lot was fairly large, sloping downwards from the street and covered with dirt, broken glass, sticks, stones and tin cans--although there had been an evident attempt to clear it out. It was surrounded on two sides by high metal fences topped by barbed wire and on the other two by high brick walls. Neither the height nor the barbed wire deterred the children from climbing all over the place. We set up the theater at the far end and used electricity from a nearby apartment to hook up the microphones. The children were remarkably good during the show, and many of them also watched the film. Others, of course, succumbed to the outdoor temptations of fences to climb, rocks to throw and fights to fight. Dr. Eismann enthusiastically told me afterwards that though I might have thought it chaotic, he had never seen the children so well behaved or so enthusiastic. [1]

Other innovative outreach programs include telling stories on the front steps of apartment houses--in competition

with traffic noises, street games and open fire hydrants--
and showing films in a vacant lot next to the library and in
another underneath an elevated train. (It was discovered to
be under the flight path of airplanes also.) This last program was successful in spite of the difficulties. The films--
which had proven successful in other outdoor programs--
were Liquid Jazz (Joseph Kramer), Judoka (CRM/McGraw-Hill),
¡Que Puerto Rico! (CRM/McGraw-Hill), Anatole (CRM/McGraw-
Hill), Glass (CRM/McGraw-Hill), and what turned out to be the
surprise hit of the evening, Pigs (Churchill).

Some libraries have taken programs and other services to the camps of migrant workers. The Cumberland
County (N.J.) Library has provided films, lectures, music,
and games at migrant camps during the summer. Films
have, once again, proved to be popular. They have also
developed an "English Language Survival Information Course"
for the Spanish-speaking workers. There are films on pesti-
cides, food stamps, job hunting, and family planning, and
there is a course book that is suitable for both individual
and group instruction. They have found it essential to gain
the support of the farmers, crew chiefs, and public officials,
and they have found it necessary to gain the trust of the
workers. Certainly sympathy and understanding are important, and speaking the language of the workers would be
practical, as well as helpful, in eliminating distrust.

The Plainfield (N.J.) Public Library has taken their
outreach programs into a great variety of places. They
have gone to neighborhood centers, senior citizens' centers,
convalescent homes, housing projects, YM and YWCA's,
playgrounds, churches, barbershops and laundromats.
Wouldn't people waiting in a laundromat welcome a film
program, though? It seems to us they would welcome almost any relief from that most boring of jobs. And there
are many good, short films available for showing to people
who are waiting for the washer or dryer to stop spinning.
You can always tie it in with an announcement or even a
sign about the library's other services.

Another Staten Island library is little-used by residents of the immediate area, but there is a heavily-used
park across the street. During the summer, the library
staff have begun taking their programs into the park. In
some cities, street fairs sponsored by block associations
and other neighborhood groups have become popular. Libraries can participate in these events to advantage. They

can set up tables with books, recordings, booklists and any special materials. They can play cassettes (even without electrical outlets), tell stories and give puppet shows. If there are electrical outlets, they can show slides or films with a rear screen projector. Above all, they can talk about the library.

Another group that doesn't go to libraries is that group confined to institutions; prisons, drug rehabilitation centers, homes for the mentally retarded, hospitals, nursing homes and homes for the elderly are all desirable places to have library programs. All the more desirable, perhaps, because many of the residents of these places desperately need and want the kinds of recreational activities that libraries can provide. A number of years ago a drug rehabilitation center was established in a suburban, middle-class community. It was met by overt hostility and a campaign to get rid of it on the part of the community's residents. Since it was hoped that the former addicts would be able to return to a normal life as members of a community, this reception was exactly what they didn't need. The authors decided at least to introduce them to the library's services. They gave an afternoon program to about eighty of the center's residents, showing a film, Rhinoceros (CRM/McGraw-Hill), playing a recording of poetry and jazz, and giving two book talks. This program resulted in the establishment of a bookmobile stop at the center, and eventually bookmobile stops at a variety of other institutions; these bookmobiles now also give programs in some of those institutions.

Many people, of all ages, are homebound. Probably the ultimate in outreach is to take programs to them. The library in Gloucester City, New Jersey has done just that. With the help of a grant, they have been able to visit homebound children who range in age from five to ten, who are either physically or emotionally handicapped, and are unable to visit the library. Five "home visitors" serve thirty children for an hour a week. The children are selected by the city school system, and they are told stories, see filmstrips, and work with arts and crafts. These activities are selected according to the needs and desires of each child, and the child requests the activity for the next session.

The "home visitors" take an intensive two-week storytelling training program, and are selected for their warmth and enthusiasm, as well as their ability to relate to the children and their families. The latter are of particular

importance. The parents of many of the children clearly
have little education, and some are fuctionally illiterate--
people who are not likely to be library-users and who are
very likely to put up a wall between themselves and any
official visitor. Each storyteller has stayed with the same
child since the beginning of the program. There have been
side benefits too. Younger siblings frequently listen to the
session, and the parents' understanding of their children
has increased.

Publicity for this program was kept at a minimum,
and limited to a statement of fact. This was to prevent
unnecessary labeling of the children involved. Reports are
written after each visit, weekly staff meetings are held, and
parents are interviewed weekly. The program is thus continually evaluated.

The primary goals of this particular program have
obviously been realized. They are "to bring pleasure to
children whose lives have been hemmed in by illness and
loneliness, to broaden their interests and to motivate them
to visit the library whenever physically possible." There
has been one additional benefit: as is usual with such programs, the visitors have found their own lives enriched,
and found their jobs to be most satisfying.

In addition to minority groups, the homebound, and
people in institutions, there are many people who would be
able to go to a library, and who would feel free to go to a
library, but who do not go. They may never go. But if
you take a program to them, they may learn something.
They might find out that you have a record or a film collection, a financial service, or a book that will help them repair their leaky pipes. And the program itself may benefit
them. Librarians have long given book talks to community
groups, but many of the programs that are done in libraries
could be done elsewhere in the community. The public library of Elyria, Ohio developed a series of slide-lectures
that they take to groups; a staff member prepares a script
and the audio-visual department makes up the slides. They
have done programs on local history, local culture and other
subjects. [2]

Most librarians have seen worthy books on foreign
relations or Congressional reform sitting on their shelves
untouched, or they have waited with increasing disappointment while few or no people showed up to see a powerful

film on the evils of stripmining or on the dangers of the invasion of privacy. A Detroit librarian expressed this disappointment when she said, "Detroiters were showing themselves more responsive to programs of a cultural nature than those concerned solely with public issues."[3]

Maybe if you take those worthwhile books and films (they can also be interesting, even engrossing, as you know but the public doesn't) to a Rotary Club meeting, a church group, or a PTA meeting, a few members of your captive audience will be shocked, startled, amazed, or made to think about something new; and maybe one or two of them will go to the library. Think of the broad field you have to choose from; there are innumerable meetings in every village and town in the country, not to mention the alabaster cities.

If a program, or programs, are to be held outside the library, a lot of trouble can be avoided by thoroughly checking the situation before the program. The first thing to do is to make sure you have a thorough understanding with the people who actually run the place. The president of a club or the central administrative office of a large organization may make plans that are not practical or they may neglect to inform local people. One library in New York State indicated some of these problems in a recent report. They planned a summer storytelling program for the playgrounds. The times and places for the whole summer were planned centrally. Unfortunately, the central playground planner did not say anything about the plans to the local people. Furthermore, the librarians were not given the names of the local people and had difficulty contacting them when things went awry. Even the schedule proved inaccurate. In one case, the librarian went to the first afternoon program--in the rain--only to discover that it had been held that morning. There were several other delays, because the planning had not been coordinated with local officials.

The premises should be checked for electrical outlets, chairs, and other equipment. The timing of the program should be discussed with members of the organization. If it is an institution, such activities as lunch, recreation, the rounds of doctors and nurses, and others will have to be considered when planning the program. Subject matter, the length of the program and other factors will have to be carefully thought out. Old people and sick people may not

have the attention span of those who are younger or healthier.
Although it is difficult to generalize about a subject when a
large group is involved, some subjects may be more or less
suitable or interesting for the old, the sick or other groups.
Talk to various people who deal with those groups.   When
we planned a program for a drug rehabilitation center, for
example, we discovered that they wanted materials dealing
with moral and philosophical problems, because they tied in
with the rehabilitation program.

In the Library

Meanwhile back at the branch (library), we find this
is where most programs will be held.   After all, that's
where the books are, and the films, and the records, and
everything else.   And if you can get people to go there,
that is still the ideal.

Whether you are having the program in the library,
or anywhere else, many things must be taken into consideration.   One of the first things to think about is what time of
day to have it.   The physical space, the location of the library in the community, the kind of community, and what
people do with their spare time are all considerations.

Time of Day

One library felt the need for a program, but the small
staff and small meeting room, which adjoined a busy children's room, severely limited their choices.   Evening programs would mean scheduling staff to work extra evenings,
and afternoons were too busy.   Mornings, however, were not
busy and a full staff was in attendance in any case.   Furthermore, since children would not be there, the meeting room
would be quiet.   They decided on an adult book discussion
group, which would fit into the small room and would require
the attendance of only one staff member.   The choice of
mornings limited the kinds of people who could attend, but
since the investment in time was small, it seemed worth
trying.   It was.   The group, consisting of housewives and
one or two men, has grown over the years to about twenty
participants, and, judging from the evolution of their readings,
their horizons have expanded considerably.   As of this writing, it is in its twelfth year and going strong.

A similar library, with an equally small staff, and no meeting space, has run morning film programs in the rear of the public area. The small inconvenience to the few morning readers was worth it in an area where such attractions were non-existent.

Another library had tried a number of evening programs with little response. Late afternoon programs, however, drew both adults and young people. Apparently people had been afraid to go out in that area after dark. Some libraries have had success in business areas with noontime programs, and there have even been breakfast programs. The point to remember is that one must be flexible and think of the time that fits your conditions. We haven't heard of a midnight program in a library, but don't count it out. Even the exact hour is important. If many of the potential audience are commuters returning to your community, a later start in the evening would be desirable.

The day of the week and the season of the year must be considered. People may shop on Friday evenings or on Saturdays. During good weather, they may garden on Saturdays and weekday evenings. Sunday afternoons should be considered as potential program times. The days preceding major holidays may be bad times for programs. School and church activities might occupy your public at certain times; examination periods for example, or the evenings of regular church group meetings, may be important in a community. Find out about any special events before you do any scheduling and decide if they will take people away from your program. In some towns there are community calendars, so that events can be coordinated.

Regular Schedule

If there is going to be a series of programs, a regular schedule is important. The difficulties involved in canceling a program or changing a date are great, so the schedule should be carefully thought out beforehand. When something has been widely publicized, it is difficult to counteract it. And if people come to a program that isn't there, they will be annoyed, undoing the goodwill that would have been created by the program. Rather than cancel a program, or change a date, it might be better to find a substitute speaker, performer or film. It will be best if you have thought of that before it becomes necessary to cancel, and have a substitute program ready. If the particular speaker or film was what the public was coming to see, it would then be better to change the date. Unfortunately, such things often happen at the last minute, so it is always wise to have alternatives. A small group, like a discussion group, can be more easily notified of changes, but even then you never know who will show up for a publicized program and angrily confront you. It is better to think carefully about changes.

Details

Forgetting to pay attention to detail can spoil a good program. All equipment should be checked beforehand, and it should be checked early enough so that you can have it replaced if necessary. You can't buy a light bulb if the stores are closed. Extras, like a projector bulb, should be provided for everything that might give out during the program. If projectors, films, props, or display materials are going to be delivered, a pre-program check must be made. One can't count on messages being delivered, records being kept correctly, or mail being delivered promptly. Performers and speakers need to be reminded and any necessary transportation arranged for. Remind them a day or two before the program. A tactful way to do it is to ask them if they need transportation, or if there is anything else you can do for them. If the speaker has a secretary, a check with him or her will be sufficient.

Think about audience comfort. Rest rooms are important. Are they conveniently located, or will a staff member have to conduct people to them? Are they unlocked, or has the custodian locked them and gone off for the evening with the key? If you are going to allow smoking, ash trays must be provided. You may want to provide coat racks, especially if the room is likely to be crowded. Ventilation and temperature are important. A room full of people can get very hot. On the other hand, you don't want a cold breeze blowing on the necks of the audience. Exits and exit lights must be checked. When P. T. Barnum wanted to get people out of his show quickly, he is said to have put up a sign that read, "This Way to the Egress." You will want to have your egresses clearly marked and unlocked.

Related Exhibits and Displays

These can give a program an added dimension. They might be put into outside display windows, or in various parts of the library during the weeks preceding the program; then they would give the event extra publicity. A display might be set up at the site of the program for the audience to look at or handle. Sometimes understanding is helped if an audience can examine objects that a speaker is talking about or if they can look closely at pictures, maps or other visual materials. Books, periodicals, and recordings related to the subject are especially useful to display, particularly when there is a how-to-do program. If library materials are displayed, you may want to charge out books and recordings on the spot, or take reserves for them. This will create some small problems, but hack away the red tape; public service is more important than a charging system. There will have to be enough staff on hand to take care of the routines. Pencils, daters, and whatever else you need will have to be ready. Extra time must be allowed. Objections from the staff may have to be overcome (We can't do that! It's against the rules!). In spite of these minor annoyances, such service is worthwhile for the goodwill it creates, and such a display is worthwhile. It will bring to the attention of the audience materials they may never have otherwise discovered.

Lists of appropriate books, recordings and films can be distributed to the audience, introducing them to a wider range of materials than can possibly be brought together for display. Such lists might already be in existence (a list might even spark the idea for a program) or you might want to compile one for the occasion.

Speakers and Performers

A number of things must be arranged with speakers and performers. Speakers may want, or not want, a lectern or a microphone. They might want lights turned on or off at particular times. Someone might be needed to run a slide projector. The length of the performance must be discussed. The speaker should be told what kind of talk (formal, informal) you would like, and the level of the potential audience should be discussed. One lecturer, on Chinese poetry, in a library program, not only went on much too long, but talked above the heads of most of the audience, marring what was otherwise an excellent and enjoyable program. Musicians, actors, and dancers will want to examine the performing space, and they may want to rehearse in that space. Actors need dressing rooms, and since most libraries don't have theatres in them, temporary dressing rooms must be arranged. Workshop leaders will want to make sure there are tables set up, equipment arranged, or other needs filled. At the time of the program, be on hand in plenty of time to greet the performers. Find out if they have additional requests. Make them comfortable; show them where the rest rooms are and where they can hang their hats; offer them a cup of coffee. One group of actors at a library program came directly from work, without eating. Sandwiches were bought and the actors were given a room in which to eat them.

There are several things that can be done before, during, and after the program. The program and the performers have to be introduced. At the same time, books and other materials related to the program can be mentioned, or briefly talked about. The library's services can be described, and future programs announced.

Add to the Mailing List; Evaluate the Program

This is a good time to add to the mailing list. Put a 3x5 card on each chair before the program--have a supply of pencils handy--and announce your intention. Tell the participants to put the essential information (name, address, telephone number and special interests) on the card, and that the cards will be collected after the program. That's one way to do it. This is also a good chance to test the efficiency of various forms of publicity and to ask the audience to evaluate the contents of the programs. Simple forms, the simpler the better, can be devised for the audience to check. (See the two representative forms on the following page, reproduced at about one-half real size. The form on the right was a dark pea-soup green.) If it is a small group, you can ask them directly. Both methods have virtues. It is possible to add to the mailing list, test the publicity, and get reactions to the programs on a single form.

Many comments from the audience, either written or verbal, will be merely polite. But some will be worth noting ("It's too hot." "The speaker talked too long." "The subject was too difficult.") and will help you improve future

please, tell us...

WHAT DID YOU THINK ABOUT THIS PROGRAM?
WHAT DID YOU LIKE OR DISLIKE?

FOR OUR INFORMATION FOR FUTURE PROGRAMS -

What are your special interests, talents, ideas for programs?

NAME _____

HOME ADDRESS _____

BOROUGH _____ ZIP CODE _____

ORGANIZATION or SCHOOL _____

WOULD YOU LIKE TO BE ON OUR MAILING LIST? _____

OFFICE OF YOUNG ADULT SERVICES
THE NEW YORK PUBLIC LIBRARY
8 East 40th Street
New York, N. Y. 10016

HELP

US PLAN BETTER PROGRAMS

WHERE DID YOU HEAR ABOUT THIS PROGRAM?

Newspaper _____
Flyer _____
Poster _____
Friend _____
Other _____

HOW DID YOU LIKE IT?

Excellent _____
Good _____
Fair _____
Poor _____

WHAT OTHER PROGRAMS WOULD YOU LIKE?

DO YOU WANT TO BE ON OUR MAILING LIST?

Name _____
Address _____

The New York Public Library

programs. Audience reactions are useful to have when you are writing reports (if you have a grant, you will certainly have to report on your activities) and they may help the morale of those giving the program.

In addition to obtaining information from the audience, it will be important for the programmer to do some evaluating. Evaluation of library services has always been important, but let's face it, we did less of it when times were good. In recent years, library administrations and library boards have, of necessity, been taking hard looks at everything. Therefore, the costs of programming in terms of staff time, supplies, postage, fees for performers, and other items must be carefully considered. That is not to say that a program attended by a few people is one the library shouldn't ever repeat. Library service can't be measured entirely by statistics. Perhaps a supermarket can count the number of cans of peas sold in a particular brand and decide not to carry that brand. But who is to say that a half hour answering a reference question is any less valuable than charging out fifty mysteries, or that a program attended by ten people should be abandoned in favor of some more broadly popular service.

Nevertheless, the usefulness and cost of a program must be considered. Maybe it should be abandoned, or maybe it can be improved. It's probably helpful to make some kind of checklist of points to be evaluated. How did the program benefit those who attended? Study the questionnaires now that you have taken the trouble to use them. Mingle with the audience, talking to as many as possible. Observe them. Watch for any use of the library by program-attendees. Don't forget to ask the rest of the staff. And what is a benefit? Maybe it just helped a lonely, old (or young) person pass the time. Maybe it gave pleasure to some of those attending. (How much pleasure makes a program "profitable"?) Maybe it created some library users. Programs have sometimes done that. Maybe somebody learned something that started a hobby, got them a job, or helped them save heating oil. Clearly, this evaluation won't be scientific, and computers will be of little help.

The staff time used on a program is, unfortunately, something most of us must think about more than ever now. Remember the time used to design and distribute the publicity, including time spent stuffing envelopes and going to the post office. Think of the time spent planning the pro-

gram, contacting performers, arranging for equipment,
setting up the room, as well as attending the program.
Who did all those things? Pages? Custodians? Librarians?
You? Could fewer staff members have been used? (Were
there enough?) Could less highly paid employees have been
used for some tasks? Were there things that did not need
doing, or that could have been done more efficiently? Would
those staff members have been doing anything more useful,
or would they have been doing anything at all? Finally,
what was the relation between staff time and the value of
the program? Ay, there's the rub, as Hamlet said in
another context. (Don't commit suicide, however, even if
nobody attended the program.) Well, you can make a judgment, just as you make a judgment about which book to
select--or more to the point, discard. If a film program
required possibly two staff members to attend and was seen
by only seven people, including one of the pages and the
husband of one of the clerks, it probably wasn't a useful
program. We say "probably" because it might have been
useful. Maybe it was an unusual film that had great impact
on the audience. Maybe the library is just beginning film
programs and is trying to build an audience.

The actual money spent on the program is another
point to consider. Postage can get very expensive; maybe
there's a better way. Telephoning mounts up and programs
sometimes require a lot of it. Perhaps supplies had to be
bought for the publicity, or for some other aspect of the
program. Performers frequently want to be paid. Ways of
cutting down on these expenses must be considered, or perhaps ways of raising additional money to pay for them.
Some libraries charge for some kinds of programs, and fees
for various library services is a subject that is agitating
the library world. The authors don't agree with this method
of raising money. One of the key features of the public
library idea is that programs should be free. A program
is another medium, just as books, films, newspapers, maps
and records are media. If a library service--or material--
is worth providing, it must be free--so that all can avail
themselves of that material or service.

Consider all the miscellaneous aspects of programming. In addition to the information you got from the
audience, make you own checklist of things to remember.
Consider the temperature of the room, the external noise,
the functioning of equipment, the availability of supplies,
the proximity of restrooms. In spite of planning, something
unexpected often occurs. Learn from it!

Evaluate the publicity. If the program was a rousing success, it's probably not necessary. On the other hand, for some kinds of programs, audiences seem to appear almost without publicity. As we have suggested, you will need to get this kind of information from the audience. But then it has to be studied. Why didn't the newspaper article draw more? Were the flyers put into the right places? Was the rest of the staff sufficiently aware of the program so they could talk it up across the desk? Could any other means of publicity have been used? Below are two forms created and used by the Prince George's County (Md.) Memorial Library: one for program evaluation and the other a checklist for planning a program.

PROGRAM EVALUATION

1/17/80
DATE

PROGRAM   Star Trek Day

Saturday   January 12, 1980   Bowie
DAY   DATE   LOCATION

PLANNER(S) M. Hargrove, M. Smith, J. Losinski
BR/DEPT   YA/CS
   OTHERS INVOLVED   M. Bauer--CS

SPEAKER(S)/COMMUNITY RESOURCE(S)   Randallstown
   Assoc. of Star Trek (RAST)--Kim Drapkin contact person

TARGET AUDIENCE   All ages
   ATTENDANCE _____ + _____ + _____ = 350+
              CS   YA   AS   TOTAL

PROMOTION

   TYPES: FLYER x   (attach sample) POSTER x   RADIO x
           TV _____ NEWSPAPER x   TTY ____
           OTHER (list) word of mouth and PA announcement
                        in schools, booktalks

   USES/DISTRIBUTION: INSIDE LIBRARY posters, flyers

OUTSIDE LIBRARY ___ schools ___

RESULTS: HOW THE AUDIENCE LEARNED ABOUT THE PROGRAM

RADIO WPGC: WRC: WMAL (which stations)

TV _____ (which channels) TTY _____

NEWSPAPERS (which ones) Wash. Post, Wash. Star, BW Blade, and BW News

OTHER (list) ___ at school ___

FLYER ___ x ___ POSTER ___ x ___

MATERIALS USED (list attached)
Star Trek Books--75 books and 4 records
Circ. all records and 30 books

GOALS: To provide an outlet for "Star Trek" fans of all ages.

Consider the effectiveness of each of the factors in reaching your goals. Describe critically.

PLANNING: J. Losinski did the bulk of the planning and coordination necessary. M. Hargrove and M. Smith provided needed local services. It was too bad that the episodes were not started on time.

CONTENT & FORMAT: Episodes were the most popular. People were disappointed because blooper reels were of such poor quality. Computer games were a real hit-- always had a crowd.

STAFFING: fine--worked well to divide day between two staff members.

PROMOTION: did all it should--we have as many as could handle.

LOCATION & ARRANGEMENTS: BW's meeting room was more than adequate--lots of room but needed. Could have used more chairs set up.

CO-SPONSORSHIP: No Problems

SPEAKER(S) COMMUNITY RESOURCE(S): Worked quite well.
Very handy that RAST was handy with AV equipment.
RAST really had their act together and everything went
off on their revised schedule and with split second timing.

AUDIENCE RESPONSE: ENTHUSIASTIC!!! Wanted to do it
again soon.

RECOMMENDATIONS: Break for lunch. Keep episodes on
published schedule. Do again.

EVALUATION PREPARED BY M. Hargrove and M. M. Smith

PGCML/PS 163 10/76

PROGRAM WORKSHEET/CHECKLIST

Date submitted _____

(Submit to Coordinator's Office at least three months before
program date)

PROGRAM _____
BY _____
    Name   Department   Branch

GOAL/S _____
    Specify Activities/Methods_____
_____

TARGET AUDIENCE _____

DATE _____ TIME _____ LOCATION ___

SPONSORSHIP: Library Dept/s _____ Community Agency ___
  Participants (Include address & phone if non-staff) _____
_____
Transportation needed? _____

STAFF: At Program (no.)_____ no. of hours each _____
Additional help needed (no.) ___ no. of hours each ___
Approx. Time ___ Signers needed _____
no. of hours (include practice) _____

BUDGET: Item___ Amount___ Approval (Coord.)___ Date___
Item___ Amount___ Approval (Coord.)___ Date___
Item___ Amount___ Approval (PS) _____Date___

PROMOTION: Fliers___ Posters ___ Publicity Timetable___
School Papers___ Booklists____
Photographer____
Distribution Plans_____
Display (at program site) _____

EQUIPMENT: Reserve needed equipment. Consult branch
equipment list.

Projector	____	Loud Speaker	____
Screen	____	Mike/Stand	____
Films	____	Spec. Lighting	____
VTR/Tape	____	Indoor Outlets	____
Recorder/Tape	____	Outdoor Outlets	____
Cassette Player	____	Record Player	____
Podium	____	Min. Theatre	____
Stage	____	Puppet Stage	____
Ext. Cords	____	Photo Equip.	____
Bookmobile	____	Blackboard	____
Piano	____	Other (Specify)	____
		_____	____

Transportation needed for _____
Insurance needed for _____

MEETING ROOM: Reserved _____ Date ____

SIGNATURES: Branch _____
Coordinator _____Meets Standards ___
Date _____

PGCML/PS 320 2/77

In Case of Mishaps

Try to be ready in case of mishaps. The best-laid
plans of mice and men do you know what. In one library

program, a speaker telephoned from many miles away to
say that he had had a flat tire ("had had" sounds like the
bumping of a flat tire) and would not get to the program at
all. An actor was in a minor automobile accident on the
way to another program and arrived fifteen minutes late.
Sometimes, with all precautions, a projector breaks down
or a film snaps. The possibilities are, if not endless,
certainly numerous. So one has to be prepared as well as
one can. If you are losing your head when all around you
are losing theirs and blaming it on you, it certainly won't
do.

The speaker with the flat tire was a psychologist who
was going to comment on some films about raising children
and then lead a discussion on the subject. The audience was
large, partly because of the subject, and partly because the
psychologist was locally prominent. When the announcement
was made, the audience expressed considerable disappointment. But the librarian, who had had discussion group experience, showed the films and led the discussion himself.
The session was lively and the audience seemed satisfied.
No one left early and they were promised an attempt would
be made to book the psychologist for another appearance.

When the actor was fifteen minutes late, the audience
(a very large one) was kept waiting. Again, all went well.
A delay of much more than fifteen minutes would probably
have been unpleasant, and might have undone much the library was trying to do. Since there were several parts to
this program, the order of appearance could have been
changed, and the program started. If a late speaker is the
entire program, the librarian can begin by talking about the
library's services, but should certainly explain the problem.
People wait better if they understand the reason. Recorded
music is useful with a waiting audience, if the music is
picked for the particular audience. If it is the audience that
is late, don't panic. Audiences have a habit of materializing
at the last minute, and inevitably some will be a few minutes
late.

We don't want to scare you out of a year's programming, but other things can happen. Most librarians have
had to deal with drunks, troublesome children and obnoxious
adults. The same people sometimes go to programs. Potential trouble of this kind can often be foreseen. In any
case, don't leave yourself shorthanded; enough staff should
be on hand to take care of such situations. Young trouble-

makers are often bored. They can sometimes be transformed by involving them in programs as ushers, ticket-
takers or stagehands; this is especially true if they can be
interested in something that is real (not just makework),
such as stage lighting or movie projector operation. One
library solved some very difficult discipline problems by
getting just such a group of teenagers involved in a videotape
workshop. They learned how to handle delicate and expensive equipment, and they learned how to do something that
must have seemed real and useful. After that experience,
some of them tried to quiet other disturbers at programs.

If the material in the program is potentially explosive,
mentally or emotionally, one has to think of possible objections beforehand, and be ready with answers, just as one
must be ready to answer objections to material on the
shelves. Troublemakers who are drunk or otherwise extremely objectionable will simple have to be ejected. The
audience will appreciate it and so will the performers.

Anyone who has ever been to a meeting of any kind
knows that speakers frequently go on much too long. Your
programs will face the same potential problem. Speakers
should certainly be given time limits beforehand. One cynic
has suggested that they be given a time limit of ten or fifteen minutes less than you really want, on the theory that
all speakers talk too long; he says if they don't, the audience
will be glad to have a break anyway. If the speaker does
exceed his allotted time, you can try to catch his eye;
maybe a signal should be prearranged. If that doesn't work,
walk across the stage and stand beside him. He should,
of course, be allowed some leeway.

Recording the Program

With the program running smoothly--and most of
them do--you might find it useful to record it in some way.
The medium used to record the program will depend on the
kind of program, the equipment available, and the uses you
intend for the record. You can take still photographs that
can be used for further publicity and for reports; they are
useful for help in obtaining grants. Children and adults like
to see themselves in pictures, as performers or as members
of the audience. A photograph album of programs will build
goodwill among those who participated and stimulate the
interest of others. A children's librarian who keeps such

an album says the children are constantly asking to see the
pictures. You could record the sound alone or you could
record both the sound and the picture on film or on videotape. Such records can be used in future library activities
or for radio or television programs; they can be sent around
the community for use with groups or they can be used for
the training of librarians. The actual recording, sound or
visual, must be carried on unobtrusively so that neither
audience nor performers will be disturbed. Fortunately,
they quickly become accustomed to cameras, cables, and
lights. As with other aspects of programming, plan ahead
and try to create a minimum of fuss.

Receptions

        For some special programs, you might want to try a
reception after the event, and serve refreshments. It will
add work, difficulties and probably expense to the program,
and you probably won't want to do it every time. But, such
a reception serves several purposes: it allows the audience
to meet and talk to speakers and performers; it lets you and
your staff talk to the audience about the program and about
the library; and it lets them look around the library. Not
incidentally, eating, drinking and talking informally with the
public creates goodwill. A reception is really an informal
continuation of the program. For a program on Chinese
culture, shrimp chips, lotus pastries, lichee punch and
jasmine tea were served, and they occasioned a discussion
of Chinese food. A t'ai chi demonstrator was questioned
further about his subject, and the musicians were asked
about their instruments. Thus, the program was given added
depth. In another library, the auditorium is used as an art
gallery. The refreshments, served after the program, allow
the audience to have a leisurely look at the paintings, drawings and photographs that have surrounded them during the
program.

        In this same library, the Friends of the Library
organization takes care of the preparation and serving of
the refreshments, as well as cleaning up, and that eases
the staff burden. Extra staff for such an event can be a
problem, but in our experience staff members are often
eager to be involved in a special event. Food, drink, and
utensils should be kept very simple to avoid problems in
serving and cleaning up. A reception need only cost a few
dollars. Sometimes interested staff members, performers

or members of the public will offer to bring in utensils or
prepared food, and the reception will cost even less.

Long-term Scheduling

All the foregoing has been concerned with planning
one program or a series of programs. For several reasons,
it is desirable to plan programs for a period of time, say a
year or a season, depending on the type of library. If programs are a regular occurrence in a library, people will
get in the habit of going to them and watching for them. If
planning is not done, scheduling tends to be haphazard. There
may be several programs in a month, and then none for
several months. Of course planning should be flexible enough
to allow for the inclusion of unexpected programs and the
removal of others. Frequently one hears of a new program
source, or a subject becomes popular, and these things cry
out to be included in your schedule.

Another reason for planning a year ahead is that
everything has limits; projectors, films, rooms, and staff
members must be scheduled, and there will be fewer disap-
pointments if they are scheduled well in advance. If money
is involved, its spending must also be scheduled. If several
people are involved in planning programs--adult and young
adult librarians, for example--the overlapping or repetition
of programs can be avoided by planning ahead.

A year's plan should provide for all ages, any other
significant groups in the community, a variety of subjects,
and several types of programs. One might want to have a
discussion series for adults, several series of film programs
for different age levels, two different musical programs or
series, some poetry readings or plays, one or two craft
workshops for different ages, two or three puppet shows and
a story-hour series. For particular kinds of audiences (film,
music) it is useful to have the programs on the same day
and time, so that audience comes to expect them; one might,
for example, have concerts once a month on Sunday afternoons at 2:30, or have films for children on the first Saturday of every month at 10:30 a. m.

NOTES

1. Conwell, Mary K. The New York Public Library. South

Bronx Project.   Children's Services Report, June-
Dec. 1969, pp. 19-20.
2.   Library Journal, April 15, 1969, p. 1570.
3.   Mansfield, Jewell. "A Public Affairs Program--The
Detroit Public Library," Library Trends, July 1968,
pp. 58-61.

13 ★ PUBLICITY

Successful attendance at a program has two ingredients: some group of persons must be interested enough in the content to go to wherever the program is being given, and that group must find out about it in time to plan to attend. The second ingredient is not as easy to supply as it might seem. Invariably, after a program is over, somebody will tell you they hadn't heard about it in time, and if they had known they certainly would have come. Although such remarks must be taken with several grains of salt, it is true that reaching people with publicity is difficult. One has only to think of the number of flyers, posters, signs and notices with which one is bombarded, and the radio and television that assault one's ears, to realize what sensory overkill we face; one also realizes that the defense against these assaults is to block much of it out.

Publicity, therefore, requires some careful thought and some hard work. We have seen too many libraries that put inconspicuous flyers on the charging desk and thought they had done their publicity work; that might do for some programs in some places, but most programs would die of malnutrition in such circumstances. In contrast, the libraries of The New York Public Library's North Manhattan Project used every available means of publicity. For teenage programs, for example, announcements were made in the New York Times, the New York Amsterdam News (a community newspaper), and on a local radio station. Posters and fliers were placed in the library and in community agencies. Fliers were mailed to teenagers, to teachers, to persons in charge of community organizations and to other libraries. Fliers were distributed on the streets near the library. Every teenager who registered for a library card was told about the programs. On the day of the program, telephone calls were made to individuals in community agencies and schools as reminders.

The Audience to Be Reached

One would not necessarily need publicity that widespread. But one must think about the potential audience and how they can be reached. The audience may be the general public or it may be a specific segment: the young, the old, housewives, blacks, whites, radicals, reactionaries, farmers, artists, or bubble gum salesmen. The pitch should primarily be made to that group; the publicity should be designed to appeal to them, and it should be distributed in places where it will reach them.

When we were fortunate enough to get Edward Field for a poetry reading, we were sure he would appeal to the young. His photograph--sweat shirt, beads, long hair--confirmed that opinion, and we used it on a poster in the library. (The photograph of another poet made him look like a middle-aged insurance salesman and we knew we wouldn't use that one with a young audience.) For the Field program, we also used excerpts from some of his poems, "Frankenstein" and "Curse of the Cat Woman," on fliers; these too we thought would appeal to teenagers, and they might draw the attention of those not familiar with his work.

The Finkelstein Memorial Library in Spring Valley, New York has a unique way of reaching teenagers. They publish a small magazine that is written by and for teenagers. It contains reviews, letters, articles and poems and it is distributed to the teenagers in the community. Sprinkled through the magazine are announcements of all the library programs likely to be of interest to this group. Thus the publicity gets into the hands of those most likely to attend.

For a program on Charles Dickens, we aimed at, and drew, a largely older audience. Publicity was sent to literary societies, women's clubs, college faculties and similar groups. Some general publicity is also necessary, since one can never be really sure who will show up. One poetry discussion group was led by a young, bearded poet and discussed no one much older than John Ashbery; it was attended by mostly elderly people, thus proving the wisdom of assuming nothing.

Physical Form of Publicity and Its Design

Having decided on the probable audience, one must

decide what forms the publicity will take (flyers, posters, newspaper articles, etc.), and who will design it and who will execute the design. As with other aspects of programs, there is probably no, or little, money available for publicity. Fortunately there is some free material available. If an author is part of your program, or you are featuring the books of a particular author, call the publicity department of his or her publisher. They can usually send you photographs, book jackets or other promotional materials. The author may have some of these items himself. Sometimes performers, or cosponsoring organizations, will have their own publicity, or will agree to create some. That will save you some work, but you should examine it before it is distributed. You won't want the library's name on anything that is tasteless, offensive or shoddy, and if it is any of those things, it won't be good publicity anyway.

If the publicity is not readymade and must be designed, explore the talents of the library staff, your friends, and members of the public. There are often staff members who can do simple lettering or have other art skills, and many people will have imaginative ideas, when they put their minds to a project. Sometimes school art classes, or other teenagers, will be interested in such a project; one possibility is to hold a contest and to offer a small prize; that should generate interest, give the programs added publicity (you can also publicize the contest), and get you some reasonably good art work. Try designing the publicity yourself. Even if you think you are unoriginal and have no talent, you might surprise yourself. Designing it yourself will also insure that you get it the way you want it.

Materials, Design Sources, Reproduction

Although you may be able to get somebody to design your publicity for nothing, the materials and the reproduction will probably cost something. Fortunately, the cost can be small. Dry transfer letters and symbols are available from stationery and art supply stores. Their use makes good-looking copy a simple matter, and for three or four dollars you can get a good supply in a variety of sizes and styles. There are several brands on the market and they vary somewhat in quality, so you might want to experiment.

There are some simple ways to get ready-made elements for the copy. If you are working with a group that

has a letterhead or a publicity brochure, you can cut from
them pictures, symbols, decorations and unusual lettering.
These items can be pasted on the mock-up and can be reproduced, if they don't have fine shading or more than one
color which make reproduction expensive.   Discarded library
books and periodicals can be useful for this purpose, provided the items are not subject to copyright.   For a program
on Charles Dickens, several sources were used.   A flyer
that evoked a Pickwickian atmosphere was wanted.   A Christmas card was found with a black and white scene from Pickwick Papers, and we cut that out.   Then we searched through
a book of designs, bought for the purpose, and found one
that seemed Victorian in style.   We cut that out too, and
pasted both these items on our mock-up.   Dry transfer letters were used for the large print.   A striking flier had been
produced, with no artistic talent--fortunate for us since
none was available.

     Sometimes pictures or symbols will be found that
can't be clipped from their source.   When we found a silhouette of Charlie Chaplin on the cover of a book, we also
found a staff member with drawing ability.   The silhouette
was so successfully copied, and was such a useful symbol
for film programs, that it has been borrowed many times by
other libraries.   Another way of using unclippable pictures
is to have them photocopied; the photocopy is then pasted on
the mock-up.   They must be illustrations that will reproduce
well.   The paper should be very white, and the drawing dark
with little shading.   We had good success, for example, with
a line drawing of a hand that we found in a book on how to
draw.

     A number of publishers now produce collections of
copyright free art.   These include animals, old engravings,
cartoons, alphabets of all kinds, plants, and decorative
borders, to name just a few.   One can simply make a photocopy of the illustration desired and paste it on your master
copy.   Thus these illustrations can be used many times.
Some of the large publishers that issue such work are Arco,
Crown and Dover.   Dover Pictorial Archives, for example,
is a series of more than 250 titles.   Some of the other producers of these graphics are Art Directions Book Co. (19
W. 44th St. , New York, N.Y. 10036), Dick Sutphen Studio
(P.O. Box 628, Scottsdale, Arizona 85252), Library Educational Institute, Inc. (P.O. Box 687, Bloomfield, N. J.
07003), Universe Books (381 Park Avenue South, New York,
N. Y. 10016), and Words and Pictures (Box R, East Schodack,
N. Y. 12063).

When creating publicity, there are some simple rules
that one can benefit from following. Sharon Orienter of the
Rochester (N. Y.) Public Library has compiled the following
list, starting with the premise that " ... you do not need
to be an artist to turn out professional, or at least polished-
looking, graphics." First she recommends a list of basic
tools:

> X-acto knife with #11 blades, or sharp scissors
> fine tipped felt pen--black (Pilot Razor Point)
> small dispenser can of rubber cement
> rubber cement pick-up eraser
> non-reproducing (also called non-photo) blue pencil
> good eraser--art gum, plastic, soft rubber, kneaded
> opaque white (Liquid Paper, Pelikan Graphic White)
> Ruler-- 6" to 12"--metal and centering if possible
> T-square--18" to 24"
> Triangle--30/60 or 45--12"
> small, good quality paint brush--#3 or smaller--red
>   sable
> frosted tape and/or masking or drafting tape
> tracing paper
> sketch pad
> bond paper--standard #20 office

She has also recommended a list of more "serious" tools,
among which are three essential additions to the basic list:

> drawing board--18" by 24" is a good size
> styles for rub-off lettering and designs
> drafting tape

Now Ms. Orienter gets down to work. For a typewriter she recommends an IBM Selectric with dual pitch
feature. However, that old library typewriter will do. All
you need, she says, is clear type and a good, black ribbon.
Carbon ribbons smear easily, so use a fixative on the type
before the paste-up, if that kind is being used. Ms. Orienter's rules follow:

Typesetting with a Typewriter

1. Break copy into logical lines.
2. Count number of spaces in each line and note at end
    of line.
3. Note lines or words to be set in another type style or
    as headlines.
4. Outline or cut paper to size of finished piece--type on

one side only.
5. Clear all margins and tabs on your typewriter.
6. Set margins at edges of paper or outline.
7. Set one tab at center.
8. Leave sufficient space for headline or design.
9. Tab to center.
10. Backspace half the number of spaces in first line.
11. Begin typing.
12. Back spacing half the spaces in each line and starting to type at that point will give you a centered typing job.
13. Double space when possible--it makes for clearer, easier reading copy.
14. Space the copy to fill available space vertically.

Shortcut: If your typing is all correct and straight and centered, simply paste on your illustration, decoration, or headline and use your typed sheet as a paste-up.

Once you have clear, correct copy you are ready to begin your paste-up, mechanical or camera-ready artwork.

Basic Procedure

A) Find a clean, clear work space--preferably where the square corner of a table can be utilized.

B) Assemble all the elements you need.
1. Tools and supplies
2. Copy--typed or typeset and carefully proofed

C) Decide if you will use headlines. If so, set in rub-off lettering.
1. Draw light line with non-photo pencil
2. Line up first letter to be rubbed off with guide line below letter on blue line
3. Rub off letter and part of guide line that matches edge of right side of letter
4. Line up second letter by matching part of guide line that is under left side of second letter with guide line already on paste-up
5. Rub off second letter (Note: use a stylus or a dull #2 pencil to rub off lettering; a ball point pen will ruin your sheet)
6. Repeat steps 2, 3 and 4 until headline is complete. Headlines can also be effectively produced by hand lettering, or cutting type elements from newspapers or magazines.

D) Decide what sort of art you will use--original, clip art, rub-off, printed source.

1. Cut out clip art
2. Transfer rub-off art to sheet of paper
3. Draw or obtain original art; if you don't feel confident making original art, don't do it; ask pages, patrons, friends
4. Make necessary copies from printed sources
5. Trace photos to make line drawings--using photos directly will require halftone reproduction which is expensive
6. Crop high-contrast photos

E) If you have a drawing board or a square table corner, place your T-square tightly and evenly against the vertical edge.

F) Line up horizontal edge of bond paper or bristol board against horizontal edge of T-square. TAPE SECURELY.

G) If you do not have a square table or drawing board, put as many sheets of bond or bristol as necessary to bring the sheet you are working on to the level of the T-square's horizontal under your work sheet. TAPE.

H) If finished size of printed piece will be less than size of sheet you are working on, outline finished size.
1. Draw line for bottom or tip edge with T-square
2. Draw left or right edge with triangle (place base of triangle firmly against T-square)
3. Measure width from corner on horizontal line and mark.
4. Measure height from corner on vertical line and mark.
5. Using T-square and triangle as in steps 1 and 2 lined up with respective marks, complete shape that defines finished shape of your publication.

I) If you wish to have more than one copy to a page or wish to have folds:
1. Outline size of page on paste-up sheet as in steps 1-5 above
2. Using a T square or triangle draw in edge lines or fold lines and mark either "cut" or "fold."

J) Basic set-up is very important! Check at this point to

make sure all measurements are correct and all lines straight and square.

K) Arrange all elements of paste-up on paste-up sheet. Rearrange until best combination is found. Don't be afraid to discard or re-do if something doesn't look right.

L) When satisfactory arrangement is found, rubber cement elements down one at a time. (Apply cement to one surface only.) Check each element to make sure it is straight, before pasting down next element; use T-square and triangle for this--don't guess.

M) When all elements are arranged and pasted down, wait a few minutes for cement to dry. Remove excess cement from edges of elements with rubber cement pick-up eraser. Be careful not to touch any rub-off elements with pick-up. Typewriter copy can also be damaged by pick-up.

N) Touch up any mistakes or corrections.
1. Use opaque white over any black areas
2. Use black ink or felt tip on any white spots

You now have a piece of camera-ready art in your hands. It can now go to the printer, duplicator or copier for reproducing. If the publicity is being sent out for reproduction, make note of the following:

Color, weight and size of paper
Color(s) of ink
Size of finished piece, after folding, cutting, etc. and where it is to be cut or folded
Your name, address and telephone number

If it is going to a professional printer, also add the following:

Whether artwork should be line or halftone
Type of ink as well as color
If parts are to be typeset, note which parts, and style or kind of type

Writing the Copy

There are several points that we have found to be

important when designing flyers and posters. They should
be clear and simple. If there are too many words, people
aren't going to take the time to read them, or they won't
remember them, or they will become confused. Avoid the
temptation--we know it can be strong--to be fancy or clever,
if by your cleverness you sacrifice clarity. Make sure that
all the essential facts are included before the copy is sent
to the printer. When the printer returns the copy, check
everything again; do this immediately so you will have time
to have corrections made. Such items as the time, date,
place (with address and possibly telephone number), ticket
information, and who is doing what are sine-qua-nonical.
It is often important to include, and perhaps emphasize, the
word free; many people do not seem to understand that a
public library's services are free. Finally, make sure no
eager staff member puts even one piece of publicity out before it is checked.

In short, trust no one (not even yourself), and assume
nothing. In one press release, somebody changed the spelling
of John Donne's name to Dunne, because they assumed it was
incorrect. In another flyer, the time, schedule of events
and details of the program were attractively presented, but
the location was omitted entirely. Both pieces of publicity
had been widely distributed by large organizations, and they
had been prepared by experienced people.

Make the most interesting word or phrase stand out,
and the public may stop to pick up a flyer or read a poster.
Names such as Charlie Chaplin, D. W. Griffith, Robert
Flaherty or Ingmar Bergman will attract film enthusiasts.
If the names are not well known, just the words FILM,
DANCE, or POETRY in very large letters will catch the
eye of those interested in the subject. To attract the attention of a particular group, you might want to emphasize
some special aspect of an art form, such as rock music,
horror films or black poetry. Sometimes the subjects or
titles are important or attention-getting; venereal disease
and narcotics are words that should stop the interested
passer-by, and titles like No Exit, Under Milk Wood, Hiro-
shima, Mon Amour and The Perils of Pauline will attract
those persons who are interested if the words stand out
sufficiently.

Even the day of the week or the time of day may be
the significant item. Certain times and days attract the
most people, and if nothing else seems more important,

you might want to feature Saturday Films or Sunday Afternoon Concerts. Symbols can be useful devices for attracting
attention. Drawings of musical instruments, film reels, or
a silhouette of Charlie Chaplin are all symbols that convey
messages to interested persons. Photographs of speakers
or performers can be helpful, particularly if you want to
emphasize some aspect of those persons, such as their
dress, race or age. Other pictures that indicate the content of the program may be good, if they are dramatic. A
close-up of a tarantula's face, a rattlesnake's fangs, or dead
fish in a polluted river should be stoppers. Nude bodies of
women, or even men, are too common. Don't use them.

Once you have caught attention, you have to keep it,
so the copy should also be intriguing. Biographical information can help.

> If a singer has sung at La Scala,
> or a filmmaker's "shot" an impala,
> or a dancer learned dancing in Bali,
> or a painter has studied with Dali,

you would certainly want to put those facts into your publicity.
If, as often happens, the name of the performer or speaker
isn't well enough known to attract attention, you can emphasize any prizes or awards that she or he has won, any
performance she, he or they have given, or any writings
they, he or she have published. Quotations from their
writings, when carefully selected, can give a special flavor
to the publicity.

If films are being shown, mention any special techniques or effects that are used in the film. Describe the
intention of the producer of the film, or point out any special
feature of the content. Such words and phrases as computer-
made, electrovideographic technique, experimental, rarely
seen or synaesthetic cinema might help.

When planning for publicity that must be printed by
somebody else, allow plenty of time for the printing, allow
for delays in the mail, and allow for the unforeseen. A
printer getting sick has caused us problems more than once,
and one of them died at a time that was inopportune for us
(as well as for him). Again, the principle of checking on
everything must be stressed. Call the printer before the
delivery date to remind him and to make sure everything is
going all right.

Distribution

When publicity has been designed, printed, received and rechecked, it must be distributed. Unless the program is a sure-fire success and you are afraid of being swamped, putting a poster in the lobby of the library or flyers on the charging desk probably won't be enough. Mailing lists are one of the most effective means of distribution. They are made not born. They must be compiled, usually over a long period of time, and they take staff time and cost some money for postage. But, if much programming is to be done, they are important, if not essential.

Most effective are mailing lists to individuals, but one can begin by compiling a list of schools, colleges, churches, clubs and other institutions and organizations. Mailings to them will draw some persons who can become the basis for a list of individuals. Continue to mail to organizations after compiling a list of individuals because some different people will see each new mailing. The library's readers can also serve as a basis for a list. Staff members can be trained to ask the readers if they want to receive mailings, while they are talking to them at charging desks, doing floor work, and in other situations. Another method is to take names and addresses from books that have been charged out. For a series of films on artists, one librarian compiled an instant mailing list by taking readers' names from books on art. This proved to be an effective method--the response was high--and it became the basis for an all-purpose list.

Use a card file for mailing lists. Lists are worse than useless if they are not weeded and kept up to date; the use of cards makes that easier. Also if a list is not weeded, the postage bill will become excessive, and much staff time will be wasted. Put names, addresses, telephone numbers and special interests on the card. If subject interests are indicated, selective mailings can be made, further cutting down on work and postage.

One way to keep mailing lists up to date is to periodically ask people on the list to return a form verifying their addresses, telephone numbers, interests and other information. The cards of those not responding can be withdrawn. A simple method, insuring a higher rate of return, would be to include a stamped, addressed post card in a mailing for a program. The following notice could also be included:

Dear Library User,
   The Klondike Public Library is updating its mailing
list. If you wish to continue receiving announcements
of programs and other library mail, please fill in the
enclosed post card and drop it in the mail box, or
bring it with you when you next come to the library.

And the post card might read:

Name _____

Address _____

Organization you represent (if any):

Kinds of programs that interest you:

   Take advantage of the mailing lists of other institutions and organizations. Libraries can often have notices
of programs of special interest to the members of such
organizations inserted in their newsletters or other mailings.

   One way libraries distribute publicity about programs
is through the use of newsletters. Newsletters are useful
devices in a number of ways. They convey to the public
any information you want them to have about the library, including schedules, notices of meetings, items about new staff
members, news of significant acquisitions, and so forth.
Most importantly, for our purposes, they give information
about coming programs. (Sometimes it is good publicity to
report on a program after it is over.)

   The size and kind of mailing depends on the library
and the community it is in. Some libraries, in relatively
small service areas of a few thousand households, mail
newsletters to everyone. A library in a city would probably
want to confine the mailing to a selected group, such as a
friends of the library organization. The frequency of mailing
will depend on how much you have to communicate, how much
it costs to produce, and the staff available for producing it.
Some newsletters are mailed monthly, some quarterly, and
some twice a year.

   Costs can vary a lot. Newsletters vary from a single,
typed sheet to a printed, multi-page, professional-looking
piece. Again, money, time, and the objective will govern
the choice. There are ways to cut costs and still have an
attractive newsletter. And attractiveness is important. We
are all inundated with mail, and if the newsletter looks cheap

and amateurish, it is likely it will be thrown away. Newsletters typed on electric typewriters are attractive, and cost less than those that are typeset. If headline copy is done on the typewriter in upper case letters, it can be photographically enlarged by the printer, saving even more money. Sometimes the same headline will be used in each, or many, newsletters. It can be set in type and used many times, again a saving. Transfer letters can be used for headlines. They provide a variety of type faces and sizes and are much less expensive than type.

Appearance depends on more than the method of reproduction, and costly publicity can look terrible. Some newsletters, for example, are unutterably cluttered, making many people not want to read them. Leave plenty of white space (or green space) between the lines and the columns. Remember, it is a newsletter, and should be written as such; that is, put down all the information, but nothing extraneous--as most of us are wont to do. That doesn't mean the writing can't be lively. It can be, and it should be, but mostly depend on the facts to attract an audience.

Illustrations add a lot to the appearance and interest of any publicity, and with new forms of reproduction, it doesn't cost a lot more to use them. A photograph of a dancer or musician who is coming to the library will draw attention to the text and arouse interest. And all kinds of art work can focus attention on what you want read. An illustration as a symbol of the library or the newsletter may be useful. Sometimes there is a picture of the library, or there may be drawings of books, or a printing press, or something unique to the library.

The method used for mailing needs to be determined. If items other than the newsletter are to be mailed, they can all be put in an envelope, saving multiple mailings. Most commonly though, the newsletter will be designed as a self-mailer. Part of the back or front page will be left vacant for the address, and the newsletter will be sealed or stapled together--according to your preference.

An $8\frac{1}{2}$" by 11" size seems the easiest. It can be simply folded, and as many additional pages as are wanted can be inserted. If the newsletter is to be mailed in an envelope, it would be well to make the size conform to the envelope, for ease in mailing. Probably the most useful thing to do is to look at a number of newsletters before designing one.

Word-of-Mouth

Word-of-mouth advertising is very effective, especially if it is reinforced by a printed reminder such as a flyer. Have the staff talk across the desk, to library users, about the program, handing them flyers at the same time. However, don't count on staff members doing this automatically. We have seen libraries where half the staff was unaware of, or only vaguely conscious of, a program. The staff--all the staff--must be trained to do these things. The first thing to do is to make sure they know all about the program; they must know the day it is to take place, the right time, where it will be held, and what it will be about. They can and should be made enthusiastic about the program. One way to do that is to get them involved; involve them in the planning and the production, talk to them about the subject and the problems, and get their ideas which will often be very helpful. As with other areas of library work, your own enthusiasm and good example are probably the best leadership.

In some cases, you may want to telephone a few selected persons who will probably be interested in the subject, following the call with a mailing of a flyer.

Librarians frequently speak at meetings of women's clubs, church groups, parent-teacher associations and other organizations. They also frequently belong to local groups of various kinds. These meetings are good places to distribute publicity and to talk about the programs. Even if you are not personally in attendance, arrangements can often be made to have announcements at meetings and in schools. One large New York City high school regularly announces a library's programs through its loudspeaker system, during the home room period. About four thousand students and many teachers are reached at once, in this way.

Although individual contacts and mailings are the most effective publicity methods, don't overlook any means. Posters and flyers can be put on the bulletin boards of colleges, schools, churches, stores, museums and other libraries. Since there is not unlimited money or time for publicity, they should be placed selectively. A poster advertising a poetry reading might be put in a garden supply center and attract some attention, but it would probably do better in a college.

Outreaching

Many times you will want to attract to a program a group of people who never use the library. Frequently they will be people who because of language or other reasons can't be reached through normal publicity channels. Some libraries employ a very direct approach: they go out, or send out others, to talk to people where they are. During The New York Public Library's North Manhattan Project, located in Harlem, staff members distributed flyers on street corners and at bus and subway stops. The Chicago Public Library and the public library of Plainfield, N. J. , among others, enlist children and other residents of particular neighborhoods to distribute flyers door to door and to invite their friends and neighbors to programs. Other libraries have found teenagers very good for this purpose.

A Staten Island librarian demonstrated the effectiveness of going into the streets and she did it by herself. The library was having its first Spanish-language program, but very few Spanish-speaking people had ever used that library. The children's librarian roamed the streets of the community for a few days before the program, and during the morning before the program. She had with her some very colorful flyers, in both Spanish and English, and she felt that they attracted much attention. She spoke mainly to children and teenagers who understood English (she does not speak Spanish, which is something to think about) and they brought their families. Eighty-five children and adults attended, and almost all of them were Spanish-speaking non-users of the library. She believes that her approach was important in her success. She says she quickly learned that they don't want to be regarded as "Spanish-speaking people," or they were suspicious when approached in that way; but, when she asked if they understood Spanish, they responded well. A librarian in Maryland also found going into the streets effective. She walked around ringing a cowbell, to gather children for a storytelling session.

Undoubtedly the most direct means of getting people to programs is to transport them, and some libraries are now using buses for this purpose. The Chicago Public Library, in a state and federally funded program, takes children to its Neighborhood Library Centers by bus and a New York state library takes groups of elderly people to programs in that way. Although it is expensive, libraries with a lot of programs could find this method useful. Parking and transportation problems, and the fear that many people have of going out at night or even in the daytime have eroded library use.

Press Releases

Newspapers provide a very important means for distributing publicity, and the press release is the primary means for pre-program publicity, in many communities. Local newspapers are usually read from cover to cover by a large segment of any community, and they will print-- sometimes giving excellent coverage--items about local activities. When sending out releases, don't disregard the small papers or the special interest papers. Although the number of major city newspapers has been shrinking in recent years, many small papers have been springing up. Frequently they serve a small area of a city. Sometimes they cater to a particular group such as black people. And there are many papers serving various ethnic groups, usually in the language of that group. In addition to newspapers, press releases should go to radio and television stations; they also serve both the general public and special interests.

Given the importance of the press release in attracting the attention of the community, it is also important to attract the attention of the editor. Newspaper editors are flooded with mail, and they make their decisions in seconds. Therefore, it is important to catch the eye of the editor by getting the most important or interesting point up front, just as with flyers and posters. Press releases have other points in common with flyers and posters. Strive for clarity. Avoid being fancy. Make sure the who, what, where, when and how are included; these facts should be rechecked, not only for your benefit, but for the benefit of the publication. A publication using a release becomes responsible for its accuracy, and it intensely dislikes being tripped up by someone else's mistake. So for the sake of future relations with the news media, check everything twice.

In writing the press release, give it some depth. Then the rewriteman won't be required to keep calling you, or be made to dig out his own information. Depth will also make the release more newsworthy. The kind of information that was described for flyers would be relevant here. If there is a newsworthy picture, that can be included too.

NEWS

May 17, 1980

The Klondike Public Library
110 Bonanza Avenue
Tel.   Yukon 5-0000

For Release:
Immediate

Contact:
Bill Snow
Yukon 5-0000
Ext. 3

GOLD PANNING DEMONSTRATION

Gold panning techniques will be demonstrated at the Klondike Public Library, 110 Bonanza Avenue, on Saturday, May 24, 1980 at 3 P. M.   The demonstration will be conducted by Joe Oldtimer, proprietor of the Whitehorse Saloon.   Oldtimer has panned for gold all over the Northwest Territories for the past seventy years and he will show how it is done.   He will also tell some stories of the rough, tough early days, and why his motto is "All that glitters is not gold."   Admission is free, as it is to all library programs.

(a sample press release)

Newspapers like their local stories to have some connection with the community, in addition to the fact that the event is taking place there.   It would be helpful if some person connected with the program lived in the area or formerly lived there.   Otherwise one could try to make a connection with some local place or event.   If the subject of the program is timely, that is important.   The release should be as concise as is consistent with a good story.   If you make it too long, it might end up in the editor's wastebasket.

Timing is important.   Be certain the release gets to the publication at least several days ahead of the day you

want it published. Editors like to schedule the handling of
even small stories. And don't forget that mail is often delayed. Personal delivery is the surest way. The story
should not be published too far ahead of the date of the program or too shortly before it. The timing will also depend
on whether you are requiring tickets. One editor of a daily
newspaper has told us that Monday and Tuesday are good
days for getting stories printed because the news tends to
be lighter on those days.

There are a number of other pieces of information
that should go into every press release. The name, address,
and telephone number of the library must be included, and
the name and telephone number (including extension) of the
person to contact for further information should be there.
Two dates should appear: the date the release is sent out
and the date of the requested release for publication. One
can either request immediate release or ask for a specific
date. If a story has special news value, the same release
can be sent to all media. If you want announcements to
appear in calendars of events, or you want spot announcements on radio and television, you can send those places a
separate release giving only the basic information.

Another use for the press is having them cover the
program with reporters and photographers. If the program
has news value, if they have room to print the story, and
if they have the staff to send, they will probably cover it.
Telephone the city editor if time is limited, but it is better
to send him a memorandum about three days in advance of
the event. Tell him the place, time and subject, and include
a brief description of the program, being sure to mention
local angles, names of well-known performers, or other eye-
catching information. Press coverage of a library program
can serve several purposes: it helps to build a good image
of the library and to alert people to the possibility of future
programs. Press clippings and photographs are useful at
budget time and when applying for grants or seeking funds in
any manner.

Libraries are shy, if we can be permitted to indulge
in a little bit of anthropomorphism. They are discreet,
dignified and reserved (that is, most of them are in outward
appearance). Even if all kinds of exciting things are going
on inside, outwardly they remain, or appear, the same.
One way to temporarily transform a cold exterior is to hang
out a banner. One library made an effective banner, simply

and cheaply. Two bed sheets were donated by a staff member, and they were stapled together. Stencils were made
from newspaper and cardboard and the letters, proclaiming
a week of Puerto Rican cultural activities, were painted with
a can of spray paint. This 12-foot banner, with foot-high
red and blue letters on a white background, was easily
legible a block away.

Such a device is certainly helpful when a series of
programs or a festival is planned, and an all-purpose banner
or flag might be made to be hung out whenever programs
were to take place. In Elizabethan days, because rain or
an outbreak of the plague would cancel the play, all the
playhouses flew flags when a performance was scheduled.
Rain or the plague are unlikely to cancel a library program,
but the plague of library anonymity is almost as bad.

Tickets

Directly related to publicity, and in a sense part of
it, is the use of tickets for programs. Although admission
will almost always be free for library programs, the use of
tickets can be valuable. If you are afraid the crowd might
overflow the space, tickets can be used to limit the size
of the audience. Not everyone who takes a ticket will come
and the amount of attrition can vary greatly. This is partly
dependent on how they are given out. If they are put on
the charging desk, they will be put to all kinds of uses, including the making of paper airplanes. People, especially
teachers, frequently ask for large batches of tickets to give
to friends, enemies, students and others. If, on the other
hand, tickets are carefully handed out to those persons re-
questing them, they do give some guide to the number of
people likely to attend. Another, and in a sense contra-
dictory, use of tickets is that they may increase attendance.
There is something about even a free ticket, if it is attractively printed on good paper, that enhances the value of an
event in the eyes of the public.

When tickets are used, indicate that on the publicity.
It is usually best to say that they can be picked up at the
library. Other pickup points can be designated but that
makes them harder to keep track of and to control. Post
cards can be included with individual mailings asking people
to request the number of tickets they would like held for
them, or mailed to them.

THE NEW YORK PUBLIC LIBRARY
OTHER PEOPLE'S MAIL

A Lecture
by
DR. LOLA L. SZLADITS

Tuesday, April 2, 1974 at 7:00 p.m.

ST. GEORGE LIBRARY CENTER
10 Hyatt Street
Staten Island

FREE ADMISSION TICKET

THE NEW YORK PUBLIC LIBRARY
You are cordially invited to hear

Mrs. Virginia Sloan, Arden Antique Shop
give a lecture - demonstration on

ANTIQUES

Monday   May 24, 1971   7:30 p.m.

TOTTENVILLE BRANCH
7430 Amboy Road, Staten Island

Admission Free

Two sample NYPL tickets (at three-quarters real size)

Tickets were put to good use by one library when its budget was severely limited. A Scandinavian multimedia program was being presented and there was no money for flyers. An 18-inch high straw goat, the Swedish Jul Tomte, was placed on the charging desk and hand-lettered tickets (using catalog card stock) were hung from the goat so that children could take them. This unusual, attractive object drew considerable attention and was a good publicity device. Some thought would bring to mind similar devices for other kinds of programs.

14 ★ ONE EXEMPLARY LIBRARY PROGRAM

Paul Zindel and Some of His Friends
Visit with Their Staten Island Neighbors

We began to be aware of Paul Zindel in the mid-
sixties. He was teaching science at a local high school,
and some of his plays were appearing on New York's educational television channel. They were original, humorous
and compassionate, and were bright spots on otherwise
generally tame television. When in 1968 his first teenage
novel, The Pigman, was published, we realized that we had
a library patron and neighbor who was a very good writer.
Then The Effect of Gamma Rays on Man-in-the-Moon-Mari-
golds opened in an Off-Broadway theatre to general critical
and public acclaim, winning the New York Drama Critics'
Circle Award. We began talking about how nice it would be
if we could persuade him to appear on a library program.
We continued to talk about it for more than a year. "Wouldn't
it be great if Paul Zindel came to talk," we kept saying.
We did nothing.

Ads started to appear in the New York Times. His
new play, And Miss Reardon Drinks a Little, was to open on
Broadway with a star cast. His books, it was reported,
were being made into films. He was suddenly big time. It
was too late. We could never get him now.

We decided to try anyway. The worst we could get
was no answer. So we dreamed up a program and wrote
him a letter. We suggested that if he would come and talk
about his work, we might be able to get some actors to perform scenes from his plays. We also said we would like to
have a big display in the library during the month of the
performance, and asked him if he could lend us some pictures,
manuscripts and other material. A few days later, during
a coffee break, the word came. "Paul Zindel is on the

phone. " Raced through the building. Up the stairs. Out
of breath. Answer. He would be glad to do it. This
month if possible. He would be busy later.

Now we needed actors. We had been in touch with
the Staten Island Civic Theatre, talking about possible programs, and decided to try them. It happily turned out that
Mrs. Elaine Boies, whom we called, was a friend of Mr.
Zindel's and would be glad to work on such a program.

After some more telephone calls, a meeting was arranged with Mr. Zindel and Mrs. Boies. Mr. Zindel was
better than his word. He arrived with two shopping bags
filled with manuscripts, galley and page proofs, photographs
of scenes from his plays, copies of his books in Danish,
Swedish, French and English, his awards, and various other
material for display. We agreed on a date, April 29, which
didn't conflict with anything we could think of and a time,
8 p.m., which was late enough for the commuters and early
enough to be finished at a reasonable hour. Scenes from
the plays were discussed, and it was suggested that scenes
from the novels be dramatized. A reception after the program was suggested, and Mr. Zindel said he liked receptions.
Life was becoming more complicated but we decided to go
ahead. Mrs. Boies measured the stage and would decide on
the scenes. They departed, leaving the staff in a state of
euphoria mixed with trepidation. The trepidation was to
increase as the day came closer.

A committee was set up to plan, buy, prepare, and
serve the refreshments for the reception, and we were
promised $25 (the only cash we spent) for the food. We
decided on two kinds of punch, one with wine and one without, and canapes and cookies. All were fairly easy to prepare and serve. We would have the reception in the children's room which was easily accessible, by two entrances,
from the auditorium.

Publicity was the next problem. Flyers, newspaper
publicity, and a poster in the branch along with the exhibits
would be enough. We knew that for this one, unlike some
past programs, we wouldn't have any trouble filling the
house. What we didn't yet realize was how overwhelming
the response was to be. Tickets were necessary to control
the size of the audience. In the past, the number of tickets
taken had been a fairly reliable guide, although it is often
difficult to tell how many ticket holders will show up, the

tickets being free. It seemed likely that the percentage coming would be higher for this one, and we would have to be careful about giving out tickets.

No matter how far ahead one plans a program, publicity inevitably seems to be rushed. We wanted flyers two weeks before the program to allow time for mailing them out and getting back requests for tickets. We had to figure on the time for printing and allow for delivery time. A final decision on the scenes to be performed and the rounding up of the actors delayed us somewhat, but a flyer was finally designed by the staff and printed in the Library's Letter Shop.

Meanwhile back at the branch, more mundane chores remained to be done. Mr. Zindel wanted a microphone which had to be brought from another branch. The cast needed screens at the edge of the stage which had to be found and brought in. Seating was a major problem. Only 80 folding chairs were available. Enough chairs were available in other branches, but their programming schedules proved to be so tight that they had to be transported in the last two days before the program. The cast wanted two rehearsals in the library, and the schedule was cleared. We were ready to go. All the preliminaries had been taken care of.

The publicity arrived on time, with all the spelling and information correct. Meanwhile an item had appeared in a column of the local newspaper announcing the program, with the wrong date. Fortunately only three people showed up a week early. We had compiled a mailing list of high schools, colleges, organizations, churches, and individuals, and we sent them all flyers, as well as sending flyers to all libraries. We wrote a press release, trying hard for clarity and good timing. The newspaper gave us some good space, but neglected to mention tickets. A faint foreboding of doom flickered feebly in our esophagi. Or it may have been heartburn.

Then came the tsunami of requests. Before we had time to turn around, a hundred tickets had gone. Soon it was 150. Fear struck deep within us. Fear? It was more like panic. Maybe we could leave the country. Visions of not sugar plums, but the Beatles at Shea Stadium danced in our heads. People kept calling. Begging for tickets. Can't I just have three? Five for my students? One for my aunt

PULITZER PRIZE WINNING PLAYWRIGHT AND NOVELIST

PAUL ZINDEL

MONDAY, MAY 24th
8:00 P. M.
PORT RICHMOND BRANCH LIBRARY
75 BENNETT STREET
STATEN ISLAND, N. Y. 10302

THE NEW YORK PUBLIC LIBRARY

Program flyer advertising the Zindel evening emphasized his
name because he was the recognizable element (he had just
won a Pulitzer Prize). Contents of this program/flyer shown
on next page. Both reproduced at 75 percent of original size.

PAUL ZINDEL	TALKS TO THE AUDIENCE

PAUL ZINDEL, a native of Staten Island and former science teacher at Tottenville High School, is the author of three novels for teenagers and has had his plays performed on and off-Broadway and on television. He has won the Drama Desk Award, the Village Voice Off-Broadway Award, and the New York Drama Critics Circle Award.

In May 1971 Mr. Zindel was awarded the Pulitzer Prize in Drama for The Effect of Gamma Rays on Man-in-the-Moon Marigolds.

MEMBERS OF THE STATEN ISLAND CIVIC THEATRE, DIRECTED BY ELAINE BOIES	PERFORM SCENES FROM: THE EFFECT OF GAMMA RAYS ON MAN-IN-THE-MOON MARIGOLDS
	I NEVER LOVED YOUR MIND
	AND MISS REARDON DRINKS A LITTLE
	MY DARLING, MY HAMBURGER

Novels:

I Never Loved Your Mind

My Darling, My Hamburger

The Pigman

Plays:

And Miss Reardon Drinks a Little

Let Me Hear You Whisper

The Effect of Gamma Rays on Man-in-the-Moon Marigolds

MOLLY SHEREN
ANGELO DeSIMONE
SARAH MODEN
PAM MAMAY
JOHN CARLSON

THE AUDIENCE	TALKS TO PAUL ZINDEL

from Tottenville? Why don't you get a bigger auditorium?
It had never happened to a library program before. Almost
200 tickets had been given out a week before the program,
and the most we had ever been able to seat was 150. For
a normal program, attrition would have taken care of the
difference. But we weren't so sure for this one. Every
movable object had to be cleared from the auditorium. With
some careful scheming we managed to put in 170 chairs,
even putting two in the projection booth for some staff members who were clamoring for tickets.

The Big Night came. Two strong-willed, stout-
hearted staff members were stationed at the doors to collect
tickets and to keep out those without them. The thought had
formed, and was now growing, that we should repeat the
program if the principals were willing. We decided to take
the names and addresses of people without tickets, just in
case we could pull it off. Not to keep you in suspense,
everything turned out all right. About thirty people were
turned away, although many who had telephoned had been
discouraged. All seats were filled and a few standees
managed to crowd in. There was some, slightly warm, discussion with one man who left because he didn't like the
plays we were presenting. The auditorium was pretty warm,
too. We must remember to open more windows next time.
The performances went off almost without a hitch, considering the crowded conditions and some difficulties with the
directions for switching on and off the lights. The performances and the reception, with some heroic work by the
staff, were enjoyed by all.

Four days later, Mr. Zindel was awarded the Pulitzer
Prize for drama. There is a sequel. We hesitantly asked
Mr. Zindel if he would be willing to give a repeat performance. He was again most agreeable and willing. The whole
thing was repeated in another branch, with better facilities,
in front of about 230 people. This second performance had
to be presented within a month, because of various commit-
ments. As it was, two new members of the cast had to be
found, and rehearsed. After we were sure of them, the
publicity had to be rewritten and reprinted. The only hitches
this time were one member of the cast who had an automobile accident on the way to the performance, which only
caused a ten-minute delay, and a heckler in the back of the
auditorium, who was taken in stride by everybody. We
taped the entire performance and had pictures taken, since,
in Mr. Zindel's remarks, and particularly in the dramatizations from the novels, we had a unique program.

There now seemed to be nothing left to do but retire. We had run out of Pulitizer Prize winners.

APPENDICES

A ★ SAMPLE LISTS OF BOOKS FOR DISCUSSION

Women's Rights
    Ibsen: A Doll's House
    Strindberg: The Father
    Woolf: A Room of One's
        Own
    Greer: The Female Eunuch

War
    Heller: Catch-22
    Brecht: Mother Courage
    Killens: And Then We
        Heard the Thunder
    Vonnegut: Cat's Cradle

Conscience of the Playwright
    Eliot: The Cocktail Party
    Brecht: Galileo
    Dürrenmatt: The Visit
    Ionesco: The Rhinoceros

Lure of the East
    Hesse: Siddhartha
    Bhagavad-Gita
    Watts: Spirit of Zen
    Lao-tzu: Way of Life

Love or Will
    May: Love and Will
    Albee: Who's Afraid of
        Virginia Woolf?
    Nabokov: Lolita

Friedan: Feminine Mystique

The Catholic Family
    O'Neill: Long Day's Journey
        into Night
    Gilroy: The Subject Was
        Roses

The Jewish Family
    Odets: Awake and Sing
    Simon: Come Blow Your
        Horn

Fathers
    Innaurato: Gemini
    Gardner: A Thousand Clowns

The Midwestern Family
    Inge: The Dark at the Top of
        the Stairs
    Kaufman and Hart: The Man
        Who Came to Dinner

The Black Family
    Hansberry: Raisin in the Sun
    Bullins: In the Wine Time

Families After War
    Miller: All My Sons
    Rabe: Sticks and Bones

Families Facing Death
    Cristofer: The Shadow Box
    Mosel: All the Way Home

Following are the lists for the Adult Great Books Discussion
Program, which is sponsored by The Great Books Foundation (307
North Michigan Ave., Chicago 60601) and is reprinted here by per-
mission. Librarians can order paperback sets of these readings

from the Foundation, or they might wish to use these lists as bases for compiling their own lists of readings. The Foundation also sponsors the Junior Great Books Discussion Program. The asterisk (*) denotes selections only.

FIRST SET
1. The Declaration of Independence
2. Sophocles: Antigone
3. Plato: Apology; Crito
4. Thoreau: Civil Disobedience; Walden*
5. Machiavelli: The Ruler
6. Plutarch: Pompey
7. Shakespeare: Macbeth
8. Locke: Of Civil Government
9. Aristotle: Politics*
10. The Federalist Papers*
11. Adam Smith: The Wealth of Nations*
12. Marx and Engels: The Communist Manifesto
13. Tocqueville: Democracy in America*
14 The Gospel of Matthew
15. Tolstoy: The Death of Ivan Ilych
16. Joyce: Dubliners*

SECOND SET
1. Melville: Billy Budd, Foretopman
2. Plato: Euthyphro
3. Sophocles: Oedipus Rex; Oedipus at Colonus
4. Aristotle: Ethics*
5. St. Augustine: The Confessions of St. Augustine*
6. Shakespeare: Hamlet
7. Freud: A General Introduction to Psychoanalysis*
8. Racine: Phaedra
9. Homer: The Odyssey
10. Descartes: Discourse on Method
11. Hobbes: Leviathan*
12. Pascal: Pensées*
13. Mill: On Liberty
14. Swift: Gulliver's Travels*
15. Poincaré: The Value of Science*
16. Gogol: The Overcoat

THIRD SET
1. Freud: Civilization and Its Discontents
2. Dostoyevsky: Notes from Underground
3. Mann: Death in Venice
4. Aeschylus: Oresteia
5. Thucydides: The Peloponnesian War*
6. Aristophanes: Peace; The Birds
7. Aquinas: Treatise on Law*
8. Rousseau: The Social Contract*
9. Kant: Perpetual Peace
10. Voltaire: Candide
11. Aristotle: Poetics
12. Shakespeare: King Lear
13. The Book of Job
14. Gibbon: The Decline and Fall of the Roman Empire*
15. Nietzsche: Twilight of the Idols
16. Shaw: Heartbreak House

FOURTH SET
1. Chekhov: The Three Sisters; The Cherry Orchard
2. Veblen: The Theory of the Leisure Class*
3. Montaigne: Essays*
4. Mill: The Autobiography of John Stuart Mill*
5. Henry James: The Pupil; The Beast in the Jungle
6. Henry Adams: The Education of Henry Adams*
7. Molière: The Misanthrope; Tartuffe
8. Berkeley: The First Dialogue Between Hylas and Philonous
9. Diderot: Rameau's Nephew
10. Plato: The Republic*
11. Hume: An Enquiry Concerning Human Understanding*

12. Calderón: Life Is a Dream
13. Bernard: An Introduction to the Study of Experimental Medicine*
14. Vergil: The Aeneid
15. The First Letter to Corinth; The Letter to Rome
16. Conrad: Heart of Darkness

FIFTH SET
1. Ibsen: The Wild Duck
2. Epictetus: The Manual
3. Chaucer: The Canterbury Tales*
4. Dante: The Inferno
5. Euripides: Medea; Hippolytus
6. Bergson: Time and Free Will*
7. Goethe: Faust
8. William James: Psychology: Briefer Course*
9. Spinoza: On the Improvement of the Understanding
10. Plato: Symposium
11. Kierkegaard: Works of Love*
12. Boccaccio: The Decameron*
13. Kant: Foundations of the Metaphysics of Morals*
14. The Book of Genesis
15. Darwin: The Origin of Species*
16. Turgenev: Fathers and Sons

SIXTH SET
1. Aeschylus: Prometheus Bound
2. Plato: Phaedrus
3. Aristotle: Metaphysics*
4. Longinus: On the Sublime
5. St. Augustine: On Nature and Grace; On Grace and Free Will
6. Aquinas: Existence & Simplicity of God*
7. Chaucer: Canterbury Tales*
8. Shakespeare: Richard II
9. Cervantes: Don Quixote*
10. Spinoza: Ethics*
11. Hume: Dialogues Concerning Natural Religion

12. Voltaire: Philosophical Dictionary*
13. Hegel: Philosophy of History*
14. Darwin: The Origin of Species*
15. Melville: Billy Budd, Foretopman
16. Henry James: The Turn of the Screw

SEVENTH SET
1. Plato: Gorgias
2. Aristotle: On the Soul
3. Bhagavad-Gita
4. Boethius: Consolation of Philosophy
5. Maimonides: Guide for the Perplexed*
6. Donne: Holy Sonnets
7. Molière: Tartuffe; The Misanthrope
8. Leibniz: Discourse on Metaphysics
9. Kant: Fundamental Principles of the Metaphysics of Morals
10. Goethe: Faust
11. Schopenhauer: The World as Will and Idea*
12. Kierkegaard: Concluding Unscientific Postscript*
13. Dostoyevsky: Notes from Underground
14. Conrad: Heart of Darkness
15. Freud: The Interpretation of Dreams*
16. Shaw: Man and Superman

EIGHTH SET
1. Aristophanes: The Birds; Peace
2. Plato: Phaedo
3. Aristotle: Physics*
4. St. Paul: Epistle to the Romans; First Epistle to the Corinthians
5. Galen: On the Natural Faculties*
6. Shakespeare: Henry the Fourth, Part One
7. Shakespeare: Henry the

Fourth, Part Two
8. Harvey: On the Motion of
the Heart and Blood
9. Descartes: The Passions
of the Soul
10. Milton: Samson Agonistes
11. Fichte: The Vocation of Man
12. Byron: Don Juan*
13. Mill: Utilitarianism
14. Nietzsche: The Genealogy of
Morals
15. Henry Adams: The Education of Henry Adams*
16. Yeats: Fourteen Poems

NINTH SET
1. Homer: The Iliad
2. Herodotus: The History*
3. Plato: Sophist

4. Aristotle: Posterior Ana-
lytics*
5. Tacitus: The Annals*
6. Plotinus: The Fifth Ennead
7. Luther: A Commentary on
St. Paul's Epistle to the
Galatians*
8. Galileo: Dialogues Concerning Two New Sciences*
9. Racine: Phaedra
10. Vico: The New Science*
11. Balzac: Père Goriot
12. Marx: Capital*
13. Ibsen: The Wild Duck
14. William James: The Principles of Psychology*
15. Baudelaire: Flowers of Evil*
16. Poincaré: Science and Hy-
pothesis*

N. Y. P. L. 's SIGNIFICANT MODERN BOOKS
FOR DISCUSSION, 1979-80

Abe, Kobo. Woman in the Dunes
Albee, Edward. American Dream
& The Zoo Story; Seascape;
Who's Afraid of Virginia
Woolf (see also Gassner 5th);
Zoo Story (see Kernan)
Anderson, Robert. Silent Night,
Lonely Night (see Gassner
5th)
Anderson, Maxwell. Lost in the
Stars (Famous Am. Plays,
40s); Winterset (Halline)
Anouilh, Jean. Becket
Aristophanes. Lysistrata
Arnow, Harriet. The Dollmaker
Barry, Philip. Philadelphia Story
(Gassner, 2nd)
Beckett, Samuel. Endgame; Wait-
ing for Godot
Behrman, S. N. The End of
Summer (Famous Am. Plays,
30s)
Bellow, Saul. Humboldt's Gift
Bettelheim, Bruno. The Uses
of Enchantment
Belli, Ugo. Corruption in the
Palace of Justice (Kernan)
Bolt, Robert. A Man for All

Seasons
Brecht, Bertholt. Caucasian
Chalk Circle; Galileo;
Mother Courage and Her
Children (Kernan)
Bullins, Ed. Goin' a Buffalo
(Couch); In the Wine Time
(Lahr)
Bush, Josef. French Gray
(Hoffman)
Camus, Albert. The Fall; The
Myth of Sisyphus; The
Stranger
Carr, Donald E. Energy and
the Earth Machine
Carroll, Lewis. Alice's Ad-
ventures in Wonderland &
Through the Looking Glass
Castaneda, Carlos. A Separate
Reality
Chayefsky, Paddy. Gideon
(Gassner, 2nd)
Cheever, John. Falconer; The
World of Apples
Comfort Alex. A Good Age
Commager, Henry Steele.
Freedom and Order
Conrad, Joseph. Typhoon

(Flower)

Coover, Robert. The Kid (Lahr)

Couch, William, ed. New Black Playwrights: Bullins, Ed-- Goin' a Buffalo; Elder, Lonne III--Ceremonies in Dark Old Men; Kennedy, Adrienne--A Rat's Mass; Mackey, William--Family Meeting; Ward, Douglas Turner--Happy Ending; Day of Absence

Crane, Stephen. The Monster (Flower)

Cristofer, Michael. Shadow Box

Crouse, Russel. (See Lindsay)

Crowley, Mathew. The Boys in the Band

Curtin, Sharon R. Nobody Ever Died of Old Age

Davies, Robertson. Fifth Business; World of Wonders

De Beauvoir, Simone. A Very Easy Death

De Tocqueville, Alexis. Democracy in America, vol. 2

Dey, James Paul. Passacaglia (Hoffman)

Doctorow, E. L. Ragtime

Dostoyevski, Fyodor. The Grand Inquisitor on the Nature of Man

Drabble, Margaret. The Needle's Eye

Elder, Lonne. Ceremonies in Dark Old Men (Couch)

Eyen, Tom. The White Whore and the Bit Player (Hoffman)

Famous American Plays of the 1940s. Anderson, Maxwell-- Lost in the Stars; Laurents, Arthur--Home of the Brave; McCullers, Carson--Member of the Wedding; Miller, Arthur --All My Sons; Wilder, Thornton--The Skin of Our Teeth

Famous American Plays of the 1930s: Behrman, S. N.-- End of Summer; Odets, Clifford--Awake and Sing!; Saroyan, William--The Time of

Your Life; Sherwood, Robert E.--Idiot's Delight; Steinbeck, John--Of Mice and Men

Fast, Howard. The Immigrants

Faulkner, William. As I Lay Dying; The Sound and the Fury

Fitzgerald, F. Scott. Three Novels: Great Gatsby; Last Tycoon; Tender Is the Night

Flower, Dean S. , ed. 8 Short Novels: Conrad, Joseph-- Typhoon; Crane, Stephen-- The Monster; James, Henry--The Pupil; Lawrence, D. H.--The Fox; McCullers, Carson--The Ballad of the Sad Cafe; Melville, Herman --Benito Cereno; Porter, Katherine Anne--Pale Horse, Pale Rider; Wharton, Edith --Bunner Sisters

Forster, E. M. A Passage to India

Frank, Anne. The Diary of a Young Girl

Freud, Sigmund. Outline of Psychoanalysis

Friday, Nancy. My Mother, My Self

Frings, Ketti. Look Homeward Angel (Gassner 5th)

Fugard, Athol. Sizwe Bansi Is Dead & The Island

Garcia Lorca, Federico. Blood Wedding (Kernan)

Gardner, Herb. A Thousand Clowns (Gassner 5th)

Gardner, John. October Light

Gassner, John, ed. Best Plays of the Modern Am. Theatre, 2nd Series, 1939-1946: Barry, Philip--Philadelphia Story; Gow, James--Tomorrow the World; Hellman, Lillian--Watch on the Rhine; Kanin, Garson--Born Yesterday; Kaufman, George S. & Moss Hart--Man Who Came to Dinner; Kesselring, Joseph--Arsenic & Old Lace; Kingsley, Sidney--The Pa-

triots; Laurents, Arthur--
Home of the Brave; Lindsay,
Howard & Russel Crouse--
Life with Father; Patrick,
John--The Hasty Heart; Rice,
Elmer--Dream Girl; Saroyan,
William--The Time of Your
Life; Sherwood, Robert E. --
Abe Lincoln in Illinois; Thur-
ber, James & Elliott Nugent
--Male Animal; Van Druten,
John--I Remember Mama;
Voice of the Turtle; Williams,
Tennessee--Glass Menagerie
Gassner, John, ed. Best Ameri-
can Plays, 5th Series, 1958-
1963: Albee, Edward--Who's
Afraid of Virginia Woolf?;
Anderson, Robert--Silent
Night, Lonely Night; Chayefsky,
Paddy--Gideon; Frings, Ketti
--Look Homeward Angel;
Gardner, Herb--A Thousand
Clowns; Gibson, William--
Two for the Seesaw; Inge,
William--Dark at the Top of
the Stairs; Kerr, Jean--Mary,
Mary; Kopit, Arthur--Oh Dad,
Poor Dad....; MacLeish,
Archibald--J. B.; Mosel, Tad
--All the Way Home; O'Neill,
Eugene--A Touch of the Poet;
Saroyan, William--The Cave
Dwellers; Vidal, Gore--The
Best Man; Williams, Tennes-
see: The Night of the Iguana;
Orpheus Descending; Wishen-
grad, Morton--The Rope
Dancers
Genet, Jean. The Balcony
Gide, Andre. The Counterfeiters
Gibson, William. Two for the
Seesaw (Gassner 5th)
Gilroy, Frank D. The Subject
Was Roses
Golding, William. The Lord of
the Flies
Gordon, Mary. Final Pay-
ments
Gordone, Charles. No Place
to Be Somebody
Gow, James. Tomorrow the

World (Gassner 2nd)
Gray, Simon. Butley, A Play;
Otherwise Engaged and
Other Plays
Great Books Foundation. Be-
coming Human; Search for
Meaning, Vol. 1: Chekhov,
Anton--A Dull Story; Less-
ing, Doris--Temptation of
Jack Orkney; Böll, Hein-
rich--Murke's Collected
Silences; The Thrower-
away; Melville, Herman--
Bartleby the Scrivener;
Kafka, Franz--The Meta-
morphosis; Sillitoe, Alan--
The Loneliness of the Long-
distance Runner, Search
for Meaning, Vol. 2:
Greene, Graham--The De-
structors; O'Connor, Flan
nery--A Good Man Is Hard
to Find; Tolstoy, Leo--
Father Sergius; Dostoyevsky,
Fyodor--A Nasty Story;
Calvo, Lino Novás--Dark
Night of Ramón Yendía;
Mann, Thomas--Mario and
the Magician; Sartre, Jean-
Paul--The Wall; Crane,
Stephen--The Open Boat;
James, Henry--The Figure
in the Carpet; Nabokov,
Vladimir--The Visit to the
Museum; Signs and Symbols
Guare, John. Cop-Out (Lahr);
The House of Blue Leaves
Guest, Judith. Ordinary People
Haley, Alex. Roots
Halline, Allan G., ed. Six
Modern American Plays:
Anderson, Maxwell--Winter-
set; Heggen, Thomas &
Joshua Logan--Mr. Roberts;
Hellman, Lillian--Little
Foxes; Kaufman, George S.
& Moss Hart--The Man Who
Came to Dinner; O'Neill,
Eugene--Emperor Jones;
Williams, Tennessee--Glass
Menagerie
Handke, Peter. Kaspar and

Other Plays: Offending the Audience; Self-Accusation

Hansberry, Lorraine. A Raisin in the Sun

Hart, Moss. (See Kaufman)

Heggen, Thomas. Mr. Roberts (Halline)

Hellman, Lillian. Little Foxes (Halline); Pentimento; Scoundrel Time; Watch on the Rhine (Gassner 2nd)

Hemingway, Ernest. Three Novels: A Farewell to Arms; The Old Man and the Sea; The Sun Also Rises

Herndon, Venable. Until the Monkey Comes (Hoffman)

Herr, Michael. Dispatches

Hesse, Hermann. Demian; Narcissus and Goldmund; Siddhartha; Steppenwolf

Hoffman, William, ed. New American Plays, Vol. II: Busch, Josef--French Gray; Dey, James Paul--Passacaglia; Eyen, Tom--The White Whore and the Bit Player; Herndon, Venable--Until the Monkey Comes; Kennedy, Adrienne--The Owl Answers; Maljean, Jean Raymond--A Message from Cougar; Molinaro, Ursule--The Abstract Wife; Owens: Rochelle--Futz

Huxley, Aldous. Brave New World Revisited

Ibsen, Henrik. Ghosts (Kernan); Three Plays: A Doll's House; Hedda Gabler; The Wild Duck

Inge, William. Dark at the Top of the Stairs (Gassner 5th)

Innaurato, Albert. Gemini

Ionesco, Eugene. Chairs (Kernan); Rhinoceros

Irving, John. The World According to Garp

Jackson, Shirley. The Lottery

James, Henry. The Golden Bowl; The Pupil (Flower)

Jones, LeRoi. Slaveship (Lahr)

Joyce, James. Portable Joyce: Portrait of the Artist; Dubliners

Jung, Carl. Undiscovered Self

Kafka, Franz. The Penal Colony: Stories and Short Pieces including The Metamorphosis

Kanin, Garson. Born Yesterday (Gassner 2nd)

Kaplan, Abraham. The New World of Philosophy

Kaufman, George S. The Man Who Came to Dinner (Halline)

Kennedy, Adrienne. The Owl Answers (Hoffman); Rat's Mass (Couch)

Kernan, A. B., ed. Classics of the Modern Theatre: Albee, Edward--Zoo Story; Brecht, Bertholt--Mother Courage & Her Children; Betti, Ugo--Corruption in the Palace of Justice; García Lorca, Federico--Blood Wedding; Ibsen, Henrik--Ghosts; Ionesco, Eugene--Chairs; Pirandello, Luigi--Six Characters in Search of an Author; Shaw, George Bernard--Arms and the Man; Strindberg, August --Fathers & Ghost Sonata

Kerr, Jean. Mary, Mary (Gassner 2nd)

Kesey, Ken. One Flew Over the Cuckoo's Nest

Kesselring, Joseph. Arsenic and Old Lace (Gassner 2nd)

Kingsley, Sidney. The Patriots (Gassner 2nd)

Kingston, Maxine Hong. Woman Warrior

Kopit, Arthur. Oh Dad, Poor Dad ... (Gassner 5th)

Kübler-Ross, Elisabeth. On Death and Dying

Lahr, John. The Great American Life Show: 9 Plays from Avant Garde Theatre: Bullins, Ed--In the Wine Time; Coover, Robert--

The Kid; Guare, John--Cop-
Out; Jones, LeRoi--Slaveship;
Malina, Judith & Julian Beck
--Mysteries and Other Pieces;
Oldenburg, Claes--Injun: A
Happening; Shepard, Sam--
Operation Sidewinder; van
Itallie, Jean-Claude--The Ser-
pent; Williams, Heathcote--
AC/DC

Laurents, Arthur. Home of the
Brave (Famous 40s & Gas-
sner 5th)

Lawrence, D. H. The Fox (Flower)

LeGuin, Ursula. The Left Hand
of Darkness

Leonard, Hugh. Da

Lessing, Doris. The Golden Notebook

Levinson, Daniel J. Seasons of
a Man's Life

Lindsay, Howard. Life with
Father (Gassner 2nd)

Logan, Joshua. (See Heggen)

McCullers, Carson. Ballad of
the Sad Cafe (Flower)
The Heart Is a Lonely Hunter;
Member of the Wedding (Famous 40s)

Mackey, William. Family Meeting (Couch)

McPhee, John. Coming into the
Country

MacLeish, Archibald. J. B. (Gassner 5th)

Malina, Judith. Mysteries and
Other Pieces (Lahr)

Maljean, Jean Raymond. A Message from Cougar (Hoffman)

Mamet, David. American Buffalo;
Sexual Perversity in Chicago
and Duck Variation

Mann, Thomas. A Death in
Venice and Other Stories

Melville, Herman. Benito Cereno
(Flower); Moby-Dick

Miller, Arthur. All My Sons
(Famous 40s); The Crucible;
Death of a Salesman; The
Price

Mitford, Jessica. Kind & Usual
Punishment

Molinaro, Ursule. The Ab-
stract Wife (Hoffman)

Morrison, Toni. Song of Solo-
mon

Mosel, Tad. All the Way Home
(Gassner 5th)

Murdoch, Iris. Accidental Man

Nabokov, Vladimir. Lolita

Nugent, Elliott. (See Thurber)

O'Casey, Sean. Three Plays:
Juno and the Paycock; The
Plough and the Stars; Sha-
dow of a Gunman

O'Connor, Flannery. Three by
Flannery O'Connor: A Good
Man Is Hard to Find; The
Violent Bear It Away; Wise
Blood

Odets, Clifford. Awake and
Sing! (Famous 30s)

Oldenburg, Claes. Injun: A
Happening (Lahr)

O'Neill, Eugene. Emperor
Jones (Halline); The Ice-
man Cometh; The Later
Plays: Ah, Wilderness;
Hughie; A Moon for the
Misbegotten; A Touch of the
Poet (See also Gassner 5th);
Long Day's Journey Into
Night; Three Plays: Desire
Under the Elms; Mourning
Becomes Electra; Strange
Interlude

Orwell, George. Animal Farm;
1984

Owens, Rochelle. Futz (Hoffman)

Paton, Alan. Cry, the Beloved
Country

Patrick, John. Hasty Heart
(Gassner 2nd) The Home-
coming; No Man's Land;
Old Times; Two Plays--
The Caretaker & The Dumb
Waiter

Pirandello, Luigi. Six Characters in Search of an
Author (Kernan)

Porter, Katherine Anne. Pale
Horse, Pale Rider (Flower)

Potok, Chaim. In the Beginning;

My Name Is Asher Lev

Pym, Barbara. Quartet in Autumn

Rabe, David. Basic Training of Pavlo Hummel & Sticks and Bones

Rand, Ayn. Virtue of Selfishness

Rhys, Jean. Sleep It Off, Lady

Rice, Elmer. Dream Girl (Gassner 2nd)

Russell, Bertrand. Power

Saroyan, William. Cave Dwellers (Gassner 5th); Time of Your Life (Famous 30s & Gassner 2nd)

Sartre, Jean-Paul. No Exit and Three Other Plays: Dirty Hands; Flies; Respectful Prostitute

Shaffer, Peter. Equus

Shange, Ntozake. For Colored Girls....

Shaw, George Bernard. Arms and the Man (Kernan); Bernard Shaw's Plays: Heartbreak House; Major Barbara; Saint Joan; Too Good to Be True; Man and Superman (contains Don Juan in Hell); Plays Unpleasant: Philanderer; Mrs. Warren's Profession; Widowers' Houses

Sheehy, Gail. Passages

Shepard, Sam. Operation Sidewinder (Lahr); Angel City & Curse of the Starving Class

Sherwood, Robert E. Abe Lincoln in Illinois (Gassner 2nd); Idiot's Delight (Famous 30s)

Singer, Isaac B. Enemies; Shosha; Spinoza of Market Street

Skinner, B.F. Beyond Freedom and Dignity

Sontag, Susan. Illness as Metaphor

Sophocles. Oedipus Cycle of Sophocles: Antigone; Oedipus at Colonus; Oedipus Rex

Steinbeck, John. Of Mice and Men (Famous 30s)

Stitt, Milan. The Runner Stumbles

Stoppard, Tom. Travesties

Storey, David. The Changing Room (including): Home; The Contractor

Strindberg, August. Fathers (Kernan); Ghost Sonata (Kernan)

Szilard, Leo. Voice of the Dolphins

Terkel, Studs. Working

Theroux, Paul. Family Arsenal

Thomas, Lewis. Lives of a Cell

Thurber, James. The Male Animal (Gassner 2nd)

Toffler, Alvin. Future Shock

Tolstoy, Leo. Great Short Works of Leo Tolstoy (includes): The Death of Ivan Ilych; The Kreutzer Sonata

Tyler, Anne. Earthly Possessions

van Druten, John. I Remember Mama (Gassner 2nd); Voice of the Turtle (Gassner 2nd)

van Itallie, Jean. The Serpent (Lahr)

Vidal, Gore. The Best Man (Gassner 5th)

Vonnegut, Kurt, Jr. Slaughterhouse Five

Ward, Douglas Turner. Happy Ending (Couch); Day of Absence (Couch)

Warren, Robert Penn. All the King's Men

Weiss, Peter. Marat/Sade

West, Jessamyn. The Woman Said Yes

Wharton, Edith. Bunner Sisters (Flower)

Wilder, Thornton. The Skin of Our Teeth (Famous 40s)

Williams, Heathcote. AC/DC (Lahr)

Williams, Tennessee. Glass Menagerie (Halline & Gassner 2nd); Night of the Iguana (Gassner 5th); Orpheus Descending (Gassner 5th); A Streetcar Named Desire

Wilson, Lanford. Hot L Baltimore; Lemon Sky

Wishengrad, Morton. The Rope Dancers (Gassner 5th)

Woolf, Virginia. Mrs. Dalloway;

A Room of One's Own

Zindel, Paul. The Effect of Gamma Rays on Man-in-the-Moon Marigolds

B ★ SOME FILMS FOR DISCUSSION

Ain't Nobody's Business 52 min. Mountain Moving Pictures Co. 1977
    An examination of female prostitution, including interviews
    with prostitutes and others.

Appalachia: Rich Land, Poor People 59 min. Indiana Univ. 1969
    Study of Appalachian poverty. Interviews with local family,
    mine owners, and others.

Banks and the Poor 58 min. Indiana University 1970
    Probes banking industry and its exploitation of the poor.
    Variety of viewpoints.

Before the Mountain Was Moved 59 min. CRM/McGraw-Hill 1968
    Efforts of West Virginia residents to have law passed controll-
    ing strip mining.

The Black Cop 15 min. Indiana University 1969
    Explores attitudes of Blacks toward policemen, and attitudes
    of Black policemen.

Bottle Babies 26 min. Tricontinental Film Center 1975
    Multinational food corporations and world hunger are linked
    in this documentary of the causes and effects of Third World
    mothers feeding their infants powdered milk.

Bulldozed America 25 min. Carousel 1965
    Plea for conservation of America before it is despoiled by
    mining, lumber and real estate interests.

Controlling Interest 45 min. California Newsreel 1978
    Deals primarily with the social and economic impact of the
    policies of multinational corporations on Third World nations
    and with the displacement of American workers when the
    multinationals move their plants to more profitable locales.

The Cost of Cotton 30 min. Unifilm
    Explores the effects of the international demand for cotton
    on a developing nation (Guatemala), and the grave health and
    environmental problems that have resulted because of the
    large amounts of pesticides used by the cotton industry.

Eye of the Storm 25 min. ABC News 1970
> Third grade teacher tries to help children understand preju-
> dice. There were strong community reactions to this
> teacher's methods.

The Hand 19 min. CRM/McGraw-Hill 1965
> Animated allegory of totalitarianism.

Heart of Loisaida 30 min. Unifilm 1979 (Spanish dialog with
English subtitles)
> Depicts the efforts of the Latino residents of New York's
> Lower East Side who have taken over their own buildings
> after they were abandoned by their landlords and how they
> are renovating them.

How Yukong Moved the Mountains: The Fishing Village 102 min.
Cinema Perspectives 1977
> One film in a series of 12 documentaries on life in China
> today.

I Am Somebody 28 min. CRM/McGraw-Hill 1970
> Record of strike of hospital employees in South Carolina.
> Most of the strikers were black women.

It Happens to Us 30 min. New Day Films 1972
> Women speak about abortion experiences. Medical and
> moral problems.

Last Grave at Dimbaza 55 min. Unifilm 1975
> A powerful film on South Africa's controversial policy of
> apartheid. Photographed clandestinely and smuggled out of
> the country.

Nell and Fred 28 min. CRM/McGraw-Hill 1972
> Nell, over 80 and Fred, over 90 must choose between caring
> for themselves or moving into old people's home.

Of Broccoli & Pelicans & Celery & Seals 29 min. Indiana University 1969
> Report on the harmful effects of pesticides.

Paul Robeson: Tribute to an Artist 29 min. Janus Films 1979
> Portrait of this controversial genius who was a Shakespearean
> actor, singer, sports figure, and champion of human rights.

A Place to Live 24 min. Lumen-Bel 1978
> Report on the building of energy-efficient homes in Maine
> from local materials, using innovative techniques.

Rana 18 min. Wombat 1977
> A young Moslem college student in India describes her home
> life and traditional customs.

Shepherd of the Nightflock   59 min.   Museum of Modern Art Dept.
of Film   1978
> Profile of a Lutheran minister who serves needs of the New
> York City jazz community.

This Child Is Rated X   53 min.   Films Inc.   1971
> Treatment of child criminals.

Tokyo: 51st Volcano   52 min.   Time-Life Films   1972
> Problems of pollution, over-population and consumerism.

Toys   7 min.   CRM/McGraw-Hill   1967
> Children's toys come alive and fight a war.   Intercut of
> faces of children.

Women Who Have Had Abortions   29 min.   Martha Stuart   1972
> American women of all classes discuss their abortion ex-
> periences.

C ★ SAMPLE FILM PROGRAMS

THE FAMILY (Changing Relationships)

Chris and Bernie color 25 min.
The Focuses on the special needs and problems of single parents.
1975. New Day Films.

Window Water Baby Moving color (silent) 11 min.
The thoughts and feelings of the filmmaker are dramatically
demonstrated during the last portions of his wife's pregnancy
with their first child. 1959. Stan Brakhage.

Not Together Now color 25 min.
A documentary about a married couple that is separated.
They speak with candor about why they married and events
leading to their separation, their careers, their feelings about
their children, and hopes for the future. 1974. Polymorph.

GROWING OLDER

Nell and Fred 28 min.
Nell, over eighty, and Fred in his nineties, must choose
between doing for themselves as best they can, or moving
into an old people's home. 1972. CRM/McGraw-Hill.

Love It Like a Fool color 28 min.
Folk singer Malvina Reynolds at age 76 as she composes,
records an album, performs in concert and rehearses with
young musicians. She gives her views on aging and dying,
romance and social changes. 1977. Red Hen Films.

Bubby 5 min.
A teenage filmmaker's view of his grandmother. 1968.
Young Filmmaker's Foundation.

DANCE

Adagio 14m.
In a Paris rehearsal studio, dancers of the Paris Opera
Ballet rehearse an adagio. Made in tribute to Heine whose
short story inspired the ballet "Giselle." 1965. Radim.

Watching Ballet   35m.
New York City Ballet dancers Jacques d'Amboise and Allegra Kent discuss and demonstrate ballet style and techniques using excerpts from the ballets of Balanchine. 1964. Association-Sterling.

Circles II   color   14m.
Dancers perform with circle sculptures. The patterns are manipulated videographically to form new colors and kaleidoscopic designs in this multi-media experience. Sculpture and concept by Doris Chase; choreography by Mary Staton. 1972. Doris Chase.

FOOD

Look Before You Eat   color   22m.
Critical examination of our eating habits and their relation to our health. Sugar, salt and fat in our diet is looked at in detail. Nutritionists comment on the relation of diet to several major diseases, and how food industry promotion affects our food choices. 1977. Churchill Films.

Crock of Gold   color/b&w   19m.
Recreates, often in humorous fashion, the way the McDonald's hamburger chain may have begun. 1977. Dennis Lanson.

For Tomorrow We Shall Diet   color   24m.
A young woman decides to lose 20 pounds and discovers the need for proper nutrition and exercise, the dangers of fad diets, and the relation of calories to energy output. 1977. Churchill Films.

WOMEN

Diane   color   30 minutes
"Semi-documentary" featuring a young would-be actress from South Dakota who tries to find success in New York and battles loneliness, frustration, exploitation and despair. 1969. Mary Feldhaus-Weber.

Domestic Tranquility   7 minutes
A young woman, bound by her children and a demanding husband, reflects on what life might have been like had she the opportunity to develop her individual talents. 1973. Women Make Movies.

Nobody's Victim   color   20 minutes
A film on self-defense for women which outlines lifesaving precautions and demonstrates simple defense methods that anyone can use to fend off attackers. 1972. Ramsgate Films.

NATURE STUDIES

Birth of the Red Kangaroo   color   21 minutes
Fascinating description of the reproductive process and birth
of this Australian marsupial.   1968.   International Film
Bureau.

Way of a Trout   color   25 minutes
Exceptional underwater and nature photography depicts the
life cycle of a trout.   1970.   James Wilkie.

White Throat   color   10 minutes
The nature of the forest is explored in this journey in the
wake of the whitethroated sparrow.   1965.   AV Explorations.

POTPOURRI

Solo   color   15 minutes
Photographed on twenty-two different climbs, located across
the North American continent, climber Mike Hoover captures
the beauty, danger, and challenge of this very special sport.
1971.   Pyramid.

Frank Film   color   9 minutes
Superbly animated autobiography of the filmmaker, Frank
Mouris.   An Oscar winner.   1973.   Pyramid.

Popcorn Lady   color   11 minutes
A gentle lady's popcorn business started at the turn of the
century is threatened by modern business enterprises.   1973.
Warren Schloat.

It Ain't City Music   color   14 minutes
A light-hearted celebration of grassroots America and its
music.   1973.   Tom Davenport Films.

Invasion of the Teacher Creatures   6 minutes
Designed as a humorous "trailer," young filmmaker, Henry
Parke, gives us glimpses of ghoulish teachers rampaging
through a school.   1974.   Youth Film Distribution Center.

ADULTS/TEENAGERS

THE FAR NORTH

Eskimo Artist Kenojuak   color   20 minutes
A semi-impressionistic study of Eskimo wife and mother,
Kenojuak, her ice bound country, and the art she creates to
celebrate it.   National Film Board of Canada.   1964.   CRM/
McGraw-Hill.

Land of the Long Day   38 minutes
 The life of an Eskimo family living near Baffin Bay.   Na-
 tional Film Board of Canada.   1952.   International Film
 Bureau.

THE RACES

Vive le Tour   color.   19m.
 A stirring documentary by Louis Malle of the 1962 Tour de
 France Bicycle Race.   New Yorker.

Spider and the Frenchman   color   22 minutes
 Downhill ski racing competition in various locales around the
 U.S.   1974.   Film Forum.

Lizzies of the Field   silent   12 minutes
 A Mack Sennett comedy ending with a free-for-all road race.
 1924.   Blackhawk.

MOVIE CLASSICS

Leave 'Em Laughing   silent   20 minutes
 A Laurel and Hardy classic, in which Laurel develops a
 toothache that results in a wild bout with the dentist and
 laughing gas.   1927.   Blackhawk.

Musketeers of Pig Alley   silent   13 minutes
 Lillian Gish plays her first feature role in this story of the
 slums and rival gangs.   1912.   Museum of Modern Art Film
 Department.

Cops   silent   15 minutes
 Buster Keaton tangles with the police department, and the
 resulting riot is the grandest chase scene ever filmed.
 1922.   Blackhawk.

Rudolph Valentino--Idol of the Jazz Age   10 minutes
 The life of this famous star with scenes from his most
 famous films.   Creative Film Society.

SILENT HORRORS

Dr. Jekyll and Mr. Hyde   silent   45 minutes
 John Barrymore plays the split personality in this first
 great American horror film, made in 1920.   Blackhawk.

The Phantom of the Opera   silent   25 minutes
 "Great Moments" from this famous film, starring Lon
 Chaney as the phantom who unleashes a reign of terror.
 Blackhawk.

TEENAGERS

SPORTS

Fabulous Harlem Globetrotters 9m.
A humorous and fast-paced demonstration of the dexterity of
this famous basketball team. Blackhawk.

Willis Reed: Center Play (Pts. I & II) color. 10m.
Willis Reed demonstrates some of the basketball techniques
that have made him famous. Schloat Productions.

Great Moments in Sports 30m.
Traces the career highlights of many sports professionals.
Among them are Jack Johnson, Joe Louis, Mildred "Babe"
Didrikson, Silky Sullivan, Jesse Owens, Joe Namath and
Olga Korbut. 1976. Time-Life Multimedia.

YOUNG LOVE

I'm a Fool 38m.
Ron Howard plays a young man who feels he has to put on
an act to get along with women. Will his deception cause
him to lose the girl he loves? 1976. Coronet Films.

Make-Believe Marriage color 33m.
Will they stay married or get divorced? A documentary
drama depicting a group of high school students who pair
off for practice marriages, and have to contend with the
practicalities--budgets, employment, and parenthood. 1978.
LCA.

SPACE

La Jetée 27m.
A gripping science-fiction fantasy. 1963. Pyramid.

Hardware Wars color 13m.
A very funny take-off on Star Wars. Uses live action and
special effects as household appliances battle. 1978. Pyramid.

K-9000: A Space Oddity color 11m.
A dog transported through space in a spoof on 2001: A
Space Odyssey. 1971? Creative Film Society.

FILMMAKING

Bambi Meets Godzilla 2m.
Animated spoof on film credits. 1969. Pyramid.

The Stuntman   color   10m.
   A day in the life of a stuntman.   He shows how he performs
   his stunts, and tells why he works in films.   1973.   Pyramid.

Special Effects   color   13m.
   How such effects as rain, fog, fire, snow, bullets and
   flaming arrows are created for films.   Humorous narration
   by Jonathan Winters.   1973.   Pyramid.

Super Bug   color 6m.
   A tiny Volkswagon pits its cleverness, size and flexibility against
   a mob of monster cars in this classic chase film.   Demonstrates
   special effects.   1972.   Youth Film Distribution Center.

Godfather Comes to Sixth Street   25m.
   Behind-the-scenes look at the filming of The Godfather.
   Demonstrates on-location filming techniques.   1975.   Mark
   Kitchell.

PRE-SCHOOL CHILDREN
(three 4-film programs)

The Smallest Elephant in the World   color   6 minutes
   The adventures of an elephant the size of a house cat and
   his attempt to find a home.   Based on the book by Alvin
   Tresselt.   1964.   Sterling.

Gilberto and the Wind   color   6 minutes
   Harry Belafonte reads from Marie Hall Ets' book in a warm
   and pleasant manner with pictures from the story interwoven
   into the visuals.   1967.   CRM/McGraw-Hill.

I Know an Old Lady Who Swallowed a Fly   color   6 minutes
   Burl Ives sings this animated version of the popular folk
   song.   1964.   International Film Bureau.

Curious George Rides a Bike   color   10 minutes
   Led by his curiosity, a small monkey gets into trouble but
   emerges triumphant.   1958.   Weston Woods.

Patrick   color   7 minutes
   A man buys an old violin and discovers that his music
   transforms everything it reaches; fish fly through the air,
   become multicolored; cows dance, their black spots become
   colored stars.   1973.   Weston Woods.

Dick Whittington and His Cat   color   15 minutes
   An animated puppet film about Dick Whittington and the
   fortune that he receives as a result of his kindness to a
   cat.   1965.   Sterling.

Fiddle-de-dee   color   4 minutes
>Gay color combinations form an abstract design to the
Mocking Bird.   1947.   International Film Bureau.

Ashlad and His Good Helpers   color   15 minutes
>Puppet animation of Norwegian folk tale.   No date.   Modern
Learning Aids.

Madeline   color   8 minutes
>The popular picture book by Ludwig Bemelmans about Made-
line and her appendectomy is animated for the screen.   1955.
Columbia.

Cirkus, The Merry Circus   color   10 minutes
>An interpretation of circus acts animated by Jiri Trnka.
1951.   CRM/McGraw-Hill.

Hen-Hop   color   4 minutes
>Animated film by Norman McLaren in which a hen and an
egg dance to barn-dance music.   1943.   International Film
Bureau.

Morning Zoo   color   10 minutes
>A young woman zoo keeper talks about her work and shows
us the animals she looks after.   1972.   Trend Films.

SCHOOL-AGE CHILDREN

HALLOWEEN FILMS

Dragon Stew   color   14 minutes
>A con man cook whose speciality is dragon stew is put on
the spot when a dragon is captured.   A delightful cartoon
for middle to older children.   BFA.

The Seventh Master of the House   color   13 minutes
>Puppet animation of Norwegian folk tale in which a lone
traveler deep in a forest asks for shelter from a strange
family of men who live there.   U.S. release 1969.   Modern
Learning Aids.

Dr. Jekyll and Mr. Hyde   silent   10 minutes
>This early silent version of the classic tale was made in
1911.   Blackhawk.

FEATURE STORY

Blind Bird   color   45 minutes
>A young Russian boy takes his blind pelican to an eye

specialist in Moscow who restores the bird's sight. 1963.
CRM/McGraw-Hill.

WINTER-CHRISTMAS STORIES

Snow (British Railways)   color   10 minutes
One of Lotte Reiniger's charming silhouette films based on
the Grimm fairy tale.   No date.   CRM/McGraw-Hill.

Ti-Jean Goes Lumbering   color   16 minutes
A little boy mysteriously appears on a white horse at a
lumber camp, performs remarkable feats and then rides
away.   1953.   International Film Bureau.

CHILDREN AND CITIES

Tadpole Tale   color   16 minutes
A warm tale about a boy who catches a tadpole in a pond
in New York's Central Park but finds he must let it go when
it becomes full-grown.   1967?   Universal Education.

My Own Yard to Play In   7 minutes
An unusual and moving document of children playing, singing
and talking among the tenements and cluttered vacant lots of
New York City.   1959.   CRM/McGraw-Hill.

The Red Balloon   color   34 minutes
The moving and beautifully photographed story of a young
boy in Paris who makes friends with a magic red balloon.
1956.   Audio/Brandon.

AFRICAN FOLK TALES

Anansi the Spider   color   10 minutes
An African folk tale from the Ashanti tribe about the origin
of the moon.   1969.   Texture.

Why the Sun and the Moon Live in the Sky   color   11 minutes
This Nigerian legend relates how the Sun and the Moon, who
used to live on land, were forced to move into the sky.
1970.   ACI.

The Magic Tree   color   10 minutes
Animated version of a tale from the Congo about an unloved
son who runs away and finds a magic tree whose leaves
become people.   1970.   Texture.

AT THE CIRCUS

Circus Town   color   48 minutes
Follows non-professional youngsters through training to the
final performance in a circus in Peru, Indiana.   Film, Inc.

NATURE AND MYTHOLOGY OF THE NORTH AMERICAN INDIAN

The Loon's Necklace   color   11 minutes
The Indian legend of how the loon, a water bird, obtained
his neckband of white feathers.   1948.   EBEC.

Navajo Rain Chant   color   2 minutes
Animation based on the designs of Navajo blankets which
shows how these patterns were inspired by natural phenomena.
1971.   Creative Film Society.

Paddle to the Sea   color   28 minutes
The adventures of a little wooden Indian in a canoe, carved
by a young boy in Northern Canada.   1966.   National Film
Board of Canada.

COMEDY AND SLAPSTICK

Apple Thieves   color   9 minutes
A very sophisticated but funny cops and robbers spoof acted
out by inanimate objects, animated.   Audio/Brandon.

One A. M.   14 minutes
A Charlie Chaplin classic.   1916.   Blackhawk.

The Ride   color   8 minutes
A chauffeur's dream about putting his employer on a runaway
toboggan comes true in part when he allows the car brakes
to slip.   A slapstick comedy.   1963.   CRM/McGraw-Hill.

When Knights Were Bold   color   20 minutes
The Magnificent 6-1/2 in a slapstick adventure full of
screaming women and pies in the face.   1972.   Sterling.

D ★ VIDEO PROGRAMS

DOCUMENTARIES

Vietnam: Picking Up the Pieces (Vietnamese aftermath) 60 mins.

Health Care: Your Money or Your Life 60 mins.

Cuba: The People 90 mins.

Third Avenue (lives of six people living on Third Avenue in New
York City) 60 mins.

Chinatown (in New York City) 60 mins.
Downtown Community Television Center
87 Lafayette St.
New York, N.Y. 10013

Police Tapes (a verité portrait of the work of New York City
Police) 85 mins.

Bad Boys (a three-part study of juvenile delinquency in high school,
in a minimum security center, and in a maximum security
center) 90 mins.
Video Verité
927 Madison Ave.
New York, NY 10021

You Do The Crime; You Do the Time (a two-part study of youth
gangs in the South Bronx, New York City) 93 mins.
Martine Barrat
The Chelsea Hotel
222 West 23 St.
New York, NY 10011

The Wheels on the Bus (portrait of a three-year-old child dying
of cancer) 60 mins.
Nan Jones
137 West 86th St.
New York, NY 10024

Family Planning Is No Private Matter (birth control in China)

315

30 mins.
Electronic Arts Intermix
84 Fifth Ave.
New York, NY 10011

Windcatchers (wind as alternative energy source) 30 mins.
Evelyn Messinger
Coriolis
519 Castro St.
San Francisco, CA 94114

VIDEO AS ART

Pictures of the Lost by Barbara Buckner 20 mins.
Barbara Buckner
344 East 9th St.
New York, NY 10003

Bubbling by Tomiyo Sasaki 20 mins.
Tomiyo Sasaki
118 Forsyth St.
New York, NY 10002

Interpolations by Kit Fitzgerald and John Sanborn 29 mins.
Fitzgerald/Sanborn Video
125 Cedar St.
New York, NY 10006

Windows by Gary Hill 8 mins.
Gary Hill
Stationhill Road
Barrytown, NY 12507

Search for Tomorrow 5 mins.
Shalom Gorewitz
310 West 85th St.
New York, NY 10024

Iris 5 mins.
Ernest Gusella
118 Forsyth St.
New York, NY 10002

E ★ FILM AND VIDEOTAPE SOURCES

Below are some of the major sources of free-loan films, filmstrips, slides, videotapes and recordings. One should also try some of the more general and more local sources that are mentioned in Chapter 2, "Film Showings." The three following companies are the major distributors:

Association-Films, Inc.
866 Third Avenue
New York, N.Y. 10022

> Their free catalog lists 16mm films, filmstrips, videocassettes, slides and recordings (there is also a section of rental films). Gives running times, color, a descriptive paragraph and terms of borrowing. Subject and title indexes. Subjects of films include Americana, conservation, science, sports, travel, and women's interests. Of interest to all ages. There are regional offices in various parts of the country.

Modern Talking Picture Service
5000 Park St. North
St. Petersburg, Fla.   33709

> The free catalogs list running times, color, give brief annotations and terms of borrowing. There are catalogs for adults and for schools covering many subjects. There are regional offices in many cities in the United States and some in Canada. These are 16mm sound films.

West Glen Films (A division of West Glen Communications, Inc.)
565 5th Avenue
New York, N.Y. 10017

> The free catalogs for high schools and for adult organizations list running times and color, give annotations and terms of borrowing. Includes sports, travel, health, economics, and films dealing with contemporary problems. Lists are shorter than the first two companies but many good films and film strips are available. They also have regular showings.

The following two books are guides to the sources of free films:

Educator's Guide to Free Films $12.75
Educators Progress Service, Inc.
Randolph, Wisc.   53956

>   This is a very useful guide for anyone running regular film
>   programs, and not having access to a large film library.   The
>   emphasis is on school age but some films would interest adults.
>   The entries indicate whether the film is 8 or 16mm, sound or
>   silent, title, running time, date of release, terms and condi-
>   tions of loan, booking time required, probable availability, and
>   names and addresses of sources.   There are indexes by title,
>   subject, source and availability.   Almost 5,000 titles are in-
>   cluded in the 1979 edition.   Publication is annual.   Films are
>   from government agencies at all levels, industry and many
>   other sources.   Subjects include arts and crafts, consumer
>   education, environmental education, history, science, music,
>   religion, and sports.

United States Government Films; A Catalogue of Motion Pictures
and Film Strips for Sale by the National Audiovisual Center
National Audiovisual Center
Washington, D.C.   20409

>   When one finds a title of interest listed in this book, it may be
>   borrowed--in many cases--free, directly from the agency that
>   owns it.   Updated periodically.

FILM DISTRIBUTORS

>   There are a vast number of film distributors.   The following
>   are those that we feel would be the most useful to libraries.   Al-
>   though some of them tend to specialize in a particular area (e.g.
>   New Day Films with its films on women's issues, International
>   Film Foundation with its documentaries on other countries, and Uni-
>   film with its films on the Third World and social commitments),
>   they all distribute films on a broad variety of subjects.   The only
>   exception is Weston Woods which deals only in children's films and
>   films having to do with work with children.   Those which also
>   distribute feature films are indicated by an asterisk.

*Audio/Brandon Films Inc.
  (see Macmillan Films Inc.)

Benchmark Films
145 Scarborough Rd.
Briarcliff Manor, NY 10510

Carousel Films
1501 Broadway
New York, NY 10036

Churchill Films
662 North Robertson Blvd.
Los Angeles, CA 90069

CRM/McGraw-Hill Films
110 Fifteenth Street
Del Mar, CA 92014

*Films Inc.
733 Green Bay Rd.
Wilmette, IL   60091

Icarus
200 Park Ave. South
New York, NY 10003

International Film Foundation
475 Fifth Ave., Rm. 916
New York, NY 10017

Killiam Shows, Inc.
6 E. 39th St.
New York, NY 10016

*Learning Corporation of America
1350 Ave. of the Americas
New York, NY 10019

*Macmillan Films Inc.
34 MacQuesten Pkwy. S.
Mt. Vernon, NY 10550
(Distributes foreign feature films
    under Audio/Brandon)

*The Museum of Modern Art
    Dept. of Film Circulating
    Programs
11 West 53 Street
New York, NY 10019

National Film Board of Canada
1251 Avenue of the Americas
16th Floor
New York, NY 10020
(Many of their films are now
    distributed by CRM/McGraw-
    Hill and Films Inc.)

New Day Films
P.O. Box 315
Franklin Lakes, NJ 07417

*New Yorker Films
16 West 61st Street
New York, NY 10023

*Paramount Communications
5451 Marathon Street
Hollywood, CA 90038

Phoenix Films
470 Park Avenue South
New York, NY 10016

Pyramid Films
P.O. Box 1048
Santa Monica, CA 90406

Texture Films
1600 Broadway
New York, NY 10019

Time-Life Films
1271 Avenue of the Americas
New York, NY 10020

Unifilm
419 Park Avenue South
New York, NY 10016

Weston Woods Studios
Weston, CT 06880

Wombat Productions
Little Lake, Glendale Rd.
P.O. Box 70
Ossining, NY 10562

Young Filmmakers Foundation,
    Inc.
4 Rivington Street
New York, NY 10002

VIDEOTAPE DISTRIBUTORS

Anna Canepa Video Distribution, Inc.
429 West Broadway
New York, N.Y. 10012
(Art)

Art Metropole
217 Richmond Street West
Toronto, Canada M5V 1W2
(Art)

Castelli-Sonnabend Tapes and
  Films, Inc.
420 West Broadway
New York, N.Y. 10012
(Arts)

Downtown Community Television
  Center
87 Lafayette St.
New York, N.Y. 10013
(Documentary)

Electronic Arts Intermix

84 Fifth Avenue
New York, N.Y. 10011
(Art, documentary)

PBS--Video
475 L'Enfant Plaza, S.W.
Washington, D.C. 20024
(Art, documentary)

Synapse
103 College Place
Syracuse, N.Y. 13210
(Art, documentary)

Sources of videotape distributors and their tapes:

The Video Log
Esselte Video, Inc.
Dept. 14
600 Madison Ave.
New York, N.Y. 10022

The Video Source Book
The Video Programs Index
The National Video Clearing-
  house Inc.
P.O. Box 3
Syosset, N.Y. 11791

F ★ SAMPLE FLYERS AND POSTERS

The following pages show various sample promotional materials developed by different libraries.

ANN McCAFFREY'S
DRAGON SERIES

DRAGONSINGER
DRAGONSONG

THE DRAGON RIDERS OF PERN:

VOL. 1 DRAGON FLIGHT
VOL. 2 DRAGON QUEST
VOL. 3 THE WHITE DRAGON

MAY 16, WEDNESDAY 7:00 p.m.
STORY HOUR ROOM

FANTASY AND SCIENCE FICTION
DISCUSSION GROUP
SPONSORED BY YOUNG ADULT DEPT.
SALT LAKE CITY PUBLIC LIBRARY

FILM

THE BEST YEARS OF OUR LIVES

THURSDAY, September 21, 8 p.m.

172 minutes

Winner of 7 Academy Awards
including Best Picture, Best
Actor (Frederic March) Best
Actor in a Supporting Role
(Harold Russell) and Best
Director (William Wyler).

The Best Years of Our Lives has
rightly been described by Variety
as "one of the best pictures of our
lives". Based on the novel, Glory
for Me, by Mac Kinlay Kantor, it tells
of an airforce captain, an army sergeant,
and a sailor, who return together to the
same hometown in middle America, and who
must face the rehabilitation and readaptation
to civilian life, and the resumption of
family life.

WANTAGH PUBLIC LIBRARY
3285 PARK AVENUE • WANTAGH, N.Y. 11793
516 CA 1-1200 • ALBERT MONHEIT, DIRECTOR

brown bag concerts

thursdays at noon
city library   plaza~east
209 east fifth so.
june 22 ~ august 31

This flyer was printed on a brown paper bag.

Fall Film Festival

Children 1st - 6th grade

A flyer from The Rockville Centre Public Library.

COOKING FOR SPECIAL DIETS

HYPERACTIVITY AND THE INFLUENCE OF DIET

WEDNESDAY, APRIL 4 AT 8 PM

...PROGRAM COORDINATED BY

ROCKLAND COMMUNITY ACTION COUNCIL

GARDENS FOR NUTRITION PROGRAM

IN THE ANNEX AT THE FINKELSTEIN MEMORIAL LIBRARY

19 S. MADISON · SPRING VALLEY · NY

© 1979 DONNY DONALD

3/79

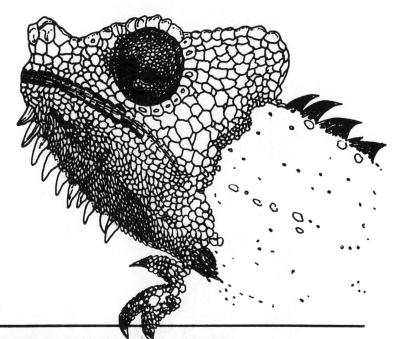

FANTASY AND SCIENCE FICTION
DISCUSSION GROUP   STORY HOUR ROOM

Aug. 15	Ben Bova	COLONY
Sept. 19	Piers Anthony	A SPELL FOR CHAMELEON
		THE SOURCE OF MAGIC
Oct. 17	free film	SECONDS
Nov. 21	Samuel R. Delany	BABEL-17
		NOVA

Sponsored by the YA Dept.   Meets each month on the
third Wednesday at 7:00 p.m.

A flyer from the Salt Lake City
Public Library

AVIATION OPEN HOUSE

MAY 23 8:00PM

SLIDE TALK
MODEL ANTIQUE AIRCRAFT
FLIGHT SIMULATOR

Sponsored by
99'S OF LONG ISLAND
AVIATION COUNCIL OF L.I.
L.I. EARLY FLYERS
CIVIL AIR PATROL
ANTIQUE FLYERS   and
BOCES

FREEPORT MEMORIAL LIBRARY
So. Ocean Ave. & Merrick Rd., Freeport, N.Y.
YOUNG ADULT SERVICES   Tel. 379-3274

THUMBNAIL HISTORY OF THE DEAF ACTION WEEK

1974 –Dedication of Teletypewriter/Phone Service
–Initiation of Deaf Awareness Week
–Bringing deaf awareness to the library and
 library awareness to the deaf community

1975 –Bicentennial year
–Recognizing contributions of deaf people to
 American history
–First workshop for local libraries at the
 District of Columbia Public Library

1976 –Programs held by deaf people for the first
 time at the Library on the beauty of sign
 language; and, of insights of deaf people
 as citizens
–Cooperative action of local library systems
 for serving the Washington area deaf population considered for the first time

1977 –"Awareness" now replaced by "Action"
–Seven deaf local leaders spoke about their
 favorite deaf heroes at different library
 areas on the same evening
–Director of D.C. Public Library spoke about
 the public library in general for the deaf
 community

1978 –American Sign Language and its linguistic
(current) heritage awareness
–Motivating Black pride in deaf Black Americans
–Full community involvement

The back and front of a flyer (unfolded).

DEAF ACTION WEEK

DEAF ACTION WEEK

DEAF ACTION WEEK

DEAF PRIDE
DEAF CULTURE
DEAF HERITAGE

DECEMBER 4-9, 1978

DISTRICT OF COLUMBIA PUBLIC LIBRARY

FOOD FOR THOUGHT

FRIDAY
OCT. 6
12:00 noon

**BRING YOUR LUNCH
DESSERT 'N COFFEE
SERVED**

BOOK DISCUSSION

THINGS
FALL
APART

BY

CHINUA ACHEBE

FREEPORT MEMORIAL LIBRARY
SOUTH OCEAN AVE. & MERRICK RD., FREEPORT, N.Y. TEL. 379-3274 ···

AMERICA, Where Are You Going ?

A Course for Senior Citizens

presented by
THE NEW YORK PUBLIC LIBRARY
and
INSTITUTE OF STUDY FOR OLDER ADULTS

A project in continuing education as
a life-long process, highlighting the
sense of potential growth throughout
life.

At
VAN NEST BRANCH
2147 Barnes Avenue
829-5864

ADMISSION FREE

This course is presented in cooperation with BRONX
COMMUNITY COLLEGE, CENTER FOR AGING and NEW YORK
CITY COMMUNITY COLLEGE, DIVISION OF CONTINUING
EDUCATION.

★ BIBLIOGRAPHY

GENERAL

Audiovisual Market Place: A Multimedia Guide. Bowker. Annual.
    An annual publication that covers AV Software and Hardware
    (including producers, distributors, periodicals, etc.).

Boyle, Deirdre, and Stephen Calvert. Children's Media Market
    Place. Gaylord Professional Publications (Neal-Schuman Pub.),
    1978.
    Directory of sources locating children's materials including
    animated films.

Duran, Daniel F. Latino Materials: A Multimedia Guide for Chil-
    dren and Young Adults. Neal-Schuman and ABC-Clio, 1979.
    An annotated list of 400 books and 75 films suitable for
    young persons that deal with Latinos in general, Mexican-
    Americans and Puerto Ricans. Suggestions of possible uses
    for the material.

Edwards, Margaret A. The Fair Garden and the Swarm of Beasts,
    rev. and expanded. Hawthorn Books, 1974.
    Excellent section on book talks to high school students--the
    objectives of giving book talks, how to prepare them, and
    techniques of delivery. Also includes section on how to lead a
    book discussion program for teenagers.

The Foundation Directory, 7th ed. Compiled by The Foundation
    Center, Marianna O. Lewis, ed. Published by The Foundation
    Center, New York, 1979. Distributed by Columbia University
    Press.
    Lists over three thousand foundations, arranged by state.
    Includes purposes, financial data, high and low grants, officers
    and trustees, and application procedures. Indices include:
    fields of interest, donors, trustees and administrators, list of
    foundations. Essential for successful grant-getting.

Foundation News. The Council on Foundations, 1828 L Street NW,
    Washington, DC 20036.
    Bi-monthly periodical that keeps information on grants up-

to-date.   Each issue contains a Grants Index of current grants
put out by The Foundation Center.   These are later compiled
in an annual volume by the Center.

Greene, Ellin and Madalynne Schoenfeld, comp. & ed.   A Multimedia
Approach to Children's Literature; A Selective List of Films,
Filmstrips, and Recordings Based on Children's Books, 2nd ed.
American Library Association, 1977.
In addition to the annotated lists, includes sources of other
materials for programmers, and a list of articles, books and
films of help to those doing programming.   Techniques are
presented and programs described.

Library Journal.   R. R. Bowker Company, 1180 Avenue of the
Americas, New York, NY 10036.
This periodical and School Library Journal do articles pertaining to programming.   The July 1972 issue has an article
on preparing and applying for a grant.

Moran, Irene, comp.   Prepare!   The Library Public Relations
Recipe Book, Public Relations Section, Library Administration
Division, A. L. A. 1978.
News releases, graphics, newsletters, TV and radio announce-
ments.

Schroeder, Don, and Gary Lare.   Audiovisual Equipment and Materials;
A Basic Repair and Maintenance Manual.   Scarecrow Press, 1979.
A simple, well-illustrated guide to AV equipment maintenance
and minor repairs that can be done with basic tools and little
experience.

Sigler, Ronald F.   "A Study in Censorship: The Los Angeles 19,"
Film Library Quarterly, Spring 1971.
A detailed description of what happened when the censor
came to a film program, and how the library handled the situation.

Top of the News, Children's Services Division and the Young Adult
Services Division of the American Library Association.   50 E.
Huron St. , Chicago IL 60611.
This periodical frequently has articles pertaining to pro-
gramming for children and teenagers in the public library.

VOYA (Voice of Youth Advocates), bi-monthly magazine published by
Dorothy Broderick and Mary K. Chelton, P. O. Box 6569, University of Alabama, AL   35486
Occasional articles on programming for teenagers.   The Feb.
1980 issue has an article by YA librarian Susan Rappaport on
a videotape workshop and a music workshop which she ran for
teenagers in The New York Public Library.

Wilson Library Bulletin.   H. W. Wilson Co. 950 University Ave. ,
Bronx, NY 10452.

This periodical includes articles on programming in the public library for various ages.

FILMS AND FILMSTRIPS

Booklist. American Library Association. 50 E. Huron St., Chicago IL 60611.
This bi-monthly periodical contains reviews of films, filmstrips, and video for all ages.

Film Library Quarterly. Film Library Information Council, Box 348, Radio City Station, New York, NY 10019.
Contains articles, news and reviews of interest to programmers. The Vol. 10 # 3 & 4 1977 issue is devoted primarily to articles on films and video for young adults including an annotated list of short films used with book talks in schools by YA librarians at Alameda (CA) County Library.

Film News. Film News Co., 250 W. 57th Street, Suite 1527, New York, NY 10019.
A quarterly which has articles on and reviews of nontheatrical films and filmstrips and AV equipment. Listing of programs currently going on in libraries, museums and film societies.

Films: A Catalog of the Film Collection of The New York Public Library. May be purchased by mail prepaid from the Office of Branch Libraries, 8 East 40th Street, New York, NY 10016. New edition in process.
An annotated list of hundreds of films for adults, teenagers, and children. Gives producer, distributor, running time and color; subject index and index to directors.

Films for Children: A Selected List. Prepared by the New York Library Association, Children's and Young Adult Services Section, 4th ed., 1977.
Annotated list, includes running time, distributor, date, price and ages appropriate for. Sample film program using different visual techniques, sample multimedia program for primary children and for older children (ages 9-12) and list of films from books.

Friedlander, Madeline S. Leading Film Discussions: A Guide to Using Films for Discussion, Training Leaders, Planning Effective Programs. League of Women Voters of the City of New York (817 Broadway, N.Y., NY 10003), 1972.
A list of free, rental and purchase sources; notes on how to preview, how to conduct a discussion, training discussion leaders, planning a program; and an annotated list of discussion films.

Gaffney, Maureen and Gerry Bond Laybourne. What to Do When
    the Lights Go On. Oryx Press, 1980.
        A guidebook for film programming for children featuring
    "recipes" for specific activities (painting on stone, in sand and
    on walls, mask making, starring in one's own radio show and
    others) designed to follow film showings and inspired by them.
    Includes an annotated bibliography of over 300 short films.

In Focus: A Guide to Using Films. Cine Information, P.O. Box
    449, Planetarium Station, N.Y., NY 10024.
        How to select, promote and screen films in a non-commercial
    setting. Choosing topics and speakers, examples of press re-
    leases, budgets and publicity, diagrams and illustrations for
    technical trouble shooting, effective after film discussions.

Limbacher, James L., comp. and ed. Feature Films on 8mm,
    16mm and Videotape, 6th ed., Bowker, 1979.
        A directory of feature films available for rental, sale and
    lease in the United States and Canada.

Parlato, Salvatore J. Films-Too-Good for Words: A Directory of
    Nonnarrated 16mm Films. Bowker, 1973.
        Annotated list of 16mm nonverbal films, many of which are
    appropriate for deaf audiences.

Previews: Audiovisual News & Reviews. Phyllis Levy Mandell,
    ed., Bowker.
        Reviews videocassettes, 16mm films, filmstrips, slides and
    kits. Describes and evaluates all kinds of equipment, including
    projectors, microphones, screens, splicers and headphones.
    The March 1980 issue contains an annotated list of best film-
    strips, slides, and kits of the year.

Rehrauer, George. The Short Film: An Evaluative Selection of
    500 Films. Macmillan Information, 1975.
        Covers all subject areas from 1930's to present. Suggested
    audience and area of use.

Semkow, Jules. "Film Programs for Senior Citizens," The Book-
    list, May 15, 1976, pp. 345-48.
        Kinds of films senior citizens enjoy, pointers on how to make
    the program successful, and an annotated list of suggested
    titles.

Sightlines (a quarterly). Educational Film Library Association, 43
    W. 61 Street, New York, NY 10023.
        Annotated lists of films and articles of interest to programmers.
    Focus on nontheatrical films. Reviews.

Top of the News. Children's Services Division and the Young Adult
    Services Division of the American Library Association.
        Occasional articles on films for children and young adults

and filmmaking by both. Also prints annually ALA's Notable
Children's Films, Notable Children's Filmstrips, and Selected
Films for Young Adults.

VOYA (Voice of Youth Advocates), bi-monthly magazine published by
Dorothy M. Broderick and Mary K. Chelton, P.O. Box 6569,
University of Alabama, AL 35486
Each issue contains reviews of films, filmstrips, and slides
with the teenage audience in mind.

Wilson Library Bulletin (monthly), H.W. Wilson Co.
Each issue contains reviews of 16mm films and video on a
particular subject. The Jan. 1980 issue highlights films on the
treatment of mental illness.

Young Viewers (quarterly), Media Center for Children, Inc., 3 West
29 Street, New York, NY 10001.
Quarterly magazine devoted to reviewing and reporting on
children's films and video, with ideas on how to use them in
libraries, schools and museums. Gives reactions of children
to some of the films and video.

SUGGESTED BOOKS AND FILMS FOR USE WITH RETARDED TEENAGERS*

Some of the following books are not that easy to read, but
they have lots of photographs or illustrations and deal with subjects
of great interest to teenagers and therefore can be introduced by
the librarian in programs.

YOUNG ADULT BOOKS

Blitz, Marcia. Donald Duck. Harmony, 1979.
From bit parts to superstar--a fun history.

Cameron, Betsy. Lisanne, a young model. Potter, 1979.
A lavishly photographed book about the life of a 14-year-old
model.

Charlip, Remy. Arm in arm. Parents, 1969.
Word games and endless tales.

Cole, William, editor. A book of love poems. Viking, 1965.
Both funny and romantic.

Gruber, Terry Deroy. Working cats. Lippincott, 1979.
Photos of them on the job.

*Compiled by Rhonna Goodman, YA Specialist, The New York Public
Library.

Hogarth, Peter, and Val Clery. Dragons. Viking, 1979.
   Beautifully illustrated (although difficult to read) book of
   dragons from Tramet to the Loch Ness Monster.

Jackson, Reggie. Reggie Jackson's Scrapbook. Dutton, 1978.
   His life in pictures.

Johnson, Eric W. Love and sex in plain language. Lippincott, 1977.
   A clear, easy-to-read, responsible introduction.

Lee, Stan, and John Buscema. How to draw comics the Marvel
   way. Simon and Schuster, 1978.
   Using the Hulk and the Thing as examples.

Lustgarten, Karen. The complete guide to disco dancing. Warner,
   1978.
   Easy step-by-step instruction.

Mendelson, Lee, and Charles Schulz. Happy Birthday, Charlie
   Brown. Random, 1979.
   Celebrating 30 years of Peanuts.

Morrison, Lillian, ed. Best wishes, Amen. Crowell, 1974.
   Autograph verses, with some in Spanish.

Morrison, Lillian, ed. Touch blue. Crowell, 1958.
   Signs and spells, love charms and chants.

Murphy, Jim. Weird and wacky inventions. Crown, 1978.
   Simple, clear explanations and illustrations with a non-
   challenging but fun quiz.

Nilsson, Lennart and others. A child is born. Delacorte, 1977.
   A photo essay on the human embryo.

Schwartz, Alvin, editor. Cross your fingers, spit in your hat.
   Lippincott, 1974.
   Superstitions to laugh and shudder at.

Simon, Hilda. Easy identification guide to North American snakes.
   Dodd, 1979.

CHILDREN'S PICTURE BOOKS

Aguirre, Carlos Antonio Llerena. Sticks, Stones. Holt, Rinehart
   & Winston, 1977.
Asbjornsen, Peter Christen and J. E. Moe. Three billy goats
   gruff. Harcourt, 1957.
Ets, Marie Hall. Little old automobile. Viking, 1948.
Gag, Wanda. Millions of cats. Coward, 1977.
Galdone, Paul, illus. The gingerbread boy. Seabury, 1975.
Galdone, Paul, illus. The monkey and the crocodile. Seabury,
   1969.

Galdone, Paul, illus. The three wishes. McGraw, 1961.
Hoban, Russell. Bread and Jam for Frances. Illustrated by Lillian
    Hoban. Harper & Row, 1964.
Hogrogian, Nonny. One fine day. Macmillan, 1971.
Marshall, James. George and Martha. Houghton Mifflin, 1972.
Mosel, Arlene. The funny little woman. Illustrated by Blair Lent.
    Dutton, 1972.
Munari, Bruno. The elephant's wish. World, 1959.
Rey, H. A. Curious George. Houghton Mifflin, 1941; pap. 1973.
Slobodkina, Esphyr. Caps for sale. Addison-Wesley, 1947.
Tolstoy, Alexei. The great big enormous turnip. Watts, 1969.
Yashima, Taro. Crow boy. Viking, 1955.
Zion, Gene. Harry the dirty dog. Harper & Row, 1956; rpt.
    1976.

SONG PICTURE BOOKS

Quackenbush, Robert M. She'll be coming 'round the mountain.
    Lippincott, 1973.
Quackenbush, Robert M. Skip to my lou. Lippincott, 1975.

PARTICIPATORY STORIES TO TELL ALOUD

"The bed" in Tiger and the Rabbit by Pura Belpré. Lippincott, 1965.
"Did you feed my cow" in Did you feed my cow? compiled by
    Margaret Taylor.
"The king with a terrible temper" from With a deep sea smile by
    Virginia Tashjian. Little, 1974.
"The Snooks family" in Juba this and Juba that by Virginia A. Tash-
    jian. Little, 1969.

FILMS

Anansi the spider. Texture, color, 10 minutes, 16mm
A chairy tale. International, b&w, 10 minutes, 16mm
The concert. Pyramid, color, 12 minutes, 16mm
Dance squared. National Film Board of Canada, 4 minutes, 16mm
The foolish frog. Weston Woods, color, 8 minutes, 16mm
Georgie. Weston Woods, color, 6 minutes, 16mm
I know an old lady who swallowed a fly. International, color, 6
    minutes, 16mm
Kick me. Little Red Schoolhouse, color, 8 minutes, 16mm
Legend of John Henry. Pyramid, color, 11 minutes, 16mm
Mr. Frog went a courtin'. Films, Inc., color, 5 minutes, 16mm
People soup. Learning Corporation, color, 13 minutes, 16mm
Strega Nonna. Weston Woods, color, 9 minutes, 16mm

PUPPET SHOWS

Batchelder, Marjorie. The Puppet Theatre Handbook: A Complete Guide for the Puppeteer. Harper, 1947.
How to make all kinds of puppets. Design and construction of costumes, stages, scenery and lighting. Choosing and writing plays. Producing the show.

_____. Puppets and Plays: A Creative Approach. Harper, 1956.
Puppetry as drama. Values and use of the puppet theatre. Making puppets. Creating the play. Staging and producing the show.

Boylan, Eleanor. How to Be a Puppeteer. McCall, 1970.
Writing the play, making scenery and stages and manipulating the puppets. Includes six plays from traditional stories.

Engler, Larry and Carol Fijan. Making Puppets Come Alive: A Method of Learning and Teaching Hand Puppetry. Taplinger, 1973.
Very clear and easy-to-understand guide.

Hutchings, Margaret. Making and Using Finger Puppets. Taplinger, 1973.
Instructions for making animal, Nativity, Eskimo, baby, clown, and many other finger puppets by sewing, knitting, and gluing.

Luckin, Joyce. Easy to Make Puppets. Plays, Inc., 1975.

Mahlmann, Lewis and David C. Jones. Puppet Plays for Young Players: Twelve Royalty-Free Plays for Hand Puppets, Rod Puppets or Marionettes. Plays, Inc., 1974.
Includes Wizard of Oz, Frog Prince, Snow White, and Pinocchio.

Renfro, Nancy. A Puppet Theater in Every Library. Renfro Studios, 1117 W. 9th St., Austin, TX, 1978.

Ross, Laura. Finger Puppets: Easy to Make, Fun to Use. Lothrop, 1971.
How to make many puppet characters from very simple materials. Includes rhymes, poems and stories to use with them for young children.

STORYTELLING

Baker, Augusta and Ellin Greene. Storytelling: Art and Technique. Bowker, 1977.

A basic book on the subject. Includes storytelling to children with special needs (mentally retarded, blind and partially sighted, emotionally disturbed, with impaired hearing, etc.), storytelling on radio and television, and sample multimedia programs.

Bauer, Caroline Feller. Handbook for Storytellers. American Library Association, 1977.
　　Includes many new media suggestions to enrich storytelling programs. Covers use of puppets, flannel boards, silhouettes. A guide for the amateur, the inexperienced and the skilled.

Cathon, Laura, Marion McC. Haushalter, and Virginia A. Russell, eds. Stories to Tell to Children: A Selected List. 8th ed., rev., University of Pittsburgh Press, 1974.
　　One of the standard lists, first published in 1916 by the Carnegie Library of Pittsburgh. Stories for preschool, ages six to ten, and for older children. A classified list that includes such subjects as Afro-American, American Indians, Ecology, Ethical and Social Values, Blindness, Jews, Action Stories and Tall Tales. Also includes a list of stories for holiday programs.

Compton's Encyclopedia. F. E. Compton Co., Division of Encyclopaedia Britannica, Inc.
　　The article on storytelling includes a section entitled "How to Tell a Story." There is also a list of "Folk Tales from Many Lands."

Iarusso, Marilyn Berg, comp. Stories: A List of Stories to Tell and to Read Aloud. The New York Public Library, 7th ed. 1977.
　　Also includes poetry for reading aloud and a sample of storytelling recordings.

Moore, Vardine, Pre-School Story Hour, 2d. ed., Scarecrow Press, 1972.
　　Ideas for story tellers, many ideas on planning programs and related activities. Includes lists of books and recordings.

Oldfield, Margaret J. Tell and Draw Stories. Creative Storytime Pr., Arts and Crafts Unlimited, Box 572, Minneapolis, Minn. 55440.

Pellowski, Anne. The World of Storytelling. Bowker, 1977.
　　An overview of storytelling and its techniques around the world.

Sawyer, Ruth. Way of the Storyteller, rev. ed. Penguin, 1977.

Shedlock, Marie L. The Art of the Story-teller, 3d ed. rev. (foreword by Anne Carroll Moore, with a new bibliography by Eulalie Steinmetz). Dover, 1951.
　　This title and the Sawyer are the classics in the field.

They tell how to select a story and give the tricks of the trade. Both books contain sample stories and lists.

Schimmel, Nancy. Just Enough to Make a Story. Sisters' Choice Press, Berkeley, 1978.
Philosophy, different ideas, excellent bibliography.

Walter, John and Sarah Long. "Story Hours for Children with Learning Disabilities," Top of the News, Summer 1979, pp. 385-88.
Mr. Walter, director of services to the blind and physically handicapped at the Public Library of Columbus and Franklin County, Ohio, and Ms. Long, director of the Fairfield County Public Library, Lancaster, Ohio describe the storytelling program they set up for learning-disabled children of first, second, and third grades and what they learned from it.

STORYTELLING--ON FILM AND VIDEO

Creative Storytelling Techniques: Mixing the Media with Dr. Caroline Feller Bauer. 30 min. color 3/4-inch "U" standard videocassette, or ½-inch VHS. PBS-Video, 475 L'Enfant Plaza, S.W., Washington, D.C. 20024.
Storyteller Dr. Bauer demonstrates the use of a variety of media--hand-craft items, puppets, toys, and other simple props --in storytelling and tells more than a dozen stories, each dramatized in a different way.

The Pleasure Is Mutual. 16mm. film 24 min. color William D. Stoneback. Six Cobble Hill Road, Westport, Conn. 06880.
Designed to help adults conduct effective picture book story hours. Tells how to present them and how to control the group. Used by libraries in training programs. Comes with a list of sample programs.

★ INDEX

Adult education (literacy) classes
83-84
Adult Great Books Discussion
Program 293-96
Adults, programs for see Pro-
grams; individual kinds of
programs
Advisory board for selection of
programs 223-26
Alexander Graham Bell Associa-
tion for the Deaf 179
Altoona (PA) Area Library 184,
185, 186
Anniversary celebrations 207-
08
Art discussion groups 22
Art Festival, Children's 145-
50, 205-06
Art show, senior citizens 172
The Arts see the individual
arts
Arts and crafts
Programs: adult and teen-
age 100-01, 203-04;
children's 145-53; on
television 203-04; the
mentally retarded 186-
88
Workshops 108-09, 112
See also Ethnic programs
Audience 2, 3
Comfort of xi, 249
Evaluation of program
250-53
Reaching 265

Backgammon tournament 206
Berkeley Heights (NJ) Public
Library 183, 184
Bethpage (NY) Public Library
99
Bilingual programs 15, 65

Blind, programs for the see
The Handicapped
Bloomfield (NJ) Public Library
160
Boise (ID) Public Library 205
Book discussion groups 7-8,
10, 12-18
Adult Great Books series
13, 14, 293-96
Children's 142-45
Criteria for reading selec-
tions 12-14
Films, use of with 11, 20
Lists of discussion books
293-302
Recordings, use of, with
21-22
Registration 11
Science Fiction 10-11
Significant Modern Books
(The New York Public Li-
brary) 14, 296-302
Spanish-speaking 15
Teenage 4, 5-6, 10-11, 15-
18; on radio 197-98
Book talks
Adult groups 83-84, 120,
174
High school classes 84-96,
191; books used 87-90,
92-93; scheduling 87;
tips for success 90-92
Prison inmates 191
Books, use of 97, 111
Arts and crafts programs
245-46
Book talks 83-96
Circulating at programs 250
Displays and exhibits con-
nected with programs 250
Drama programs 68
Film discussion groups 20
Music programs 71

343

See also Children's pro-
grams
Boston (MA) Public Library
111, 135
Boulder (CO) Public Library
41
Brooklyn (NY) Public Library
70, 107, 119, 156, 172,
174
Bus trips sponsored by library
208-09

Caldwell (ID) Public Library
141, 222
Captioned Films for the Deaf
Distribution Center 178
Carnegie Library of Pittsburgh
121
Chess tournaments 206-07
Chicago (IL) Public Library
118, 278
Children
Children's programs 118-67,
179-80, 187-88, 192,
244-45; art contests 205-
06; Art Festival 145-
53; arts and crafts 120,
145-53; book discussion
groups 142-45; cook-
ing 205; creative writ-
ing 147; dance 72; de-
signing games 119;
drama workshops 135-
42; dramatizing fairy
tales and picture books
139, 140, 141; Easter
120; ethnic 159-60;
film programs (sample)
311-14; film showings
150-59; filmmaking 158,
159; footsie contest 119,
165; games 169; garden-
ing 118; kite flying
118-19; multi-media pro-
grams 120, 159-65;
music 120; pet shows
119; photography 205;
puppet shows 133, 242;
puppet workshops 133-
35; radio 202-03; read-
ing clubs 121, 160;
storytelling 121-33, 202-

03, 244-45; Summer Arts
Festival 145-50; televi-
sion 202, 203-04; tongue-
twister contest 119; top
spinning contest 119
Deaf children: films for
178; storytelling to 179-
80
Early Childhood Resource
and Information Center
(The New York Public
Library) 98-99
Emotionally disturbed and
neurologically-impaired
children, programs for
187-88
Homebound children, pro-
grams for 244-45
Mentally retarded children,
programs for 118, 182-
86
Parents, programs for 120,
123
Pre-Schoolers' programs 122-
23, 150, 157-58
Prison, programs for children visiting parents in
192
Publicity 278, 284; see
also Publicity
Storytelling 121-33, 179-
80, 202-03, 244-45, 339-
41
Transporting children to pro-
grams 278
Videotaping programs 120
Children's Film Theatre 154,
155, 158, 159
Children's Theatre Conference
142
City University of New York 21
Cleveland (OH) Public Library
224
Collector's fair 207
Complaints, how to handle 236-
37
Concerts 69-72
Contests 205-06
Cumberland County (NJ) Library
243

Dallas (TX) Historical Society

152
Dallas (TX) Public Library 71-
72, 199
Danbury (CT) Public Library
194-95, 197, 201
Dance programs 251
Belly dancing 72-73
Ethnic 72-73
Folk 73
Instruction 72, 113
Tap dancing workshop 113
Dayton and Montgomery (OH)
Public Library 202-03
The Deaf 177-81
Films about 176-77
Programs for: consumer
education 180; dog
obedience 180; film
178-79; storytelling to
deaf children 179-80;
theatrical productions
179; video 179; work-
shop for deaf parents
and their children 180;
workshop for parents of
deaf children 180
Programs to promote un-
derstanding of the deaf
180-81
Sensitivity training for
library staff 181
Sign language courses 181
Deaf children: films for 178;
storytelling to 179-80
Demonstrations see Talks,
demonstrations, instruc-
tion
Discussion films 18, 303-05
Discussion groups 2-24
Books vs. films 18
Discussion leader 2, 3-6,
15-16
Kinds 16-17
Materials, print and non-
print 2, 8, 14, 17, 23
Participants 2, 3, 6-8,
11-12
Publicity 11-12
Registration 11
Resource person 2, 16,
19, 22, 33, 43, 44
Rules for participants 11-
12

Sessions 2, 8-9, 18, 23-
24
Size 2, 9
Subjects, popular 18
Techniques: for leaders
3-6, for participants 6-
8
See also Book discussion
groups; Film discussion
groups; Music discussion
groups; Play discussion
groups; Poetry discussion
groups; Science Fiction
discussion group
See also discussion groups
under Children's pro-
grams, Senior Citizens,
Teenagers' programs
District of Columbia Public Li-
brary 180, 181
Dover Pictorial Archives 267
Drama workshops 68-69, 135-
42
Dramatic presentations 65-69
Dramatic readings 67
Original plays 66
See also Children's programs;
Teenagers' programs;
Theatre company
Drug rehabilitation centers, pro-
grams at 244, 247

Early Childhood Resource and
Information Center (The
New York Public Library)
98-99
East Meadow (NY) Public Library,
22, 113
The Elderly see Senior Citizens
Elyria (OH) Public Library 245
Emotionally Disturbed and Neur-
ologically-Impaired chil-
dren 187-88
Films, effect of, on 187
Storytelling to 187-88
Enoch Pratt Free Library 92
Ethnic programs 216, 278; Af-
rican culture 112; Ameri-
can Indian culture 112;
Black culture 241; dance
72-73; drama 66, 68;
"Ethnic Heritage Studies"

170; film 17, 241; mul-
timedia 159-60; music
19, 70, 241; oral history
170; poetry 64-65, 278;
Puerto Rican culture
112; storytelling 124,
132
Sources 216
See also Children's programs;
Publicity
Evaluation forms (sample) 252,
255-59
Exhibits and displays, related
xi, 241, 250

Ferguson Library, Stamford,
CT 199, 200
Film and book discussion
groups 20
Film contests 45-46
Film discussion groups 8, 18-
21, 176-77
Books, use of 20
Criteria for selection of
films 18
Films vs. books 18
List of discussion films
303-05
Topics 19-21
See also Senior Citizens;
Teenagers
Film distributors 318-19
Film projectors 26-27
Borrowing sources 26
Buying; new 26; used
26-27
Projection Distance Tables
for Kodak Motion Pic-
ture Projectors 52
Film showings 25-60
Criteria for selection of
films 36-37
Equipment 26-27, 45, 47,
54
Guest expert 33, 43, 44
Introducing the film 32-
34
Noontime showings 35
Prisons, in 43, 189-90
Projecting 31-32
Projection Distance Tables
52-53

Projectionist 25-26
Sample film programs for
adults 306-08; adults and
teenagers 176-77 (about
the handicapped) 308-09;
pre-schoolers 311-12;
school-age children 312-
14; teenagers 310-11,
(retarded) 338
Seating guide 49-50
Showcase for young and un-
known filmmakers 45-46
Subjects, popular 39-44
Viewing space 30-31, 34-
35, 46-52
See also Children; The Deaf;
Ethnic programs; The
Mentally Retarded; Prison-
ers; Senior Citizens; Teen-
agers
Filmmaking workshops 105, 110-
12
Films
Acquisition 27-30
Books and periodicals about
334-36
Distributors 318-19
Free-loan films 28-30
Leasing 27
Purchasing 27
Renting 27-28, 29
See also Film discussion
groups; Film showings
Filmstrips 209, 265
Books and periodicals about
334-35
Projection distance tables
53, 130
Sources, free 317-18
Finkelstein Memorial Library,
Spring Valley, NY 100,
113-14
Flyers see Publicity
The Foundation Center 219
The Foundation Directory 218-
19, 332
Foundation News 219, 332-33
Foundations (for grants) 218-20
Fox Lake (WI) Correctional In-
stitution 190
Framingham (MA) Public Library
196
Free Library of Philadelphia

(PA) 135-36, 151, 180, 181
Free Public Library of Wood-
bridge (NJ) 191-92
Fund raising methods 220
Funding sources 218-20
See also Grants

Gallaudet College 179
Gallaudet Theatre Touring
Company 179
Gloucester City (NJ) Public
Library 244
Grafton (WI) Public Library
118
Grand Prairie (TX) Memorial
Library 169, 170, 171-
72
Grants, applying for 218-20,
253
Guidelines for writing pro-
posals 218-20
Use of photographs 260,
281
The Great Books Foundation
16, 293-96
The Great Books series 13,
14, 16, 293-96
See also Book discussion
groups
Greenwich (CT) Public Library
160

Half Hollow Hills (NY) Public
Library 184, 195, 199,
200
The Handicapped 175-88
See also The Deaf; Emo-
tionally Disturbed and
Neurologically-Impaired
Children; The Mentally
Retarded
Hendrick Hudson Free Library,
Montrose, NY 131
Homebound children, programs
for 244-45
Hospitals, programs at 244
Houston (TX) Public Library
159

Institutions, library programs

at 188-92, 244, 247
See also Drug rehabilitation
Centers; Hospitals; Prisoners
Instructional programs see
Talks, demonstrations,
instruction
Intellectual Freedom Committee
237
Iowa State Traveling Library
34-35
Ithaca (NY) Video Festival 55

Job-related workshops 106-07
Joice (IA) Public Library 42
Junior Great Books series 15,
294

King County Library System,
Seattle, WA 85

Lists of books, films and recordings, use of, at library
programs 250
Long Beach (NY) Public Library
108
Los Angeles (CA) Public Library
45-46, 237
Lunch time programs 35, 70

Mailing lists 251-52, 274-75,
287
Manhasset (NY) Public Library
97, 143, 153
The Mentally Retarded 182-87
Programs:
adult: crafts, 186-88;
film 183, 184; music
186; Children's: crafts
186; film 184; music
186; storytelling 184-86;
Teenage: crafts 187;
film 183, 184; music
186; storytelling 185-86
Techniques in working with
182-83
Metropolitan Cooperative Library
System, Pasadena, CA
179
Migrant workers' camps, programs at 243

Milwaukee (WI) Public Library 208
Mishaps 258-60
"Mothers' Club" for planning programs 224
Movie screen 47, 54
Multi-media programs see Children's programs
Music discussion groups 21-22, 23
Music programs 69-73
    Library as showcase for new works 71-72
    Noonday concerts 70
Music workshops 112-13

National Endowment for the Humanities 21
National Theatre of the Deaf 179
Natrona County (WY) Public Library 97, 199
New Carrollton (MD) County Library 19
New Hyde Park (NY) Public Library 144
New Jersey State Library 192
New York Library Association 164
The New York Public Library 5, 7, 10, 14, 15, 16-17, 18-19, 40, 55, 56, 65-66, 68-69, 72, 85, 87-92, 96, 98-99, 101, 107, 110, 118, 121-122, 132, 152, 155, 161-65, 169, 170, 175-77, 183, 189, 197-98, 205-06, 230-32, 242, 264, 278, 296
Newsletters 275
Newspapers
    Press coverage of programs 281
    Program publicity in 279-82

Oak Park (IL) Public Library 44
Ocean County (NJ) Public Library 195, 200

Open House 144-45, 208
Osterhout Free Library, Wilkes-Barre, PA 106
Outreach programs 188-92, 240-47, 278; Organizing 246-47
    Children's 242-43, 244-45, 246, 278
    Community organizations 246
    Drug rehabilitation centers 244, 247
    Homebound 244-45
    Hospitals 244
    Institutions 188-92, 244, 247
    Laundromats 243
    Migrant workers' camps 243
    Minority groups 241-43
    Neighborhood centers 241-42
    Parks 243
    Prisons and detention centers 188-92
    Street fairs 243
    Vacant lots 242, 243
Overhead projectors, use of 169
    Children's programs 119, 132, 159
Oyster Bay (NY) Public Library 69, 170

PBS 55
Paducah (KY) Public Library 203-04
Parents, programs for 120, 123
Performers and speakers 217, 250-51
Plainedge (NY) Public Library 109
Plainfield (NJ) Public Library 69, 72, 121, 224, 243, 278
Plays discussion groups 171
Plymouth (MA) Public Library 114
Poetry discussion groups 10, 14, 21
Poetry readings 61-65
    Ethnic 64
    Locating the audience 61
    Publicity 61

Selecting the poet 62
Poetry workshops 61, 65, 109, 171
  Bilingual 65
  See also Senior Citizens; Teenagers
Port Washington (NY) Public Library 17-18, 106, 107, 109, 113, 145, 173, 207-08, 226
Portland, Oregon libraries 159
Pre-Schoolers' programs see Children's programs
Press coverage of programs 281
Press releases 279-82
  Sample press release 280
Prince George's County (MD) Memorial Library 92-94, 106, 205, 255-58
Prisoners 188-92
  Censorship in prisons 189
  Programs for: book talks to teenage inmates 191; "Guides for Living" courses 192; film showings 43, 189-90; library skills course 191; quiz program 190-91; storytelling lessons 191; writing workshop 190
  Programs for visiting children 192
Program planning and producing --summary and checklist of preparations
  Dance 78-80
  Discussion groups 22-24
  Drama 75-77
  Film 56-60
  Music 77-79
  Poetry 74-75
  Talks, demonstrations, instruction 102-04
  Workshops 114-17
Programs
  Advisory groups for planning 223-24, 226
  Audience 249
  Charging for 254
  Complaints 236-37
  Equipment and furniture 236

Evaluating 251-59
Evaluation forms 252, 255-59
Exhibits and displays 241, 250
Location 240-47
Performers 250-51
Publicity 255, 264-84
Reasons for having vii-ix
Receptions 159, 180, 206, 208, 261-62, 286
Recording 260-61
Recordings, use of, in 68, 73
Selecting the right program 223-37
Sources 212-222
Space 235
Speakers 250-51
Staff 234, 253-54, 277
Surveys of audience program interests 228-29, 231-32
Taping 290
Tickets, use of 282-84, 286
Time of day 247-48
Volunteers, use of 221-22
See also under individual types of programs; Publicity
Projectionist 25-26
Projectors see Film projector; Overhead projector
Providence (RI) Public Library 46, 135
Public Television Library 55, 179
Publicity 61, 255, 264-84, 286-87
  Banners 281-82
  Discussion groups 11-12
  Exhibits and displays xi, 241, 250
  Film showings 46
  Flyers and posters: design and execution 265-71; distribution 264, 265, 274-76, 277, 278, 287; Dover Pictorial Archives 267; samples 288-89; 321-31; writing the copy 271-73
  Mailing lists 274-75, 287

Newsletters 275
Press releases 279-82, 287
Reaching the right audience 265
Volunteers, use of 221
Work-of-mouth advertising 277
Puppets: books about 339; shows 129, 133; use in storytelling 129; workshops 133-35

Queensborough (NY) Public Library 64, 110
Question and answer period 82-83

Racine (WI) Public Library 15-16
Radio 194-204
Commercial stations, library programs on 195-96
Library-owned stations 194-95
Programs: book discussion 197-98, 202; book reviewing 199; book talks 196-97, 199; children's 202-04; interviews 197; music 200-01; question and answer 200; quiz 201; reading to listeners 200; talks on a variety of subjects 199-200, 201
Sources of free programs 195
Taped programs 196, 197
Randallstown (MD) Public Library 45
Receptions 159, 180, 206, 208, 261-62, 286
Recording programs 260-61
Recordings, use of 68-73; in children's programs 133, 146, 147
Circulating at programs 250
Displays and exhibits at

programs 250
Music discussion programs 8, 21-22
Poetry discussion programs 21
Radio programs 201
The Retarded, programs for see The Mentally Retarded
Rochester (NY) Public Library 268, 325

Salt Lake City (UT) Public Library 10, 68, 69, 70, 113, 207, 327
Seattle (WA) libraries 207, 327
Seattle (WA) Public Library 95-96, 135
Senior Citizens 168-75
Advisory group for program planning 224
Programs: art show 172; courses 170, 171; discussion groups: film 19; play reading 171; poetry 10, 265; exercise 169; film 172-73; "Sexuality in the Later Years" program 169-70; "sing-a-longs" 169; talks on: crime prevention 169, local history 169; workshops: genealogy 170, poetry 61, 109, 171, theatre 68
Senior Assistants 174
Transportation to programs 278
Significant Modern Books discussion group 14, 296-302
Slide lectures 245
Sources for program 212-22
Free speakers and performers 212-17
Grants, applying for 218-20
Volunteers, use of 221-22
Speakers 145
See also Performers and speakers; Talks, demonstrations, instruction
Spotswood (NJ) Public Library 114
Springfield (MA) City Library

64, 69-71, 152
Storytelling 121-33
  Books about 339-41
  Criteria for selection of
    stories for: 18 months-
    3 years old 130; pre-
    schoolers 123; school-
    age children 123-24
  Film and video 341
  Learning the story 124-
    25
  Props with 129, 131-33
  Radio 202-03
  Techniques 124, 126, 130
Surveys, use of, in program
  selection 228
  Sample surveys 228-29,
    231-32

Talks, demonstrations, instruc-
  tion 82-104
  Adult literacy classes 83-
    84
  African dance 73
  Arts and crafts 100-01
  Authors 97
  Belly dancing 72
  Book talks 84-96
  Cooking 99
  Cosmetics 100
  Dance 72-73
  Food 99
  Grooming 99
  Hypnotism 100
  Money 100
  Parenting 97-99
  Sex education 101
  Summer subjects 100
  Winter subjects 100
  See also programs for in-
    dividual age groups and
    individual handicaps
Tampere Public Library, Fin-
  land 135
"Teen Age Book Talk" (radio
  program) 197-98
Teenagers
  Advisory group for selec-
    tion of programs 223-24
  Designing publicity 226
  Junior Great Books series
    15

Mentally Retarded, programs
  for 182-87
Performers, as 72
Programs: book talks to
  high school classes 84-
  96; chess tournaments
  206; contests: cooking
  and photography 205;
  dance 72; discussion
  groups: book 4, 5-6,
  9-11, 15-18, on radio
  197-98, film 19, poetry
  10, 14, 21; films: con-
  tests 45-46, made by
  teenagers 42, 45, popular
  with teenagers 41-43,
  189, sample film programs
  308-11, showings 35,
  189, workshops 110-12;
  music 72; poetry read-
  ings 66; sex education
  10, 19, 43, 101; work-
  shops: African culture
  112, American Indian
  culture 112, arts and
  crafts 100-01, 203-04,
  baby-sitting 106-07,
  backpacking 113; film
  110-12, music 112-13,
  poetry 61, 109-10, 171,
  Puerto Rican culture 112,
  summer jobs 106, theatre
  68-69, 135, videotape
  105, 114, 120, writing
  109-10; for inmates of
  correctional institutions
  43, 189, 191
Showcase, library as, for
  teenage talent 45-46,
  68-69
Survey of Program interests
  229, 231-32
Theatre company 68-69
See also Book talks; Discussion groups; Talks, demonstrations, instruction
Television 194-204
  Commercial stations, library
    programs on 195-96
  Library-owned stations 194-
    95
  Sources of free programs
    195

352 / Library Programs

Taped programs 196, 197
Theatre see Drama work-
    shops; Dramatic presen-
    tations
Theatrical groups 67
    Library-formed 68-69
    See also Children's pro-
    grams; Teenagers' pro-
    grams
Tucson (AZ) Public Library 201

United States Chess Foundation
    206
Utah Society of Science Fiction
    10

Video Catalog (The New York
    Public Library) 55-56
Video programs
    Documentaries 315-16
    Video as art 316
Videotape
    Artists 55
    Books about 317-18
    Distributors 319-20
    Sources, free 317
Videotape showings 54-56
    Differences from film
    showings 54
    Equipment 54-55
    Programs 315-16
    Sources of videotape 55

Videotape workshops 105, 114
Volunteers, use of, in programs
    221-22

Wantagh (NY) Public Library 99
Westport (CT) Public Library
    160
Workshops 105-17; African cul-
    ture 112; alternative
    energy sources 108; arts
    and crafts 108-12; as-
    tronomy 114; babysitting
    106-07; backpacking 113;
    beauty 108; dance 113;
    drama 68-69, 135; film
    105, 110-12; first aid
    108, health 108; holo-
    graphy 113; job-related
    106; motorcycle repair
    114; music 70, 112-13;
    poetry 61, 65, 109;
    reading 107; résumé-
    writing 106; retirement
    108; review for Scholastic
    Aptitude Test 107; scrim-
    shaw 113; speed reading
    107; star gazing 114;
    stop smoking 108; video-
    tape 114; writing 109-
    10, 190; see also Chil-
    dren's programs; Senior
    Citizens' programs; Teen-
    agers' programs